ArtScroll History Series®

Rabbi Nosson Scherman / Rabbi Meir Zlotowitz

General Editors

The Youngest

Published by

Mesorah Publications, ltd.

Partisan

A young boy who fought the Nazis

A. Romi Cohn
with Dr. Leonard Ciaccio

FIRST EDITION
First Impression ... November 2001
Second Impression ... May 2005

Published and Distributed by
MESORAH PUBLICATIONS, LTD.
4401 Second Avenue / Brooklyn, N.Y 11232

Distributed in Europe by
LEHMANNS
Unit E, Viking Industrial Park
Rolling Mill Road
Jarow, Tyne & Wear, NE32 3DP
England

Distributed in Australia and New Zealand by
GOLDS WORLDS OF JUDAICA
3-13 William Street
Balaclava, Melbourne 3183
Victoria, Australia

Distributed in Israel by
SIFRIATI / A. GITLER — BOOKS
6 Hayarkon Street
Bnei Brak 51127

Distributed in South Africa by
KOLLEL BOOKSHOP
Shop 8A Norwood Hypermarket
Norwood 2196, Johannesburg, South Africa

ARTSCROLL HISTORY SERIES®
THE YOUNGEST PARTISAN
© *Copyright 2001, by* MESORAH PUBLICATIONS, Ltd.
4401 Second Avenue / Brooklyn, N.Y. 11232 / (718) 921-9000 / www.artscroll.com

---

ALL RIGHTS RESERVED
*The text, prefatory and associated textual contents and introductions
— including the typographic layout, cover artwork and ornamental graphics —
have been designed, edited and revised as to content, form and style.*

**No part of this book may be reproduced
IN ANY FORM, PHOTOCOPYING, OR COMPUTER RETRIEVAL SYSTEMS
— even for personal use without written permission from
the copyright holder, Mesorah Publications Ltd.**
*except by a reviewer who wishes to quote brief passages
in connection with a review written for inclusion in magazines or newspapers.*

THE RIGHTS OF THE COPYRIGHT HOLDER WILL BE STRICTLY ENFORCED.

ISBN:
1-57819-784-8 (hard cover)
1-57819-785-6 (paperback)

Typography by CompuScribe at ArtScroll Studios, Ltd.
Printed in the United States of America by Noble Book Press Corp.
Bound by Sefercraft, Quality Bookbinders, Ltd., Brooklyn N.Y. 11232

Table of Contents

Acknowledgments

I would like to take this opportunity to thank YITZCHOK BRANDRISS, who, based on taped interviews, produced the original manuscript of this book; DR. LEONARD CIACCO, who revised and refashioned it; and RABBI YEHOSHUA DANESE who edited and refashioned the book into its final form.

I am appreciative of the invaluable assistance of ALLEN ADELSON of the Jewish Heritage Foundation, DARCY LOCKMAN, MOLLY MAGID HOAGLAND, the Ministry of Defense of the Slovak Republic, GENERAL JAN HUSAK of the Central Committee of the Slovak Antifascist Warriors, and the HON. MARTIN BOTURA, PH.D., the Slovak Republic's Ambassador to the United States of America.

MRS. CHARLOTTE FRIEDLAND, MRS. FAIGIE WEINBAUM, FRADY VORHAND, and TZINI HANOVER of the staff at ArtScroll/Mesorah did their utmost to ensure the beauty of this final product. I am grateful for their efforts.

Though I walk in the valley of the shadow of death,
I will fear no evil, for You are with me (Psalms 23:4).

Prologue:

s long as I live, I shall never lose my faith; it is the center of my being, the life of my soul. I shall thank my Creator and praise Him for every breath I take. "Though I walk in the valley of the shadow of death, I will fear no evil, for You are with me"; this has been my motto, and support for my every step.

I know that the evil that stalks the valley of the shadow of death takes many forms, from the smallest compromise to the most monstrous deeds. I also know that in a menacing way, the valley of the shadow of death is created by the choices that men make.

The author, just after World War II

Chapter 1

"Have You Seen My Father?"

In the late spring of 1945, it was all over. With the war ending I returned to my home in Pressburg, Czechoslovakia. I was determined to collect as many of the pieces of my life as I could find, to rebuild a normal existence for myself. I was only 17 years old, but for what I had been through, it seemed I had already lived a hundred lifetimes. Every familiar step I took on the streets of my childhood, I hoped, was a step toward recapturing that childhood. My first steps led me to my familial home.

I caught my breath and rubbed my eyes as I saw the house we had lived in looking as beautiful as ever. I began to run as I fantasized my family inside — my mother baking, preparing for the Sabbath, my father learning Torah, my siblings playing. But soon my feet halted; tears welled in my eyes. Pressburg's police commissioner and his large family were now cozily residing in our home.

The entrance to modern-day Pressburg. The city's famous castle can be seen in the background.

This was extremely common in the postwar reality. Jews sans family, sans hope returned to their homes, only to realize they were now also homeless, for while they had been in the concentration camps, their gentile neighbors had moved into their homes, making themselves comfortable.

I was left with no choice but to move in with a friend, Micus Sternfeld, one of the very few from my childhood who had survived the war. Though we were separated because of the war, Micus and I had shared many things during the preceding eight years, including the reality that we were both alone. Upon his return to Pressburg, Micus found that all of his family had been murdered. He, at least, was able to reclaim his family home and, for a time, I had a place to live. It was not my home, but it was near the synagogue and the community which I remembered. From there I hoped to begin my life.

Superficially, the physical appearance of the city, the buildings and the avenues were all in satisfactory condition,

The Great Synagogue of Pressburg

suffering very little destruction from the war. However, underneath the facade of normality, the city had been devastated, for I found no relatives, no friends, and no neighbors. Before the war, 20,000 Jews inhabited Pressburg. Of this number hardly anyone remained alive. The synagogues, the schools and the stores were nearly abandoned and all the people we grew up with – friends and relatives — were no more.

About a month after the war's end, trains chugged into town carrying camp survivors, between 30 and 50 in each transport. Whenever a transport would approach, the townspeople were alerted. I made it a point to be there

This hotel is built on the site our former house, on land stolen from my family.

Interior of the Great Synagogue

every time one arrived. Every transport was the same: broken people, starved, lifeless, dressed in the rags of their death-camp uniforms, sunken eyes, skin stretched over bones. It was too much for me to fathom. I had seen so much during the war, but what I was seeing now, after the war, was too much. For months, I met every train to inquire frantically of the shattered Jews who were returning whether they had news of my father and what had happened to him. No one had any information. I prayed to G-d and entreated Him that if my father were still alive he should find me.

Finally, I was given reason to hope. Among the refugees there were a few people whom I had known before the war. One told me that he had indeed seen my father in one of the camps, and he was as healthy as one could expect. My hopes soared, "Maybe my father has survived!"

After I questioned the Jews exiting one train, I began looking forward to the next transport. After months of this, though the number of trains and the number of survivors per train began to dwindle. I began to accept the inevitable, despite my hopes, despite my prayers. I could not bear to hear once again, "I do not know who Leopold Cohn is; I do not know your father." I decided I would give up my futile search. I would ask no further questions about my father.

However, despite my resolute decision, my conscience would not let me rest. I had an obligation to persevere, to continue, not to give up hope, no matter how disappointing the outcome seemed. How could I abandon my search? Once more, I resolved to try, sustained by my faith and belief in my Father in Heaven.

Each time I went to the train station, the group of survivors I met resembled the previous group and every group before. They were all dressed in ragged prison uniforms, dirty and emaciated with hardly enough strength to get off the train. Many had to be carried. They waited passively, standing listlessly, sitting or lying on the ground. Few were talking. And everywhere, healthy people intermingled in and out looking, searching for a familiar face, a cousin, a mother, a child, or a father. I inquired of everyone but no one knew of my father, no one could give me any information, no one could supply me with any hope.

I trudged home again. As I made my way through the streets, past the houses that had been so familiar and comforting to me during my childhood, I noticed a shriveled little man dressed in the ragged concentration-camp uniform, whom I must have missed, one I did not speak with. He was emaciated, little more than bones held together by skin. The flesh of his face was pulled taut like a macabre death mask. Though I did not recognize him, there was something familiar about this man. When I asked whether I knew him, he replied that his name was Shlomo Brown. This skeletal apparition was a family friend, a well-to-do merchant, and a learned man, who had lived in the large house across the street from us. The depth of my sadness shook me.

The Shlomo Brown I now saw did not resemble the healthy man of a few short years ago. How fiendish were our tormentors. It was not enough their desire to kill us; first they had to break and humiliate us, erasing any vestige of humanity before they dealt their deathblow. They desired to murder our souls.

Once again I inquired about my father.

"Yes," he responded, "I saw your father in Mauthausen.[1] We were in the barracks together." I was elated and my spirits soared, despite the fact that Mauthausen was a death camp which, because it did not have gas chambers, employed the cruelest methods to end the lives of the Jews. (After the Allies liberated Auschwitz, the Nazis took their last Jewish victims on death marches toward Mauthausen, desperately determined to finish them off there.)

"How is he? How is his health? Is he still alive? Where is he!?" I asked, overcome.

I could see his already wretched countenance deteriorate. "When I last saw him, your father was in pitiful health." Mr. Brown was at death's door himself, so if to him my father's condition seemed critical, then I had to find him immediately. Our old family friend saw that I had not understood his hint, yet he was careful to treat me with great kindness. Hoping that I would understand and accept my father's fate, he continued, attempting to be gentle, "I do not believe your father had the strength to live more than a few days. He was weaker than all the rest of us. You should look after yourself. Why loiter around the train yard?"

I was devastated. My last hope of seeing the person dearest to me in the world was shattered.

I managed to get some degree of control over my emotions. I became resigned that I would have to suffer even this. It was extremely difficult but I have learned, unfortunately, from experience, that in order to move on with my life there

---

1. Mauthausen was a concentration camp built by prisoners from Dachau and opened in August 1938. Its first inmates were mostly political prisoners, but as time went on the SS designated it and its subcamp, Gusen, to receive what they considered the most dangerous prisoners, and they were treated with exceptional cruelty. Large numbers of Jews were sent to Mauthausen from the east in 1944, and additional subcamps were built all over Austria. It was liberated by the Americans in May 1945. 102,000 prisoners were murdered there. Donald Niewyk and Francis Nicosi, *The Columbia Guide to the Holocaust*, New York, 2000, p. 204. For further reading, see Evelyn LeChene's *Mauthausen: The History of a Death Camp*, London, 1971.

were so many things I could not dwell upon. There was so much which would be detrimental for me to even think about. I occupied my mind with surviving.

Weeks later, I was returning to my apartment in Pressburg, preoccupied with thoughts of my new export/import business. I found myself walking along with a group of the ever-present refugees. "They all look the same," I thought, "the desolate concentration-camp uniform only slightly concealing a starved and abused body of skin and bones."

One refugee was more decrepit than the others were; he was a skeleton of a man, struggling with every step. I could see his bones, arms, ribs, shoulders and even the bones of his face. His shoulders were little more than sticks with a skull balanced unsteadily on top. The thinnest of ashen-gray skin was stretched tightly over the bones of his face and forehead and his eyes were sunken into two deep dark holes in his skull.

"How could the German monsters do such horrid things to a human being? How could they reduce a man to little more than a skeleton and worse?" It is one thing to kill a man, but it is quite another thing to spend years destroying the essence of a person and then kill him. This level of evil can be found only with the Nazis. These questions, and more, raced through my mind, reawakening profound feelings of anger and sorrow as I trudged on. I walked ahead, struggling to steer my mind toward the concerns of my business.

"Romi."

The sound of my name, barely audible, reverberated in my head like a distant echo. It was the sound of my childhood. Though the voice was weak and frail, it was my father's voice, exactly the way it had always sounded. I quickly assumed that my desire to see my father again was making me hear things.

"Romi." The voice was louder, more insistent this time.

For two or three seconds my mind raced. Though I knew it was an impossible dream, I turned toward the group of sur-

Leopold Cohn, my father.

vivors. I stooped in front of the wretched soul I had passed. It was my father. Tears burst from my eyes. All the love I had for my father — all my sadness, bitterness and hopelessness — came gushing forth like a geyser.

His eyes were still clear, lively brown eyes I could never forget, eyes gleaming with warmth and an over-powering desire to live. They were the only way I could recognize my father, his eyes and his voice. I fell into his arms, both of us weeping uncontrollably. They were tears of joy and they were tears of sadness over what had happened to us and to our family.

Over fifty years later, the questions still persist, still perse-cute me, demanding answers. The memories I have tried to squelch, but I have failed miserably. The questions refuse to let me rest. So many years and still the Holocaust is the first thought I awake with, it is the thoughts that deny me sleep. More and more, I delve inward, as I try to understand the inex-plicable. I pose temporary answers, but each brings up a myr-iad of even more trying questions.

When my exhaustion triumphs and sleep overtakes me, still I relive, in my dreams, the disconnected array of mem-ories. The boundless joy of a face remembered; people long buried come to visit me, trying to comfort me, a friend, a relative or an unrelenting fear... the voice of my sister... deafening pounding and screams of terror... monsters in hideous uniforms and monsters in everyday clothing... my mother calling for me... joyous holidays with wonderful foods and happy faces... the Great Yeshiva of Pressburg... holy days alone in the darkness... Jews lying dead in the street... murdered babies... tortured friends... limitless courage... magnificent faith, synagogues and Torah and my Father in Heaven.

Will I ever understand? Can anyone understand that which is inexplicable, that which is too horrible to be even imagined?

I write this story so that everyone will know what happened, and I write this story so that I might know why it happened.

Chapter 2

The Gathering Storm Clouds: Childhood Ends

I was born in 1929 in the city of Pressburg, now known as Bratislava. Nestled in the foothills of the Little Carpathian Mountains, Pressburg straddled both sides of the Danube River. It was one of the oldest cities in Slovakia, and had a history rich in the traditions of so many different cultures stretching back to antiquity — it was even the outpost of the Roman Legions. Ancient cathedrals stood side by side with the oldest of synagogues. The plethora of Greek and Roman artifacts was a constant reminder that this city had nurtured and spawned so much of the history of Middle Europe. Education and scholarship were the lifeblood of this city, touching every aspect of society. This was the city where I was raised. It was the capital of the Czechoslovakian Republic. Though it was not the largest city in Middle Europe, its history made it the center of cultural and spiritual life for everyone, especially for Jews.

Entrance to the Jewish neighborhood of Pressburg.

Pressburg was a great center of Judaism in which the study of the Talmud and the Torah, provided the life force, the essence of our everyday life. Synagogues and study houses were found on every corner, and in them Jews studied Scripture with acute intensity and with loving devotion. Jewish family life flourished in Pressburg and the city became the home of many outstanding students and scholars. In fact, the "Great Yeshiva" of Pressburg was one of the foremost institutions, not only of Central Europe, but for all of Europe. It was at that time the highest postgraduate Rabbinical school from where all the major *Rabbanim* of Europe graduated. As a result, hundreds of exceptional young scholars from many countries converged on Pressburg to study. The Jewish community embraced and supported these young men.

At 9 years old, I was a happy child and my parents and my siblings largely defined my world. My mother, Emilia, was a pious woman who maintained a perfect household. My father, Leopold, was an impressive man. He was a very well-known and successful businessman in international commerce. But most importantly, my father was a man of great trust in G-d and was devoted to the study of our faith.

A childhood picture of me with two of my sisters, Hana (at right) and Deborah, left.

My parents, like most of the Jews of Pressburg, were known for their charity and kindness, their hospitality, and their readiness to come to the aid of anyone in need of help. Their generosity was extended to both Jews and gentiles alike.

Our gentile servants stayed with us for many years and became like members of the family, for my parents were so devoted to them that they helped to provide for their needs as if they were their own children, even paying for their weddings.

Our relationships with the gentiles of Pressburg were friendly and cordial. The section of the city in which we lived was not particularly a Jewish neighborhood, yet we were always safe. Many gentiles knew my father or my mother and went out of their way to say "Hello" or to wish them a "Good day."

I had three sisters. The oldest was Hana; she was 10 years old, with beautiful jet-black hair and very dark eyes. She was a serious and responsible young lady whose biggest concern was to grow up to be exactly like her mother. Unlike myself, Hana was a "goody-goody," who always did her homework to perfection, and always did more than her chores. I still remember how proud everyone was of her when she baked her first cake. Hana was to grow up to be a very fine and beautiful young woman. Deborah was 7 and had hair and eyes just like Hana. She was a kind person who wanted to help her older sister with every chore. Sara, a baby of 3, was fair with very blond hair and blue eyes. She was the one who always looked for me and ran to hug me when she was happy and to hold my finger when she was frightened. Later, a fourth sister would join our family, Hindi, who was as fair as Sara. I had two younger brothers. David was 6, and Yaakov was 5. I like to think that they learned important things from their older brother, Romi. I know that they were willing accomplices in any mischief that I could muster.

My childhood home, constructed in the 18th century, was where I imagined I would always live. The granite stones of the two-story building were so large they must have been three to four feet thick. On the first floor was my father's office where he conducted the main interests of his international commerce business. The second floor is where we lived. Part of our home we graciously provided gratis to two outstanding yet needy younger students of Pressburg's Rabbinical School. This academy was more of a finishing school from which these young men would enter the Rabbinate. There were also four needy younger students still in pre-Rabbinical training, who were given their own suite. In our home, all their needs were attended to, leaving them free to pursue their studies uninterrupted. One wing was reserved for the household help. There was a master bedroom for my parents, adjacent to which were their own personal private rooms. The children's suite housed our rooms and a large center playroom. There was a kitchen, a living and dining-room in which we would host out-of-town guests and students from the yeshiva at every dinner meal. And finally, an official formal dining room used only for special occasions, with a fresco ceiling, imported palm trees lining the walls, rosewood furniture and a dining room table that comfortably sat thirty people.

With all the tumult and tragedy that was to take place in my life, my early childhood was a normal one. I studied in school and attended daily morning and evening services in the synagogue; I began to know and cherish the Torah; I loved and honored my parents. However, I was an impatient and precocious child who found it difficult to sit still and study.

Pressburg's Rabbinical School (first building on left) and the shul.

I did not enjoy reviewing my lessons; my biggest problem was my aversion to homework. However, even though I was a child, I had great success in solving this problem.

Giving my lunch to a fellow classmate, who would do my homework, was an easy price to pay. When the teacher then reviewed those assignments and found them to be excellent, he would sign them and send them home to the student's parents. Soon I bypassed the need to hand over my lunch because I quickly mastered the teacher's signature and I too was able to return home with "excellent" work. This skill in forgery would eventually save my life and the lives of others

Yet I was not satisfied, and I soon devised another plan to avoid the boredom of school.

Every day at noon, we were allowed to go home for lunch and were expected to return before 1 o'clock. I surmised that if I could invent a believable story, the teacher might excuse me early from school. At my first attempt at 11 a.m., I moaned to the teacher, clutching my ear, complaining about an ear-ache and asked if I could please go home early. To my surprise and delight the teacher said, "Yes"! Feigning great pain, I left school with an extra hour to spend looking around the toy stores up and down the many streets.

This proved to be a grand ploy. I was careful to vary my story and I did not ask to leave early every day, but it worked regularly. However, as always, it was my mother who found me out.

To reach one of my favorite toy stores, I had to pass in front of the windows of my father's downtown office. I successfully managed to steal by many times with no problems. I would crouch down below the level of the window and as long as I stayed close to the building no one would ever see me. Two oversights would be my undoing. First, I did not plan on my mother visiting my father's office before lunch. Second, I forgot that I had my distinctive blue knapsack on my back. My mother instantly recognized this knapsack as it moved past the window. When I reached the corner, she was waiting for my hunched-over form. Lectures were my reward. Mother brought me to the teacher and arrangements were made to insure that I would not leave school early again.

Though my mother was wise, I was resourceful. My teacher had a penchant for stamp collecting. Every day my father received mail from all over the world. Within a few days I was showing my teacher some of *my stamp collection.* This would be the basis for a truly symbiotic relationship between the teacher and myself. Every day I would bring in a new pile of canceled stamps and the teacher would excuse me from my schoolwork so that I could labor on his stamp collection.

Thus I was able to avoid the tedium of schoolwork. These skills and my knack at outsmarting others would someday be essential to my survival.

My brothers, sisters and I had only the whimsical cares of children. We understood that adults were people who whispered in hushed tones about serious matters and impending troubles. Adults always seemed to worry too much. We knew

A Jewish elementary school I attended. It is now an office building.

that the world could be difficult for Jews, but we had little sense that the world around us was changing; we understood even less about the meaning of these changes.

The first signs of the coming disaster had already surfaced when the Nazis entered Austria on March 11, 1938.[1] Looking back, there were clear indications of menacing horrors looming over the horizon. The viciousness and hatred, increasingly more overt, warned of the great tragedy that was to descend upon us.

Well before the "Angel of Destruction" swooped down upon Pressburg, stories of the terrible savagery of the Germans trickled into our community. This trickle eventually became a deluge. As refugees began pouring into Pressburg, the Jews of the city opened their doors wide to receive them.

---

1. Within two days Hitler's army annexed Austria. Most of the population welcomed the annexation with joy and this enthusiasm manifested in widespread anti-Semitic rioting. The Austrian Nazis followed the patterns established by their German counterparts, attacking and arresting Jews, seizing their property, taking away their jobs and sending prominent members of the community to Dachau. Israel Gutman, *Encyclopedia of the Holocaust*, New York, 1990, pp. 126-8.

Many of us had relatives or friends who had escaped from Austria and who brought us stories of Nazi cruelty escalating into unbelievable atrocities perpetrated against the Jews of Vienna. In every household, the children overheard the adults whisper in fearful, hushed tones about the impending trouble. Every conversation seemed to end with, "It will not be long before these sorrows reach our city."

Before 1938, under the presidencies of Masaryk and then Benesh, the city of Pressburg was considered a model of democracy and social harmony. Overt anti-Semitism and per-secutions of the Jews were against the law. With a population of 500,000, it was a city of great diversity. About 10 percent of the population was Jewish; 10 percent, Czech; 20 percent, Hungarian; 20 percent, German, and the remainder were Slovak. For the most part, we lived in harmony with these people, even with most of the Germans.

However, by 1938, our relations with the young Germans were altogether different. They were the first to enthusiastically embrace the Nazi philosophy of hate. These Germans, from 15 to 25 years old, welcomed Hitler's propaganda. Terribly anti-Semitic, they were the principal source of our difficulties. Not only did they adopt their nationalistic doctrine of hate but they also organized themselves to pursue and actualize this mon-strous ideology. The "Hitler Youth"[2] movement took many forms throughout the country, but they all shared this vision of malevo-lence and were all trained to carry out Hitler's whims and wishes.

They took advantage of every opportunity to harass a Jew. Even little children could expect to be besieged by the hatred of the Germans. On our way home or to school or even in school, we were called the vilest of names by these young

2. Hitler Youth: This National Socialist youth movement began in 1922, but was not called the Hilterjugend (Hitler Youth) until 1926. By 1935, 60 percent of Germany's young belonged. Members, aged 10 to 19, often spurned their formal education and became estranged from their families. Their training and activities taught them to hate Jews. Ibid., pp. 677-9. For further reading, see H.W. Koch, *The Hitler Youth: Origins and Development*, 1922-45, London, 1975.

disciples and it was not uncommon for me or for my brothers to be physically attacked.

Also at this time, there was a local Slovak group that was attempting to spur on a nationalist movement that would enable them to seize political power from the Czechs. Their spokesman was a man named Hlinka who wanted to break up Czechoslovakia and form an independent Slovak state with a Fascist government. Hlinka's ideas were attractive to many Slovakians who resented their second-class status in the Czechoslovakian government. Hlinka's supporters organized themselves into local action groups, which came to be known as the Hlinka Guards.[3] With the help of the Nazis they gained support for their movement and established their dominance, breaking away from the democratic Czechoslovak Republic to become an autonomous Slovak State. The agenda for the Hlinka Guards soon found common cause with the Nazi movement. They quickly became Hitler's staunch allies, resolutely adhering to all his policies. Eventually they would become synonymous with another group: the German SS.

On October 6, 1938, the Hlinka Slovak National Party issued a declaration of Slovak autonomy.[4] For the leaders of the Jewish community, this formal separation of Slovakia from Czechoslovakia was a clear indication of the future policies of the local government. Six months later, the German army occupied Bohemia and Moravia but not Slovakia. These

---

3. The Hlinka Guard emerged in October 1938, immediately after Hitler's demand for the Sudetenland was accepted and Slovakia became an autonomous country at the Munich conference. This paramilitary organization, which fostered nationalism and was meant as a counterbalance to the army and the police, operated against Jews, Czechs, the left and the opposition. Throughout its existence, the Guard competed with the Hlinka Party (from which it had emerged) for rule of the country. After the Slovak national uprising in 1944, the SS took over the Hlinka Guard. Yeshayahu Jelinek, *The Parish Republic: Hlinka's Slovak People's Party*, 1939-1945, New York, 1976, pp. 8-100. Gutman, *Encyclopedia of the Holocaust*, New York, 1990, pp. 944-52.

4. Dr. Dezider Toth, *The Tragedy of the Slovak Jews* (Slovak Republic, 1992), p. 107.

events left Slovakia an independent Fascist state allied with Hitler. Our lives changed terribly. With the government in the hands of the Slovaks, the local Germans and Nazis had de facto control. In April 1939, the Nazi State of Slovakia passed its own version of the Nuremberg Laws and they were zealous in their enforcement.[5] Under the government of President Tiso, anti-Semitism became the official policy and the persecution of the Jews became an official government objective.[6] Tiso's prime minister, Sano Mach, was ferocious in his attacks against the Jews and anyone who resisted the Fascist program. Persecutions began immediately and grew worse each day. As part of the independence of Slovakia, southern Slovakia was annexed to Hungary. Just before the Hungarians took possession of this territory, Tiso issued a decree to transport thousands of Slovak Jews to this area.[7]

Unfortunately for the Jews of Pressburg, along with the Fascist government came an onslaught of Nazi propaganda against the Jews. With this unending barrage, attitudes began to change — even among those who had not been actively anti-Semitic previously. Many of the people who usually treated Jews politely became less civil. So too, many of our gentile friends and good neighbors became people to be feared. Now, if one was a friend of a Jew, he was a Jew lover. For a gentile this meant he would be labeled, "Traitor to the State."

The Hlinka Guards were brutal oppressors in their own right, no less vicious or zealous than the Nazis. They used every opportunity provided by the Fascist regime to torment the Jews

---

5. On April 18, 1939, the Slovak state enacted its first anti-Jewish decree. Raul Hilberg, *The Destruction of the European Jews Volume II* (New York, 1985), p. 721.

6. President Jozef Tiso, ultimately executed for war crimes, was a Catholic priest and politician who ruled Slovakia throughout the war. In Marc h 1939, he declared Slovakia's independence at Hitler's behest, and brought the country into the Nazi camp. He surrendered Slovak Jews to labor camps and "resettlement" in order to deter a German invasion. The truth was that they were not being resettled but that they were being annihilated there. Hilberg, *The Destruction of the European Jews*, New York, 1985, pp. 719-21.

7. Ibid., p. 719.

and make our lives unbearable. Each day new laws were enacted designed to persecute us. Whenever a law was announced to curb our freedoms, we knew that the next day would bring yet another that would take the injustice one step further.

We began to see our plight as the fulfillment of the warning in Scripture: "In the morning you shall say, 'Would that we could go back to the evening,' and in the evening you shall say, 'Would that we could go back to the morning'" (*Deuteronomy* 28:67). As time went on, things became worse. Every day new terrors were sent our way, making us long for yesterday when things were not as bad. Fear was becoming our constant companion.

Laws were gradually passed to keep Jews from their livelihoods and to isolate them from the rest of society. One morning a decree was published in the newspaper and placards posted in public places announcing that all Jewish-owned establishments — stores, businesses and factories — had been confiscated, with no compensation to the owners, by the government. They took businesses, some of which families had built up for generations. All of our lifework was gone overnight and we were left with nothing; we had become destitute. The sense of loss was immense.

When the government took possession of a business, officials appointed a new manager whose only qualification was his membership in the Hlinka Guards. Almost always they were uneducated boors with no business experience, unable to run these establishments. Therefore, they insisted that the previous owner had to stay on to work in the very business that had been stolen from him.

One law and then another restricted the items Jews were allowed to own. Jews were barred from owning cars and telephones, and they were required to turn over all their gold, precious stones and jewelry to the government. Anyone caught with such possessions after the deadline for their surrender

The Jewish Quarter, now devoid of Jews. Today a memorial to the perished Jewish population of Pressburg stands at the head of the street.

was punished severely. Little by little, the Jews were stripped of their personal belongings and all of the usual privileges afforded citizens.

New decrees were piled upon old decrees; laws were used to cut the ties that anchored us to the community. First, houses that Jews rented to non-Jews were seized. When we learned to live with this decree, new laws evicted us from our own homes. When a non-Jew desired your house, all he had to do was to go to the authorities and they would issue a decree. The Nazis came to your house and you had to pack whatever they would allow you to keep and you had to be out of your house within 24 hours. Many Jews who were successful businessmen had fine homes in gentile areas of the city. The Nazi militia evicted these people from their beautiful homes and they became refugees who were then taken in by Jewish families still lucky enough to have a place to live. Eventually, the Jews were living mainly in the poorer parts of the city where they had to share small apartments with other families. Thus, within a few months, most Jews found themselves living in designated Jewish areas. Though not officially designated as the Jewish Ghetto, these areas began to serve the same purpose.

One of the most profound changes in our lives was the humiliation of having to wear labels that marked us as a targeted group. This was imposed upon the Jews by a decree that required us to wear the infamous yellow patches, stars with the word "Jude" on our clothes.[8] Not only had our possessions been stolen from us and given to our persecutors, but we were also branded and marked as fair game for any wanton attack by every malicious passerby.

In the city of Pressburg, these terrible tribulations were visited on the Jews only. The war was still far away; our non-Jewish neighbors lived in peace. At first some people helped by hiding Jews. However, most acted as if nothing objectionable was happening. And even if our neighbors may have felt that the treatment of the Jews was unjustified, almost no one could come to our aid openly.

More importantly, as each law reduced our status as citizens, it became easier for the gentiles to ignore the injustice of the next decree.

The Fascist government effectively suppressed all opposition by inflicting unbelievable cruelty for any offense. The instrument used to implement this policy of intimidation and destruction was the Hlinka Guards. The Guards were originally made up of ordinary citizens who conducted their meetings at the "party headquarters." They eventually became a group

8. The first suggestion that a Jewish badge be mandated probably came from Reinhard Heydrich, chief of the German Security Police at a meeting in Hermann Göring's headquarters in November 1938. The intent of the badge was to humiliate, isolate and segregate its wearer. In November 1941, the German propaganda minister Josef Goebbels described the badge imposition as a "very humane ordinance... a hygienic prophylactic in order to prevent the Jew from sneaking into our ranks without being recognized... Whoever wears a Jewish star is thus marked an enemy of the people." The introduction of the Jewish badge in countries occupied by the Germans always signaled a change for the worse. Philip Friedman, *Roads to Extinction: Essays on the Holocaust*, New York, 1980, pp. 11-17.

of young fanatics who dressed in uniforms and traveled in bands to intimidate people. They quickly identified the "Jewish problem" as their special responsibility. Once the Fascists took power, they became the agents of government policy and could act on their warped ideas with unchecked power. Even the police were subject to their authority.

After our houses and their contents were taken from us, the physical torture began. A Jew could be accosted, maliciously ridiculed and beaten savagely on the street, with no one to intercede on his behalf. Often, the tormentors would drag him to the City Square, beat him, throw him to the ground and cut off his beard and *peyos* before the jeers and cheers of the gleeful gathering crowd.

We learned that the Hlinka Guards had beaten a neighbor while he was returning home. A few days later, another neighbor was beaten while on his way to the synagogue. At first, these attacks occurred only after dark, but, as the attacks grew more frequent, Jews began to be beaten in broad daylight. Soon, the beatings were a daily occurrence.

At first, the Nazis preyed upon adult men only. Eventually, they came after the older people in the community as well. When a healthy adult Jew was beaten, he might be seriously injured; but usually, with help, the victim could get medical care and return home. When they beat an elderly person, too often he never moved again. Instead, he was returned to his family for a funeral. Soon, young girls were being attacked in the streets in this free-for-all. To walk outside in the street was to place oneself in mortal danger. If you had to travel for some urgent reason and returned home safely, the entire family offered fervent prayers of thanksgiving to G-d for your escape and good fortune.

One day, my father and I were returning home from the synagogue. Because I always had another question, we were engrossed in our usual "scholarly" discussion. We were so involved we were not paying attention and did not see the patrol of about twenty Hlinka Guards turn the corner from a side street.

The Guards, who were dressed in the official uniforms of Nazi militia, would prowl and terrorize the city. Their uniforms — the knee-high black leather boots, the swastika armbands on brown shirts, black pants — meant terror and pain to every Jew. These monsters, like the dreaded Nazi storm troopers, were so crazed with hate and viciousness, they looked less like soldiers and more like an angry, mindless mob. They were upon us before we could change direction. When they pounced upon my father, there was no possibility of escape.

Without a word — no questions, no warnings, and no explanations — one, and then a second, and then a third man began to pummel my father. They hit him with their fists; they kicked him, all the while laughing in fiendish glee. I screamed for help but no one came to our rescue. I begged them to stop. I kept on screaming with all my strength to no avail as they took turns beating him. The local police, though never overtly anti-Semitic in the past, would not help, they only looked on.

The Hlinka Guards left my father on the road, bleeding, motionless and nearly unconscious. With heroic pride, they marched triumphantly away. Only by the grace of G-d were we spared death. My father moaned softly. My first thought was that he was dying — that they had killed him. However, slowly he rose and we silently limped home. We never discussed this attack. Attacks like these had become so common that there was nothing to speak about. We thanked G-d that we were still alive.

With time, the attacks became increasingly incomprehensible. Within a few months, the Hlinka Guards and the Slovak Nazis were attacking little schoolchildren. In my school, the children ranged from 8 to 14 years old. One day, the Hlinka Guards broke the doors down. Two or three went into each classroom; first they grabbed the teacher and began to punch and kick him until he was unconscious. When they finished with the teacher, they began beating the children. They repeated their "assignment" in each classroom, continuing until they had horribly beaten even the youngest of children. These "heroes," in the name of the Führer, viciously pummeled children as young as 8 years old.

I leapt out the window before they could attack me. A few other children followed my lead. We ran from the porch along the side of the building and managed to hide in the woods behind the school. We could hear the cries and screams of the children still inside as the Hlinka Guards beat them. We stayed hidden until these monsters had finally left. I need only close my eyes to travel back through the years, and remember. I can still see the blood everywhere. It was too much to comprehend. How was I to understand a group of Hlinka Guards declaring war on these gentle, innocent children?

As frightening as it was during the daytime, the conditions at night were even more terrifying. The Nazi monsters freely invaded Jewish homes doing whatever they chose; seizing banned possessions, smashing and ruining whatever they left behind. We hid behind locked doors with the cur-

The white building in the center was my yeshiva, Yesodei Talmud, which was raided by the Hlinka Guards. I ran with my friends up the hill to hide in the woods until these monsters had finished their evil work.

tains drawn. In our dread and horror, we felt ourselves to be the fulfillment of the verse: "The sword shall destroy on the outside and terror shall reign indoors, even a young man, even a maiden, a suckling infant with the aged man" (*Deuteronomy 32:25*). When the Guards came at night, doors were smashed open, rooms were searched and people were taken hostage. Why they were taken, where they were taken, when they would return, no one ever knew. There were horrible unthinkable rumors, but it was not until the war was over that we learned what had really happened to these people. However, the worst was yet to come. If we could somehow have learned to live with our lot, we still could never have envisioned the cataclysm that awaited us. And we could never have suspected the magnitude of the conspiracy that the Nazis and the Fascists would put in place to deal with the "Jewish problem" or comprehend the horror of the "Final Solution."[9]

The "Final Solution to the Jewish Question" was the name for the Nazi plan to destroy all the Jews of Europe. Beginning in December 1941, Jews were rounded up and sent to death camps in the east. Initially, the program was disguised as the "resettlement of the Jews in Eastern Europe."

It started innocently enough. The Slovak Fascists picked leaders of the Jewish community to form a committee called the *Judenrat*, to represent the interests of the Jews. Promises were made for their safety and many Jews thought that the community could be protected if these prominent Jews could communicate formally with the government on their behalf. The

---

9. The Final Solution, the Nazis' plan to solve "The Jewish Question" by murdering every single Jew in Europe, was conveyed to the larger German government by Reinhard Heydrich at the Wannsee Conference, held in suburban Berlin in January 1942. The purpose of the conference was to effect "coordination among the various agencies with regard to the Final Solution." The conference was put together by Eichmann. Heydrich "outlined the general procedure in the Final Solution's 'practical implementation,' in which Europe was 'to be combed through from west to east' for Jews, who would be evacuated 'group by group, into so-called transit ghettos, to be transported from there farther to the East.'" Lucy Dawidowicz, *The War Against the Jews*, London, 1986, pp. 136-9.

members of the *Judenrat* were led to believe that they had some ability to bargain with the Nazis. As a result, each new decree took on the veneer of the best possible compromise. The intention was to mislead the Jewish people and they succeeded.

First, Jews were required to register at special offices set up by the *Judenrat*. Their identity papers were stamped with the distinctive "J." Soon, all unmarried young women were required to report for community service in their own town. This was not so objectionable. Next, the young women who were at least 18 years old were taken to work in labor camps. Though this was unpopular, everyone accepted this decree as necessary. The next decree required the young men to live in camps where they could work in the heavier industries that were essential to the war effort. The community was certain that they were safe and they were helping the country. However, this was only a ruse, for they were being sent to the Birkenau-Auschwitz death camp.

Before long, any Jew who was not deemed essential to the economy of the city was moved to a work camp. Entire families were moved to new towns and then, to work camps. Later, Jews were to be collected like property of the state to be "relocated" to another city to work in support of the war effort. For the most part, the Nazis did not take everyone in a given city. Rather, they took a percentage from each city. In the beginning, these people were always moved to new towns as a first step. After a few weeks, the process was repeated; the Nazis came back to round up another group of Jews. All this happened over a four-month period from late winter of 1941 until spring of 1942.[10]

Looking back, it is obvious that the Nazis wanted to implement their plan gradually so that the populace would be more accepting. In Pressburg there were non-Jews who were good people, who would never raise a hand against us. The Nazis realized that these people might resist their "program" for the Jews.

---

10. Israel Gutman, *Encyclopedia of the Holocaust* (New York, 1990), p. 697.

The key was to separate individual Jews from their friends and neighbors. The Nazis understood that if they isolated the Jews from people who knew them as real people with names and addresses and families, and placed them in towns where they were strangers, they could move the Jews anywhere they wanted. No one would object to placing strangers into work camps to support the war effort.

At the same time, the Nazis never missed an opportunity to demonstrate their total, barbarous cruelty. It was understood that this cruelty could be directed toward anyone who might raise the slightest objection, putting his life in jeopardy. All the pieces were in place.

By the middle of the summer of 1942, the Jews who were being held in the labor camps were shipped off to Auschwitz-Birkenau, Majdanek, and Treblinka. The cruelty was savage. Eventually, everyone was rounded up — men, women, and children, the elderly, pregnant women and nursing mothers — all loaded into boxcars with no food or water or sanitary facilities. Hundreds were packed into each car and forced to stand. The cars were packed so full that it was impossible to even lie on the floor. Anyone who fell to the floor, weakened by illness or exhaustion, was trampled. The journey often lasted for several days and when the doors were finally opened many were dead.

It was also becoming clear that these new concentration camps were places where the Jews were being abused horribly and systematically killed

We received letters from those being held in the concentration camps assuring us that they were being treated well. However, these letters were not the words of our loved ones. It was clear that the prisoners were being forced to pen these glowing optimistic accounts. They still managed to fool the Nazis who scrutinized each correspondence before being forwarded to us. One of my relatives sent us a letter signed, "Sincerely, *Hakol Sheker,*" which meant, "Sincerely, It's All Lies."

More than 90 percent of the Jews of Pressburg were brought to the camps. However, there were a few whose work was so essential to the economy that they were allowed to remain in the city. Many who managed the hospitals and factories or who were leaders in the field of commerce were Jews and, without their expertise and connections, the cities and their primary industries would have ground quickly to a halt. Also, the Jews largely controlled international trade and cutting these lines would drastically disrupt the region's economy. These fortunate few were issued special permits and allowed to stay in the city to continue at their work.[11] Even with this permit, they were essentially prisoners. They were not free to travel, but were confined to the sole area where their services were needed.

As my father was a successful international trader in the city, our family was granted one of those "special permits." We were not deported; we would be allowed to work in our own city and live in our own house. Though our first reaction was one of great relief, we recognized full well that the permit we were granted was a precarious guarantee of our safety. Any government official or Hlinka Guard could tear up our permit and send us to a work camp in a moment.

There was no end to our anguish and terror. During the day, we could not venture out of the house into the streets. It was even too dangerous to visit friends who lived nearby. We ate only what my father would bring home when he returned from his business. The door was always locked. My father had an iron door installed behind the original wooden one. The iron

---

11. In October 1941, 3,500 Slovak Jews still held work permits. Though their wages were fixed at a very low rate, they were privileged relative to most of their neighbors in that they were not sent to labor camps, and were exempt for some time from concentration and deportation measures. Hilberg, *The Destruction of the European Jews*, New York, 1985, p. 725.

door was closed with a heavy iron crossbar to prevent the Nazis from breaking into our home while we slept; it served to symbolize our fear and perilous condition. When we heard the Hlinka Guards marching or saw them goose-stepping down the street, our only thought was that "this time they are coming for us." When they continued on, passing our home, it was as if we had been reborn; we were spared once again. However, our joy was quickly squelched as we realized they would be stopping at some other unlucky Jewish house. This was not an infrequent event, but would occur several times, every day and every night.

As a result, we never felt safe even in our own home, even in our own beds. It became so bad that if someone simply knocked on our door, we felt certain this would be the end of our family. Now we were all finished; we were to be beaten, killed or worse.

My father realized that sooner or later the day would arrive when the Nazis would come to take one of us. He therefore hired a carpenter to build a hiding place in our attic pantry. The carpenter constructed a new wall that cut the pantry lengthwise. The inner room included a skylight that would allow us to escape onto the roof if need be. It was just big enough for one cot. On the pantry side of the new wall, the carpenter replaced all the shelves so that they hid the door seams. It was impossible to see that there was a room behind the shelves. Some of us, but certainly not all, might be saved in this tiny hiding place.

Chapter 3

A Child to Say Kaddish

By Passover 1942, most of the European conti-
nent had surrendered to or allied themselves
with, Germany. The Nazis were aggressively
fighting the war on two fronts: against the Soviet
Union, its one-time ally, and Great Britain. On March 24, the
Nazis began their deportation of Slovak Jews to Auschwitz.[1]
The situation of the few Jews remaining in Pressburg had
reached its nadir. The daily terror visited upon us by the
Nazis, who had stripped away all of our most basic civil
rights, had rendered the streets too dangerous. By this time,

---

1. Auschwitz was the largest concentration and extermination camp in Nazi-ruled
Europe, located in a part of Western Poland that had been annexed to Germany in
1939. Between May 1940 and January 1945, approximately 405,000 prisoners were
registered at Auschwitz. (Many were murdered upon arrival, and thus never registered.) Auschwitz ultimately encompassed 40 subcamps, one of which (Birkenau)
housed the machinery for mass extermination, and was designated by Heinrich
Himmler as the centerpiece for the Final Solution ... Gutman and Michael Berenbaum,
Anatomy of the Auschwitz Death Camp, Washington D.C., 1994, pp. 6-72.

A never-before-published photograph of Jewish men forced to dig their own grave before being murdered by Nazis. The photo was taken in Konin, Poland, in 1939 by a Nazi soldier for the amusement of his girlfriend.

more than 80 percent of the city's Jewish population had been forced to leave the city. There were so few Jews left, and those few who remained were so terrorized, that the community was hardly able to maintain even the barest essentials of Jewish life. Procuring food was difficult for all citizens, but for the small Jewish community it was nearly impossible to obtain kosher food. The Nazis specifically devised decrees against the preparation of kosher foods. Therefore, it was impossible to prepare even for the most basic needs for the holiday. I remember my parents' lament, "We will have no matzos for the holiday, but we have certainly had our fill of bitter herbs."[2]

By this time, even those who had special permits were being picked up by the Hlinka Guards. Any one of our tormentors could rip up this permit at whim, and without his special permit one disappeared into the work camps. Also,

---

2. One of the ceremonial dishes eaten at the Passover Seder to remind us the bitterness of our exile in Egypt.

by now, what had been an unthinkable rumor had become an undeniable truth; the so-called "work camps" were, in reality, "death camps."

In 1938, when the Germans invaded Austria, they immediately began to arrest Jews. My uncle was one of the first to be taken in Vienna by the Nazis. Without delay my mother traveled to Vienna in an attempt to secure his freedom. She spent many days meeting with various government officials, but received absolutely no help. Eventually, she met with Gestapo officers. From that moment, she knew in her heart what the Germans were preparing for the Jews. She knew they intended to kill us all.

Pressburg's Volunteer Army, though sounding like a noble outfit, was solely composed of soldiers of German descent who met up with the Nazis at the front, to join them in their objective of world domination. Returning on leave from the front in Poland, they happily brought back unbelievable tales of synagogue torchings, mass killings and incomprehensible evil perpetrated against Jews every step of the way. They bragged about the Dachau Concentration Camp,[3] of the brutality, of the Nazi obsession with inflicting humiliating cruelty before killing Jews. These stories made us reel with disbelief; such events were beyond our comprehension.

My parents realized we had to escape from this "Valley of Death." We had no choice but to flee Pressburg. Since the effects of the war had not yet reached Hungary (rather than risk invasion and conquest, Hungary allied itself with the

---

3. Dauchau was a concentration camp 10 miles northwest of Munich, opened in March 1933. Initially, it was a prison for political opponents of the Nazis. Eventually, the number of Jewish prisoners increased as the systematic persecution of the Jews intensified in Europe. Of the 206,206 prisoners at Dachau in its 12-year existence, there were 31,591 registered deaths, though the total number of victims of individual and mass executions and the final death marches will never be known. The camp was liberated by the Americans on April 29, 1945. Hilberg, *The Destruction of the European Jews*, New York, 1985, p. 1219. Gutman, *Encyclopedia of the Holocaust*, New York, 1990, pp. 339-43. For futher reading see Marcus Smith's *The Harrowing of Hell: Dachau*, Albuquerque, 1972.

Germans in November 1940), my parents felt we could find refuge there. However, we had to be smuggled past the border guards. Someone had to attempt the journey, but the Nazis would quickly note my father's absence. Therefore, it was decided that I would go alone with a guide to test the route and make contact with our relatives living there.

During the preceding weeks, my father had been investigating possible avenues of escape. He learned of a gentile smuggler of goods and contraband who resided near the border. My father met with this man, and asked whether he would be willing to take a person. The guide emphasized the extreme danger of such a trip for someone inexperienced in the art of border crossing. However, it could be done, the smuggler intimated, for the right price.

Barbed wire and electric fences covered the entire length of the border. Patrols made frequent passes. At each road the police manned checkpoints with a troop of heavily armed Nazis. He agreed to risk his life to help us for the exorbitant fee of 5,000 Slovak crowns (equivalent to about $50,000 today).

I was only 13 years old, and though it happened so long ago, that day is still clear in my memory. My mother's tears told me how difficult this decision had been. The guide would not permit me to carry any luggage, so my mother dressed me in three undershirts, three underpants, three shirts, two pairs of pants and, over it all, my best suit.

My mother took me aside to speak privately to me. She told me that she had no hope left for the survival of our family or for any of the other Jews remaining in Pressburg. I remember her exact words. "We know what our destiny is ... we are all doomed to be killed," she said. "At least one of us should survive to say *Kaddish*[4] for the rest. The family name should not be entirely wiped out." Though we talked about the

---

4. A prayer recited for a family member who has died.

family being reunited across the border in Hungary, this was a dangerous trip, a trip that had already cost many lives.

I carried all my family's hopes for survival while they remained behind. I bid farewell only to my mother and father. The pain of leaving my parents was unbearable. We cried bitterly and unrelentingly with the fear that we might never see each other again.

It was 4 o'clock in the afternoon when my gentile guide and I began our journey. Even though it was 40 miles away, the guide intended to get us across the border that night. For the first part of the journey, we traveled by train. I was disguised as a gentile, as I pretended to be the guide's son. There were many people on the train; any one could have pointed me out to the police as a Jew trying to escape the country. Both my guide and I were certain that if we were caught we would be killed. We had to be watchful of every word and action; anything might give us away.

Shortly after twilight we disembarked from the train and traveled for about five hours, walking cautiously near the roadside, toward the border in total darkness. This was a country road, a simple footpath that went over fields and through forests. We wore dark clothing, carried no light and made no sound, hoping no one would notice us. We were prepared to dash into the woods at the first hint of trouble. As we walked, the tension increased to almost unbearable levels.

At the border we would be in the most danger. It was aggressively patrolled by both the local police and by heavily armed Nazi troops. The border guards stopped all that tried to cross, carefully checking their papers. These guards were notorious for their callousness and would have no qualms about shooting anyone at the slightest provocation. Consequently, when we were a few miles from the border, the guide led me off the road into the forest. We found a way through the fences along the border two or three miles from the road into Hungary.

The dense forest made walking very difficult, but the underbrush made it easy for us to hide. We walked for miles, creeping quietly through the night, hiding at the slightest unusual sound. Often, we crawled on our stomachs. As we approached the frontier, we did more crawling than walking. The going was very difficult; every step was fraught with danger and fear. We encountered fence after fence under which we had to crawl. A number of times we crouched frantic with fear in bushes or behind logs or rocks as patrols passed close by. With each passing hour, time became more and more of a concern. If we were still traveling after sunrise, we would easily be spotted.

After many hours, my guide whispered, "When we cross this next fence we will be in Hungary." Finally, we crawled along the fence until we found a gap through which we could pass. At intervals of about three or four hundred meters, the border guards had placed searchlights, which they used to sweep the cleared area through which we had to crawl. Many had made the journey to this point, only to die in a circle of bright light and a hail of Nazi bullets.

As we moved toward the last fence, the guide threw himself on me, covering me with his coat. After about ten seconds he removed his coat and told me that he was afraid that my coat, a little bit lighter in color than his, might reflect the passing searchlight beam. I was so consumed with fear that I was afraid the patrols would hear the pounding of my heart. As I started to move forward, the guide pulled me back signaling for me to be quiet with one hand and pointing off to our left with the other. As I looked out into the darkness, I could barely discern a patrol that was marching alongside the fence. Since we knew that the patrols passed at regular intervals, we let them move by us until they were a safe distance away. We had only a few seconds to cross an expanse of bare land and reach a hiding place on the other side of the border. We scampered quickly through the gap in the fence and into the woods on the other side before the next patrol came along.

We were in Hungary; my escape was successful. It was truly a miracle that we made it across the border before sunrise. Later that morning, I reached Serdahel, a city of 10,000 people, 80 percent of whom were Jews. This was my father's birthplace. In one day I experienced a lifetime of emotions. I quickly made contact with my father's family.

My relatives, who fully understood the danger I faced crossing the border, were overjoyed at my safe arrival. I stayed in the home of my uncle, David Gandel, the husband of my father's sister. He was a pious man and a prominent businessman, renowned throughout the country for his charity and righteousness. Robust and energetic, who lived only for others, he was the owner of the town's mill. Those who were in need always found a bag of flour — clandestinely and discreetly delivered so as not to embarrass the recipients — at their door. His table was always filled with needy people and with students from the local yeshiva. My uncle and his entire family welcomed me warmly, making me feel that I was part of their family. Though I was grateful for the kindness that they had shown me, I thought constantly of my parents and siblings.

It was impossible for me to return to my family; all I could do was wait, worry and pray. From the other side of the border came only rumors of terrible disasters befalling the Jews at the hands of the Nazis.

My uncle enrolled me in the yeshiva of Serdahel, which was led by Rabbi Osher Anschel Katz. It was a fine school and I am certain my Uncle David understood that the lessons would occupy my mind and help me deal with the anxiety I was enduring. The loving treatment I received from my uncle was exactly what he extended to all those in need. Kindness was a way of life for this man and his family. (Not one member of this entire family survived the Holocaust. My uncle's son, Chaim Alter, endured many trials of hell, each of them taking a great toll. By the time he arrived at the Mauthausen concentration camp, near the end of the war, his physical condition was greatly weakened. My father, who was also imprisoned there, came upon Chaim and embraced him joyfully. My cousin gazed into my father's eyes with a look of great happiness. "Uncle Leopold," he said, "I am very tired, very tired" and died in my father's arms; dead from the combined effects of prolonged suffering and a broken heart from all he had lost.)

While I was living with my Uncle David, the local police became a problem for the Jewish community. More and more Jews were doing exactly what I had done. Since Serdahel was so close to the border, the Hungarian police patrolled the city searching for refugees. There was no official decree, but the police were afraid of incurring the wrath of the Nazis across the border in Slovakia. It was essential to keep the fact that I was a refugee from Pressburg a secret. When the Hungarian police caught a Jewish refugee they handed the poor soul directly to the Slovak border guards and the Nazis. Anyone who met this fate could expect only viciously prolonged torture and eventual death.

As the days passed, the police patrols grew more frequent as they began to search houses. At first they would knock and ask that the resident open the door, but they quickly resorted to smashing down the door. As the local people became more frightened, Uncle David realized that it was just a matter of time before someone turned me over to the police and smashed their way into his house. This profound change in Serdahel occurred over a period of two months. We knew that things would rapidly deteriorate. We decided that I should move further from the border to a town called Yarmot in the hope that there the local police would be less diligent in their hunt for foreign Jews.

In Yarmot, I stayed with another uncle, Reb Kalman Weiss, the husband of my mother's sister. Uncle Kalman, like Uncle David in Serdahel, was one of the most highly regarded and prominent Jewish citizens in the town. And like my previous foster family, this new family greeted me with great warmth and looked after my every need. I was amazed that, with all the fear and worry that beset their community, they continued to help all in need.

Though we still had to make every effort to keep my identity secret, I was much safer here than I was in Serdahel. In Yarmot, I studied in the yeshiva of Rabbi Deitch, the chief rabbi of the city. This was a well-respected school, which educated approximately 80 students who all were outstanding in their accomplishments in scholarship and ethics. Rabbi Deitch was a very kind, empathetic man who generated tremendous warmth. He knew I was living in Hungary illegally, and even though this jeopardized his entire yeshiva, he personally did everything in his power to make me feel as if I was at home. He was like a father to me.

The Hungarian Jews were G-d-fearing and devout people. They had lived for a long time in harmony with their non-Jewish neighbors. Hence, Hungarian Jews were nurtured with a sense that they were protected and not in danger. They had a steadfast faith in the government's willingness and ability to protect them. Though great horrors were being perpetrated around them in Poland, Germany and Czechoslovakia, they expected to live in peace and tranquility protected by the Hungarian government. Many Jews felt themselves so much a part of the Hungarian community that their loyalty to their country was deeply rooted, even at the expense of their religious beliefs and moral principles. Many were reluctant to break the law even for a good cause.

Consequently, as more and more Jews managed to escape the Nazis and enter Hungary as refugees, they sometimes encountered a surprising reluctance among Hungarian Jews to assist them — that is, to act illegally on behalf of the Jewish refugees. Others felt that the refugees were bringing their troubles with them to Hungary and that this would bring down the wrath of the Nazi oppressors. Many thought the refugees were endangering the lives of the native Hungarian Jews. However, the vast majority of Hungarian Jews acted heroically in their efforts to help the refugees, often placing themselves and their families at great personal risk.[5]

This was certainly the case with my uncle and his family. Even though they knew that informers were telling the Hungarian police which families were harboring refugees and that being caught would certainly lead to the most severe punishment, their devotion to me and to my family never wavered. Eventually, Reb Kalman and his family, including seven of his children, were murdered. Only his first-born son Eliezer escaped the vicious net of the Nazis.

I had been living with my uncle's family for about two weeks when I received wonderful news. My baby sister Sara had escaped to Hungary. I had begun to lose all hope that I would see any of my immediate family ever again. A few days later, she joined me to live with our uncle.

The story of Sara's escape demonstrates that, with all the trials and horrors that plagued our lives, wondrous goodness could still bless our days. With the Nazis and their vile helpers everywhere, there were still good and courageous people who were willing to risk their lives to help the Jews. One of our former servants, a gentile named Marishka, visited my parents because she was so worried about their safety. Marishka had been our housekeeper for seven years. Whenever our nanny had a day off, Marishka would volunteer to look after us. She would say our morning prayers with us making sure that we did

---

5. Between March 1942 and March 1944 over 16,000 Jews found refuge in Hungary and were not turned over to the Nazis. Dawidowicz, *The War Against the Jews*, New York, 1975, p. 381.

not mispronounce any of the Hebrew words. How she learned them I do not know. My parents had paid for Marishka's wedding to an officer in the Hungarian army. She lived with him and their two children in Hungary. Seven years had past since she last worked for us. Marishka was back because she was well aware of the fact that Slovak Jews were being shipped off to labor camps where they were being treated inhumanely.

Marishka begged my family to try to escape. My parents explained that the family could not escape as a group; there were too many of them and they would be detected and killed. They were making plans to avoid capture by the Nazis, but it was going to take some time. Their only hope was that each could escape one at a time.

Marishka was greatly upset by the thought of my family, which she regarded as her own, falling into the hands of the Nazis. She was distraught that something terrible would happen to them, especially Sara. Sara was so young that it would be impossible to take her by the route that I had traveled. On the other hand, if they tried to go through the regular checkpoint the family would likely be found out and captured.

It was a comment that Marishka made to my parents that provided the idea for an escape plan to save Sara. Marishka said, "I wish that you could use my papers and you could just walk through the checkpoint without any problems."

Sara, who had blue eyes and blond hair, looked more like the "perfect Aryan child" than did most Germans. If the guards did not look too carefully, she might pass for Marishka's baby. Furthermore, Marishka's papers listed her as having a young daughter. Marishka happily took Sara as her 3-year-old child on the journey to return to their home in Hungary — a relaxing and happily uneventful excursion — and we were reunited.

Almost immediately, Sara began to miss her mother, asking for her every few minutes. Her cries of "Mommy ... Mommy" still ring in my ears. Each night she would cry herself to sleep, her last word always, "Mommy ... Mommy ...", only to awake the next morning crying out, "Mommy ... Mommy." The only thing that would stop her crying, and sometimes even bring a smile to her face, was to hold my finger. The moment she lost hold of my finger, day or night, asleep or awake, she would cry uncontrollably.

When Sara was crying, she would ask for our mother or where mother was or any number of questions about her. This was a potential disaster because she spoke German, our language in Pressburg. In Yarmot, Jews who conversed in German were refugees wanted by the police. To keep her quiet, I let her hold my finger every minute, including during my hours in yeshiva where every day she stood at my side, my finger held firmly in her tiny hand as I concentrated on my studies. She was never restless or unhappy as long as she held my finger. Each morning, I awoke before daybreak to pray and to study. I would gently slip my finger from Sara's grasp so as not to awaken her and I would dress as quickly and quietly as possible in an attempt to sneak out of the house without her noticing. But when I arrived at the front door, she would be waiting for me, fully dressed and with her small hand raised in anticipation of my finger. Without a word, off we would go. It was weeks before she would leave my side. Fortunately, Sara eventually became more secure and would stay with others in my uncle's family.

Within a few days, I received more good news. My oldest sister, 15-year-old Hana, had been able to get through the border guided by the same gentile who had taken me. A few days later she reached Yarmot and joined Sara and me. Because she could speak German only and had dark hair and eyes, we were worried that she might be noticed if she went outside and mixed with the native Hungarians. Even in Yarmot where Hungarian Jews were still living in relative peace, there was no shortage of people who might feel it was their duty to report foreign refugees. Consequently, Hana was forced to stay in the house all the time so that the neighbors would not notice her. Only at night, under cover of darkness, was she allowed to go out to see the sky and breathe fresh air.

For a time, we felt safe in my uncle's house. I was hoping to continue to study at the yeshiva in Yarmot indefinitely. But, by then, I should have known better. The plague of hatred and evil unleashed by the Nazis in their own land was spreading like a raging epidemic from town to town and from city to city, often preceding their occupation. Borders and boundaries made no difference. The symptoms of their disease appeared in one town and only too quickly spread to the next.

So it was in Yarmot. The first searches by the local police were only half-hearted efforts. Most refugees could be hidden in the house or escape out the back door. However, the searches became more and more aggressive and systematic. The government formed special police units whose sole duty was to hunt for Jewish refugees. Unannounced, these police forced their way into each house, breaking down the door if necessary and often tearing the house apart looking for their prey.

Soon enough, someone informed on me and the police came. They looked all over the house but did not look under the bed, where I hid. Two days later they came back again. This time they looked in every room and in every nook and cranny of the house: in closets, in the basement and in the attic. Even though they were more thorough in their search this time, we were prepared, for my uncle and cousin had shown me a small door in the attic that led onto the roof. While on the roof, I could not be seen from the road. When they finally left, we were not relieved, for we knew they would be back.

A friend of my uncle who worked in the police station sent a message to him that the police would be returning because they knew that he was hiding a foreign Jew. Uncle Kalman quickly constructed a hiding place in the attic. It was a very small room, barely big enough for a single adult. From the entrance to the attic, the wall of this room looked like the outside wall. Because it was located at the dark end of the attic, no one would suspect that there was a room behind it. When the police began banging on the front door, I hid in this room with my cousin Eliezer who stayed with me so that I would not panic and kept me absolutely quiet. If I were discovered, it would be as big a disaster for his family as it would be for me.

This time the police ransacked the house. We could hear them yelling orders, banging and scraping as they over-turned furniture, emptied closets and threw the contents of the house about in their frustration. They emptied dresser drawers and looked behind bookcases for doors to secret hiding places. It seemed that the search went on for hours; I was too frightened even to breathe. But they found not the slightest hint that there was any refugee hidden in this house. They left angrily without the prisoner they sought. After another long wait, we heard the tapping signal that meant the police were safely gone from the neighborhood. Taking what seemed to be our first breaths in hours, we rejoiced to be out of our tiny hiding place and into what now seemed like an expansive attic.

Through all of this, not one question was asked about either of my two sisters. They never considered that my sisters might be refugees. Clearly, the police were searching for me because someone had informed them that I was a foreign Jew, hiding in a Hungarian home.

It was clear that I could not stay there any longer. The police had decided that my uncle was hiding refugees, so it was only a matter of time until I was apprehended. Uncle Kalman decided that I would be safer in Budapest, it being a much larger city. I was to leave immediately by train. I packed my belongings, said goodbye to my two sisters and we set off to the train station. As we approached, Uncle Kalman and I were horrified to find that it was being guarded and the soldiers were checking papers. They would immediately deduce that I was a foreign Jew. Returning to the house was not an option; surely the police would be waiting for us. Instead, my uncle hired a man who owned a motorcycle to drive me to a little village where there were no police or soldiers guarding the train station. There I boarded the train that would take me to Budapest.

Chapter 4

The Beast Strikes

While I was in Yarmot, the Nazis deported most of the Jews remaining in Pressburg to Majdanek[1] and Treblinka[2] concentration camps. Only a minute number of Jews remained in the city. There were still some Jews who had special permits because they performed some essential service. My dear uncle, Rabbi Chaim Yehuda Naftoli Yitzchok HaLevi Greenwald, known

1. Madjanek was a concentration and extermination camp established on the outskirts of Lublin, Poland in October 1941. It had several small gas chambers, but most who died there were either shot or succumbed to camp conditions. In 1943 a crematoria was built to dispose of the bodies. It was evacuated in July 1944, but most of the Jews had been shot in November of the previous year. Niewyk and Nicosia, *The Columbia Guide to the Holocaust*, New York, 2000, p. 204.

2. Treblinka was open in July 1942 northeast of Warsaw, and was the killing center primarily for Jews from the ghettos of Central Poland. An underground resistance movement planned an uprising in August 1943, but the plot was uncovered by the SS and the revolt put down. The camp was shut down in the fall of 1943, but not before more than 800,000 Jews were murdered there. Niewyk and Nicosia, *The Columbia Guide to the Holocaust*, New York, 2000, p. 210.

Uncle Yehuda Naftoli Chaim Grunwald in 1937.

to all simply as Reb Yudel, was one of the Pressburg Jews who managed to remain in the city with his family.

Reb Yudel was married to a pious woman named Raizel, who was my mother's sister. As a prominent citizen with close ties to the authorities, he was able to secure the release of many Jews. He also used his material and spiritual wealth to advance and spread Torah learning in every way he was able. Though not one member of his family survived the death camps, their good deeds and devotion remain a blessing forever.

My father had expertise and influence in the import and export of manufactured goods critical to the functioning of the economy. He was one of those "essential Jews." Despite this, in April 1942, the Nazis came for him, for he was now on the police's most-wanted list. Miraculously, he was not in his main office when they came to apprehend him. The Nazis next came to our house in the middle of the night. If their objective was to terrify, they were totally successful. While they were ferociously banging on the door, my father hid behind the false wall that he had built into the attic pantry. The Nazis managed to break down the door and ran through the house searching every corner, every closet, the attic and the cellar. As they searched, they became more and more frustrated and angry. A great deal of furniture was smashed and artwork destroyed. My mother was terrified that the Nazis would unleash their frustrations against the children, burn the house down or that one of the babies might say something that would give my father away. No matter how they took the house apart, through the mercy of G-d, they found not a trace of my father.

Eventually they gave up the hunt, announcing that they would return later to take care of Leopold Cohn. My father hid in the attic's secret room for a total of 48 hours as the Nazis returned each day. During the entire ordeal he dared not make even the slightest noise for fear of alerting the Nazis.

It was clear that this threat was to the entire family, for when the Nazis found my father, they would take everyone away for harboring him. The family knew they had to act quickly. My father had already arranged with a guide to find a way across the border for the rest of the family, as a group. Like the guide who had helped me, this man was an experienced smuggler. My father went with this guide on a trial run because he wanted to be sure that there would be no chance of anything going wrong. They followed a route that was similar to the one I had used to escape. This time, though, they entered the forest further from the border and they went deeper in before they actually crossed into Hungary. Though the resulting trip was miles longer, the chances of encountering the border guards or police were much smaller. They made it into Hungary.

Because my father had been born in Serdahel, he held Hungarian papers. Though these papers were not strictly legal, as he was not a Hungarian citizen, they enabled him to move around in Hungary more easily. In addition, he spoke the language well enough to pass as a Hungarian citizen. Once inside the Hungarian border, my father decided to go to Budapest where he had no trouble finding a small room. Here he was to wait for his family to join him. My father sent the guide back for my mother and my siblings. The group that would cross the border into Hungary included my mother, 11- year-old Deborah, 9-year-old David, 8-year-old Yaakov and 2-year-old Hindi.

I remember the pervasive fear that gripped me when I made the trip. For them it had to be incredibly terrifying. Every stranger they encountered on the train was a potential informer, eager to turn a Jew over to the Nazis. When they left the train to travel on foot, the journey was also physically demanding; they had to walk for miles over difficult terrain. Through it all, mortal danger lurked around every bend and behind every tree and boulder; every unexpected sound escalated the terror. It is difficult to imagine their relief or my mother's joy at escaping the horror that she feared was their destiny. When they had crossed the frontier into Hungary, they were certain that they had made it to freedom. However, before they had traveled even a few miles inside Hungary, the border guards apprehended the entire group.

My mother and the children were taken to Samorin, a small town very close to the border, to be interrogated. There was no doubt that the authorities, the local police, fully intended to return these "foreign" Jews to the Slovak Nazis even though they knew the fate that awaited them.

After they were interrogated, my mother and the children were imprisoned in Serdahel, where two of my uncles, — David Gandel and my father's youngest brother, David Cohn — had some influence with the local government based upon their standing in the community. My uncles convinced local officials that my mother was extremely ill and in need of hospitalization. They managed to obtain a document from a doctor that certified this. After innumerable attempts, the Hungarian authorities were convinced that my mother and the children were too sick to travel back to Slovakia. Eventually, they agreed not to deport them. Instead, they took them by ambulance directly to a hospital in Budapest. For "humanitarian reasons" they were held as dangerous prisoners under armed guard day and night.

So it was that my father, mother, my two sisters, my two brothers and I were all in Budapest at the same time (Hana and Sarah were still safely hiding in Yarmot). I was searching for a place to live, my father was living in a single rented room in the city; my mother and the children were imprisoned in a hospital, waiting to be sent back to the Nazis. We were finally together in the same city, but we were completed separated.

Chapter 5

A Prayer for Survival

Budapest had always been a large cosmopolitan city made up of diverse people where a fugitive could easily blend into the background as another anonymous face. However, for a foreign Jew, the city had become a very dangerous place.

As the possibility of a German invasion increased, the Hungarian regime became more malicious, sparing no effort in hunting down the Jewish refugees hiding in the city. This intensification in their persecution of their Jewish citizens was to assure the Nazis of their complete cooperation in Germany's war against the Jews in hopes that it would stave off any need for the Nazis to invade. The police had the authority to stop anyone. They would station themselves on a corner, carefully scrutinizing pedestrians. Whenever someone appeared even slightly suspicious, they stopped him. First, they would demand his papers. As one of the officers inspected his documents, the others would question him. If the papers looked unusual in any way, if the answers were "incorrect," or if the accent was not to their liking, the police could arrest and cart him off to the police station for interrogation. Most of those who were taken by the police were guilty of something; usually they were guilty of being foreign Jews. And those found guilty of this crime received quick justice. They were returned to the Nazis.

And, of course, the police conducted searches. They searched factories, homes, warehouses and abandoned buildings, churches and synagogues, looking anywhere that might hide a refugee. Conditions were becoming so terrifying that, increasingly, people who were once sympathetic to the plight of the refugees were becoming less willing to endanger themselves or their families. Severe punishment was meted out to any citizen who might harbor a foreign refugee. Those caught breaking these laws were arrested and imprisoned; all their money and property was forfeited to the state, and many were never to be seen again. The fear spread so that even some of the Hungarian Jews were becoming reluctant to help others if it put them at risk.

Consequently my sojourn in Budapest was fraught with great danger. Even though I had forged documents attesting to my Hungarian citizenship, it was very dangerous for me to move around in public. I spoke German and Czech, but I could not speak Hungarian. If anyone would converse with me or if a policeman would question me, my response would give me away. I had to be vigilant and avoid situations in which I might be stopped and questioned. Whenever I traveled in the city, I was careful to walk with a group of people so that I would not draw attention to myself. I avoided passing close to anyone who might be a policeman. Usually, I kept my attention on the next block so that I could change direction if I saw a policeman or someone in street clothes who might be a policeman.

I was always looking for an escape route, an alleyway between two buildings, a door, or a basement window. I was ever alert for the sound of marching feet, for shouts of "open up" or suspicious whispers, for banging on the door or the slightest movement of the doorknob. When I was asleep, the slightest noise would awaken me. Every minute of every day I was ready to run for my life; I knew that my life could end at any moment. It is a state that is impossible to describe.

For my father, it was easier to live and to move around in Budapest. No one suspected that he was not a citizen; he spoke Hungarian and had papers to prove that he was born there. As a result, he had been able to rent an apartment from a Hungarian family. Hungarian Jews were still protected as citizens by the government, and my father was able to live a relatively normal life. He was living in this apartment when my mother and the children were taken prisoner and placed in the hospital under police guard.

It had been half a year since I had seen either of my parents or siblings and I wanted desperately to see them all. Though reaching my father was a difficult and perilous undertaking, it was the first thing I did after entering Budapest. His arrival to Budapest preceded mine, and through previous correspondence I had his address. When I reached my father's room, our reunion was joyous; we hugged for a long time. I was so happy to see him. My father told me how much I had changed and I felt very comforted that he had not changed at all. But if our reunion brought us great joy, it also emphasized our great sorrow. I thought I would be able to visit my mother in the hospital. But my father refused, saying that it was far too dangerous. I begged him to let me go to her. He insisted that it was impossible. The police guarded her day and night. They would surely recognize me as a refugee and imprison me with her. It was a terrible conflict for me. Both of my parents, but especially my mother, had made it clear to me that I was to survive; I knew that they wanted me to live to carry on the family name. I had no doubt about my duty to my family.

I had no place to stay. My father wanted me to move into his apartment with him. He asked the people from whom he was renting the room if I could stay with him. I was introduced to them as a relative, because it was impossible to tell them that I was his son, for I could not speak Hungarian. They looked me over from head to toe. Suddenly, in a state of near panic, they began yelling at my father, "He cannot stay here under any condition. Your relative looks like a refugee and that will bring the police here!"

I had nowhere to go, but I had no choice but to leave. My father remembered that we had relatives on my mother's side of the family who lived nearby and who would certainly take me in. I would stay with this second cousin, Jeno Weise.

Jeno and his family seemed happy to see me and they agreed to let me stay with them. I was relieved to be safe in the home of relatives and I spent the night sleeping soundly. However, when I awoke the next morning, they were already up and waiting to speak with me. Without ceremony, they told me that I could not remain another night because they did not want to risk their lives. Again I heard, "You look like a refugee. The police are bound to investigate and we will all wind up in prison." I tried other relatives, cousins of my father and then my mother, but their reactions were all essentially the same: I could not stay with them because it was against the law to harbor Jewish refugees. They could not risk their lives even for a relative.

I was 13 years old, alone in a foreign city, hunted by the police and with nowhere to sleep. I felt a loneliness that I had never known before, but I was determined to survive; I was determined to find a place to live.

A few days earlier I had met a fellow refugee, a boy named Yacob Fried. I knew that he had found a place to live, so I decided to see whether he could help me. When I found him that evening, he immediately said he was willing.

"I am renting my room from an old man," he said. "He's nearly deaf so he will not realize that you do not speak Hungarian." I thought to myself, if his eyesight also is not too good, this might work.

My friend took me to meet the landlord. He was an elderly man well into his 80's, very feeble, who hobbled only by means of a cane. After I was introduced, Yacob used gestures to explain that I wanted to rent a bed. To my surprise and relief, the landlord agreed. For at least one night, I had a place to sleep. Never was a bed more comfortable.

I stayed with my friend for two weeks. Every morning we were woken up by our landlord's recitation of his morning prayers, which we could hear through the thin walls. Since he had no teeth, he whistled with every word of his supplication. To this tuneful whistling we arose each morning.

With each passing day, my desire to see my mother grew more intensely, as did the temptation to hazard the risk of visiting her. But each day I visited my father and each day he told me curtly: "No, it is impossible." Though I always honored his decision, my grief at not being able to see her was becoming unbearable.

Thoughts of my mother and my siblings occupied my mind day and night. I knew that they were in danger, that they could all die at any moment and that only G-d could save them. One day, while I was praying at the *Chedar Has* synagogue, I was overcome by the heartache I felt for my mother. I found myself mumbling; "Master of the Universe! Please, please help my mother and my brothers and sisters!" After everyone had left the synagogue, I poured out my heart before G-d, begging that they should not be handed over to the Slovak Nazis and certain death.

I was living on my own, praying in the synagogue as an adult. But the tears of a child that I had held back through all my troubles suddenly gushed forth. I wanted to destroy the evil men who had imprisoned my family. My muffled prayers and sobs grew increasingly louder until I found myself crying out like a little boy desperate for his mother. For me, though, there was no finger to hold for comfort.

Finally, exhausted, I turned to leave. I was startled to see a man in his 50's, a distinguished and aristocratic man, standing opposite me. He had been listening to me while I was praying and crying. He was staring at me awestruck, unable to understand why a Jewish youngster might be crying so. When he asked me who I was, I knew that I could not tell him my real identity. My face turned crimson with embarrassment. This man had no doubt heard my prayers. "Why do you need to know my name?" I asked him hastily in Yiddish.[1] My first thought was that he might be an informer and that he might suspect I was a foreign Jew. In fear, I ran quickly out the door. A great unhappiness overcame me. Was it possible that fear and mistrust would follow me even into the synagogue?

Once I was outside in the dark of the night, I was an adult again, no longer a weeping baby — an adult with the responsibility of surviving, of carrying on the family name.

---

1. Yiddish was the language of Eastern European Jews, hence, speaking it would not betray my identity as a foreigner.

Chapter 6

Into the Jaws of Death

I n the fall of 1942 the Jews of Budapest and throughout Hungary were busy preparing for the holiday of Succos,[1] secure in the relative normalcy of their lives, trusting that the laws of the country would protect them because the leaders of the government would abide by those laws.[2] The Germans were infiltrating deep into Russia, and

---

1. Succos is a holiday commemorating G-d's protection of the Jewish people during their 40-year sojourn in the wilderness.

2. Indeed for the majority of the war, the Jews of Hungary fared better than the Jews throughout the rest of Eastern Europe. Under Prime Minister Miklos Kallay, appointed in March 1942, deportations halted and Jews were "subject only to tightening employment restrictions, forced-labor conscription and more extensive expropriations. Some 16,000 Jews from Austria, Slovakia and Poland even found refuge in Hungary and were not handed over to the Germans. At the end of 1942, Kallay rejected German demands to introduce yellow badges for Jews and deport them to Poland. In May 1943 Kallay, in a public speech, rejected 'resettlement' of the Jews as a 'final solution,' so long as the Germans were giving no satisfactory answer about where the Jews were being resettled." With the German occupation in March 1944, Kallay was dismissed. Lucy Dawidowicz, *The War Against the Jews*, London, 1986, pp. 379-82.

their conquering of Africa was continuing unchecked. Himmler was ordering all of the German Jews in concentration camps to be sent to the gas chambers of the Auschwitz and Majdanek death camps. Still, the Jews of Hungary were living in total faith that the Hungarian government was the instrument by which Divine Providence would protect them from the Nazis, despite the deterioration of their rights, despite the ominous signs from around the world.

The history of the Jews in Hungary supported this view. They had grown accustomed to equal protection under the law and there seemed to be little anti-Semitic feeling among the people of Hungary. Gentile and Jew had lived in harmony for as long as anyone could remember. No one wanted to believe that Jewish blood was being spilled like water in the other countries of Europe. The mind refused to accept the reports that were filtering in about the atrocities against the Jews. Once I walked into a bathhouse as a group of elderly Jews were discussing the war between Germany and Russia. In my youthful brashness, I volunteered that in Poland there were death camps where the Nazis were slaughtering thousands of Jews every day.

Immediately, one of the men jumped up and slapped me across the face, screaming: "What kind of ridiculous lies and horror stories are you spreading?!" He was so angry and offended by what I had said that when he hit me it was with such force that I found myself sprawled, lying face down on the floor. The men all stared at me in horror, not because I had been hit so ruthlessly, but because of the awful "untruth" I had uttered. They felt that I was irresponsibly attempting to scare people. The truth was so monstrous that no one would or could believe it. It was an evil so horrible that it was beyond their comprehension.

In the face of the most unbearable hardship or terrible injustice, Jews have always found solace and strength by adhering to their faith. Leopold Cohn and his son were no different. When I visited my father on the eve of the holiday he said "This year, the first night of the holiday (Succos) falls on the Sabbath. Since we are here in the city alone, we should have a special holiday meal in a restaurant."

My father knew an elegant kosher restaurant in the city that was known to provide a sumptuous meal. He decided that we would go to this restaurant at noon to make reservations to eat our holiday meal there Friday night.

I was thrilled, both by the thought of this holiday meal and all the happy memories that it engendered; this small bit of normalcy made my spirits soar. This celebration of the plenty of the harvest season had always been such a special time. We always built a most beautiful succah[3] with wonderful harvest decorations. My mother prepared the most delicious foods which we shared with our friends, neighbors and relatives.

As we made our way to the restaurant I walked with renewed energy. I thought that there was once more another blessing that would make this a truly wonderful day: I excitedly suggested to my father that we go to the hospital to see my mother. My father abruptly halted. He stood perfectly still, quietly wrapped in the deepest of thoughts. For a moment, it seemed as though he had been frozen. Just as suddenly, he turned toward me, his forehead deeply creased with wrinkles and his eyes tightly closed. The look of pain on his face took my breath away. Slowly, he whispered words that made my blood run cold: "Your mother and the children are no longer in Budapest. We did everything we could. Despite our best efforts, we could not win their release. A few days ago, the Hungarians sent them back to the Slovak Nazis. A transport train took them to Majdanek. I do not even know if they are alive."

---

3. During the eight-day holiday of Succos, Jews dwell in a temporary structure called a succah to remind us that is not our homes which afford us shelter and protection, but Hashem.

Through all of the hardships of the past months I had been sustained by the hope that somehow we would rescue my mother and the children. Every day and at every opportunity I urged my father and every relative to act, to do something to get them out of the hands of the authorities. I was devastated by my father's words. I began to cry hysterically. I felt my entire world collapsing, spinning wildly. For a moment, I thought I would pass out. However, instantly I realized that I must control myself lest my behavior attract suspicion.

But, even with our minds in utter turmoil, we continued walking side by side, neither of us saying a word. We each bore our pain silently. I understood that my father and I would, from this point, be bound together by terrible sorrow and unrelenting pangs of guilt. We both knew what Majdanek meant.

As we had originally planned, it was about noon when we approached the restaurant. My father and I were each in our own private world of sorrow and not paying much attention to our surroundings. With thoughts of my mother and the children occupying our attention, we were less careful than usual as we entered the restaurant. The instant the glass door closed behind us, I knew that we were in trouble.

We stood in a narrow dark corridor, approximately 20 feet long, which led to the charming dining hall. To our horror, the corridor was lined on both sides with Hungarian border police and detectives from the local police. My father was instantly surrounded. Two of the border police grabbed my father by his arms and shoved him against the wall. Another group of two or three detectives aggressively questioned him, rapidly shouting questions at my father, one after another, demanding that he answer.

"Show me your papers!" As one of the guards inspected his forged papers, the others continued the barrage of questions. "What's your name? Where were you born? Where do you live? What is your mother's name?" The questions were yelled at my father so rapidly that it was difficult for him to answer. As he became confused and failed to answer quickly, the questioners became more demanding, yelling at him and repeating the questions. The more confused my father appeared the more they became suspicious of him.

In all the commotion, I realized that no one was watching me. I slipped quietly along the opposite wall of the corridor into the dining hall and hid beneath one of the tables. The hall was full of religious Jews who had come to the restaurant to eat their noon meal. The people who were sitting at the table I was hiding underneath ate their lunch, acting as if there was nothing unusual going on. They did nothing to give away my hiding place. Though no one could see me in the darkness underneath the tablecloth, I was able to watch everything that was happening in the corridor.

Everyone who entered the restaurant was stopped and interrogated. When the police were finished with them, satisfied that their papers were authentic, they were allowed to continue into the restaurant. However, no one was permitted to leave the building. So they took their place at a table and tried either to enjoy their meal or to wait quietly. I noticed a handful of people were standing in a remote corner of the restaurant under police guard.

The police were still interrogating my father, so I was hopeful that they might release him. After all, he was born in Hungary, he spoke the language, and his forged papers were near perfect. Even if he was not a citizen, perhaps he could talk his way out of their clutches.

I never found out what made my father's papers unacceptable. I watched in horror as the police shoved my father across the hall until he was one of the group of suspects under house arrest in the corner.

By this time, the Nazis were allowing people to leave the restaurant and the dining area was nearly empty; most of the diners had quietly risen from their tables one at a time and walked out. From my hiding place, I saw the policemen gesture to my father and his fellow prisoners to line up. They yelled and prodded the prisoners with the nozzles of their rifles forcing them to march single file, policemen flanking them on either side. My first thought was that this could not be happening, the police could not be taking him away. My denial died quickly as I watched them march their prisoners out of the restaurant. From my hiding place, I could see that all of the policemen had accompanied the prisoners, and no one remained in the restaurant. It was safe for me to emerge from my hiding place.

My only thought was that I had to find a way to save my father. I understood that I could not let him out of my sight because I would never be able to find him again. I knew from terrible experience that the Nazis acted swiftly. To free my father, I must know where they were taking him. I had to follow, but at a distance. When they turned the street corner, I walked to the corner and watched. Once they were out of sight, I continued after them, hoping that no one would deduce that I was following the police and their prisoners. When they turned the next corner, I walked to that corner and remained there watching until they turned another corner.

As I followed, I tried to appear nonchalant, just a young person strolling about the city. I did not want attention attracted to a youth that was aimlessly walking around upset or lost. Yet, as I walked, my mind churned and my soul was awash in anguish. I had an ever-increasing sense of dread as I realized how perilous my father's situation was. For so many Jews in Pressburg, for Jews in Serdahel and Yarmot, for countless Jews in countless towns and cities, the last sight of friends or loved ones were as the police or soldiers dragged them off. They had taken my mother, two sisters, two brothers and now my father. Would I ever see any of them again? How could I save my father ... or my mother ... or my sisters and brothers? I did not know where to turn.

I did the only thing I could do. I followed the prisoners. I kept a running inventory of escape routes of alleyways, of windows and doors, of fences, parks, and woods, of anywhere that I might run or hide. With each step, I formulated one escape plan after another, for I expected at any moment someone yelling for me to stop. I was determined that these monsters would not catch me. I had to remain free if I was to help my family.

After I had followed the prisoners for about two miles, my worst fears were confirmed. There could be no doubt where they were being led — the Rumbach concentration camp. As we approached, I could see the name, Rumbach, in bold black menacing letters over the gate with smaller warning signs written in Hungarian on either side. Even though I could not speak the language, I knew that this place meant death to any prisoner taken through that gate.

Rumbach was actually a converted armory, a large brick and stone building with barred windows. In front of the building there was a large courtyard completely enclosed by a 10-foot-high two-foot-thick brick wall. The only entrance was through two large, heavy wooden doors that could open widely enough to admit a large truck. On the left-hand side of this main entrance, there was a standard-size door to permit pedestrian passage. On each side of the gate was a small guardhouse in which lurked two or three policemen. Everyone knew that this was a collecting camp for foreign Jewish refugees and that from Rumbach, Jews were loaded onto transport trains and taken back to their native countries, to Poland or Slovakia. Every refugee knew that these Jews were never to be seen again.

Despite my fright and worry, knowing where my father had been taken, there was now some chance that I could arrange for his release provided that I acted quickly. I had not the faintest idea how to accomplish this miracle. I found a spot, 200 feet from the gate, from which I could spy out the camp entrance undetected. There were enough people walking about that I would not be noticed. I stood and waited as I thought that with G-d's help, my father would be released. He did have papers and he did speak Hungarian and he was born in Hungary and ... My panicked mind raced through the reasons why they might release him.

I had been watching for a few minutes, when the camp door opened suddenly. My heart pounded wildly as I hoped to see my father. However, disappointingly, one of the secret police arrogantly emerged. The door opened a second time, but again my hopes were dashed as a policeman strolled out. The third time the door opened, the entire platoon of policemen who had searched the restaurant came out of the camp. I watched as they goose-stepped away. The door never opened again as no one else exited the concentration camp. My father's situation could not be more serious. He was not coming out of the camp unless I, with the help of G-d, found a way to get him out.

It was Friday afternoon and soon everything would be closed for the holiday. I had only a few hours left. Once the Sabbath started, no one would be able to intervene for my father's release.

I realized that my only hope was to ask one of our relatives who lived in the city for help. It took me a few minutes to reach their home. My cousins listened to my terrible news and suggested that I contact a friend of my father's who could help. I rushed to this friend's house. After listening to my story, he told me to go to the law office of a man who was a high official, a senator of the Hungarian government. This senator might be sympathetic to my father's plight and he could be bribed for a large sum of money to secure the release of a prisoner.

I stood there, in the house of my father's friend, not knowing what to do next. I did not have a cent. Where was I to procure such an enormous sum of money? It was nearly 4 o'clock in the afternoon. I was a foreigner who did not even speak the language, a 14-year-old youth who knew no one and no one knew me.

I struggled to calm myself down and took down the address. I ran to the law office with little concern for whether I would attract attention. The day was passing too quickly. In addition, it was rumored that the prisoners held in Rumbach were to be sent out the next morning to the Majdanek death camp. I only thought incessantly about the nightmare of having my father, whom I loved so much, taken off to a death camp.

Scores of people were sitting in the large waiting room of the law office. When I realized that I was the last in line, I knew I would not see the senator for hours. I was near panic, for each second that passed my father was another second closer to boarding the train to Majdanek.

When, after a few minutes, an important-looking man came out of the conference room, I rushed forward in front of everyone else. I apologized profusely, and blurted out in broken Hungarian, "I must speak to you immediately about an urgent matter of life and death. There is no time to wait!" I added that my father was very wealthy and that we could pay any sum that he asked. To my surprise my empty promise of a substantial bribe worked, for the official agreed to speak with me in his office.

As we sat in his large austere office, I deduced that this senator was an aristocrat and a nobleman. He listened to me patiently while I related my father's dire plight. I told him that I was willing to pay any amount to secure my father's release. "Money is no object," I assured him. After I finished, he assured me with great calmness and authority that according to Hungarian law, the prison director had no right to do anything with the prisoners, one way or another, until Monday of the following week. He instructed me to return after the weekend and he would see what he could do. I adamantly told him that I had heard from reliable sources that all the prisoners would be sent to Majdanek the next day. However, he dismissed my concern. "Child, don't worry, and don't pay attention to rumors. It's impossible for this to be true because it's against the law. Come back on Monday, and I'll expedite the matter and take care of everything."

I was desperate. I could not expect any help from this senator. He might be very important but how could I take the chance that the laws of Hungary would protect my father? It was too dangerous to rely on his assurances, for once my father was on that train, he would be lost forever.

I hurried back to the home of my father's friend. I ran as fast as I could with little concern for the police who were everywhere. When I reached his home, I explained that the senator had put me off until Monday. My father's friend agreed that my assessment of the situation was probably correct. He had another idea. I should approach a Mr. Kesser, an influential businessman who had connections in the government. However, Mr. Kesser did not know me and had no reason to help. I needed someone whom he respected to convince him to intervene on my behalf. My father's friend said that there was an important rabbi who might be willing to approach Mr. Kesser for me.

As each minute passed, I grew more nervous. I was no closer to rescuing my father.

I ran the entire way to the rabbi's house. I was received immediately by a member of his staff. Trying to catch my breath, I related the situation and my father's desperate dilemma as calmly as I could. He gave me a perplexed look. I thought that I must sound and look like a wild man. My heart sank when he said, "An hour before sunset? You have no time to see the rabbi now." Before I could say anything he gave me a solution "But go immediately to Mr. Kesser and tell him that the rabbi commanded that he make every effort to help you." The assistant assured me. "Mr. Kesser will do his best to get your father out."

I had renewed hope. Off I rushed, trying to marshal all my energy as I ran to Mr. Kesser's house. As I approached, I saw him, a middle-aged, well-to-do, tall, thin man, at the back door of his home, shining his shoes in preparation for the holiday. I ran up to Mr. Kesser and hurriedly related my story. As I finished, he, too, looked at me as if I had asked him to do the most outlandish thing he had ever heard.

"Now? Right now?" he asked. "Right before the Sabbath? Right before the holiday? It is not possible, I don't have time to do what you ask." Very kindly, he said, "Come back on Monday and I will see what I can do."

I demanded, "Please do something now! If we wait, it will surely be too late!"

Patiently, but emphatically, he answered, "No, I can't do anything now. There will be plenty of time later."

I was bewildered. What could I do next? Where could I turn for help? At first, I began to cry quietly. Before I knew it, I was weeping loudly, nearly hysterically, and begging him to have compassion. "Please help a Jewish child whose father is at the threshold of death." I pleaded, "All I have is my father. He is going to be given to the Nazis to be killed." Still begging, I collapsed at his feet. I was literally on the floor crying, "Please do something. Save my father." He continued to calmly shine his shoes.

I cried for a few more minutes, his polished shoes staring me in the face. Gradually, I realized that there was no hope here either, so I ceased my useless weeping. Again all my hopes were dashed. There was no way for me to save my father. I picked myself up from the floor and left the house crushed. Once out on the street, panic gripped me again. I had wasted more time and I was no closer to rescuing my father.

I dashed back to the house of my father's friend a third time. As I was catching my breath, I related the details of my visit with Mr. Kesser. A neighbor who was visiting and listening to my story volunteered that he knew a Jewish man named Mr. Dekner who might be willing to help me. This Mr. Dekner owned a successful textile business and was said to have some influence with the prison administration.

Once more I had hope. Armed with a new set of directions, I ran with the last of my energy to Mr. Dekner's home. A man in his 40's, dressed in his holiday suit, invited me inside and listened patiently to my story. I was elated when Mr. Dekner nonchalantly told me that he could free my father. However, he said, it would cost the equivalent of $5,000 to bribe the head of the prison. "And I need to hand over the money before 10 o'clock tonight if I am to have your father successfully released."

I asked Mr. Dekner, "How can I be sure that you'll get my father out?" This was not a question of trusting him with the money. I knew he would not run off with it. He was obviously a pious man and was not planning to keep even a penny for himself. My concern was whether he could deliver what he was promising. The prison guards might gladly take my money and still refuse to release my father. How could I tell that Mr. Dekner had pull with the prison guards of Rumbach?

Mr. Dekner patiently answered me. "To ease your worries, and prove that you can trust me, I'll demonstrate to you my great influence with the guards." Mr. Dekner continued, "We will bring a meal to your father in prison. When the guards permit us to enter without hesitation, it will be obvious that I have substantial influence and respect from the guards. You will know that you can have confidence in me."

Even if I had found someone who could save my father, I was still no closer to saving him. It was already very late, the holiday had already begun. I was overwhelmed and bewildered. How could I possibly find the amount of money needed to bribe the prison guards? At that time, $5,000 was the equivalent of what the average person earned over the course of several years.

There was one possibility but I had little hope that it would work. Perhaps my relatives in Budapest could help. Though they were not particularly wealthy, they might know someone who could help raise the money I needed to free my father.

I was greatly disappointed but not surprised when my cousin told me that they could raise the equivalent of $200, maybe $500. He lamented: "How can we give you a sum like that? Only the richest men in town have that kind of money." As we talked, it became clear that even if we combined the resources of the entire family there was no possibility of procuring such an enormous sum.

In desperation, my last alternative was to go to the synagogue to seek help. By the time I arrived, the congregation had already begun the evening services. I must have looked as if I had been through some great ordeal, because a number of people asked me what was wrong. I recounted my father's capture and imprisonment, and the rumor that the entire group was to be transported to Majdanek. I received many expressions of compassion and sympathy. I told those around me that I had a contact who could secure my father's release provided I could bring him the equivalent of $5,000 for the guards before 10 o'clock tonight. I pleaded, "We are not talking simply about redeeming captives." My voice grew louder, "We are talking about saving my father's life!"

I was creating a stir in the synagogue, causing more and more people to gather around. I was startled to hear someone announce, "I will give the money!"

I turned to see who had spoken and it was the man who had witnessed my prayers for my mother in the synagogue. He gave no indication that he had ever seen me before. He simply continued to look at me with a kind expression on his face and waited for my response. (I eventually learned that his name was Yitzchok Zvi Kovesy. He was a wonderful and learned man who was one of the leaders of the Budapest community. After the war, he settled in New York and in 1965 moved to Jerusalem, where he died that same year. Though he left no children, the good that he did in this world will be an everlasting memorial.)

I remembered Mr. Dekner's admonition that he had to present the money to the guards by 10 o'clock to free my father before the prisoners were to be loaded onto the train to Majdanek. "I must have the money right away. We have to hand it over by 10 o'clock!" I blurted out.

He replied gravely, "But what should I do? I cannot desecrate the Sabbath. It is strictly forbidden to do any business transactions or to handle money." Upon hearing these words, the rabbi of the congregation jumped up and declared: "Let me be part of this *mitzvah* of saving a life! Tell me where to find the money and I will go and bring it myself!" This man was Rabbi A. Babad, a refugee from Poland who knew very well what was happening to the Jews there. He also understood the fate of any Jew who entered the train that would leave Rumbach the next morning. Years later, Rabbi Babad became very famous and widely respected in America as the Rabbi of Tartkov.

These words greatly moved Mr. Kovesy. Seeing how urgent Rabbi Babad considered this matter, he quickly told me that I should come home with him after the services and he would give me the money I needed to save my father.

As soon as the services were completed, I hurried home with Mr. Kovesy. Upon entering his house, he went into his living room. In the corner of the room was his safe. He went directly to it and opened it. I realized that he did not intend to touch the money himself. Instead, he pointed to the bundles of money saying, "Take this bundle and that one and that one."[4] I picked up each bundle and counted out the entire sum. I thanked him from the bottom of my heart but my thoughts were only on getting the money to Mr. Dekner before 10 o'clock. I knew that I must not be caught by the police carrying all that money so I ran to my room and hid it there. I then raced all the way to Mr. Dekner's house. It was almost 9 o'clock when he opened the front door. As I stood there, he asked if I had brought the full amount. Without waiting for me to answer, he pushed past me and whispered, "We must hurry if we are to get everything done by 10 o'clock." We picked up the food that we would bring to my father. As we set off for the Rumbach camp, I could not help worrying that it might already be too late to save him.

I asked Mr. Dekner if he knew when the prisoners would be moved. He responded, "The guards told me that the prisoners would not be moved until early tomorrow morning." I was greatly relieved by his answer and the fact that he seemed very confident in his knowledge. If Mr. Dekner could get this food to my father then I knew I could really trust him.

We were about ten streets from the camp when I noticed that there were many Jews on the streets, more people than you would expect this late on a Shabbos evening. Many were crying. With each street, the number increased. I stopped when I recognized a familiar face, a young woman from my hometown. She was the daughter of Mr. Adler Kemfner, the counselor at the summer camp I had attended in Pressburg. For a moment, I remembered a different, carefree life. Was it possible that I had ever gone to summer camp? Playing with friends, swimming, and hiking — did this occur in my lifetime? Did these wonderful things happen only a few short years ago?

---

4. When it is a question of saving a Jewish life, all the laws regarding the Sabbath can be broken.

Miss Kemfner pleaded, "Please, could you help me save my father?"

As we got closer I encountered more people I recognized from Pressburg. A man begged for his wife and children, "Can you help me?"

As I passed people in the street, I could hear their pleas, each a different nightmare. A woman sobbing, "They arrested my husband. They are going to kill him"; a sister whose brother had been taken, "Please get him out for me"; a brother whose sister had been taken, "Did you hear that they will be shipped out tomorrow?" It seemed to go on forever. I could even see these sorrowful people huddled up and down the side streets and adjoining alleyways. I was going to save my father but I could do nothing to help them rescue their loved ones. This reality weighed heavily on me and my heart went out to these poor souls, but I was not deterred. I had to save my father.

When we were approximately three blocks from the camp, I could hear the voices and crying of the people from behind the prison wall of Rumbach. At the same time, I noticed that this close to the camp the streets were empty. Anyone loitering near the camp could only be a relative and the guards or the police would be more than happy to add more victims to their collection of "dangerous refugees."

Two thousand terrified souls crowded the yard of the detention camp. It was their pained moaning and sorrowful weeping that made one feel the terror and suffering of the prisoners.

Suddenly, I was in front of the gate to the Rumbach camp and Mr. Dekner was pounding on the door. A guard poked his head out a window and, seeing Mr. Dekner, opened the door. Mr. Dekner gestured for me to follow him into the camp. Even though I desperately wanted to see my father, walking through that door was one of the most difficult things I have ever done. Every part of my being rebelled; entering would put me totally at the mercy of these animals. My usual ritual of planning an escape for any potential disaster would be of no help once I entered the camp.

I took a deep breath to marshal all my courage and with my father's food held firmly in my hands, I walked into a vestibule which led into a hallway lined with offices. The busy officers and guards who paid attention to us were cordial to Mr. Dekner. We were quickly escorted toward a large iron door. This creaking door was pushed open into a cold concrete prison yard. Two guards standing rigidly at attention manned this door. From the compound another guard rapidly approached us. Mr. Dekner conversed briefly with the officer, who then ordered, "Bring out Leopold Cohn."

It was obvious that the guard knew Mr. Dekner well and was used to dealing with him.

While I waited, I looked around the prison yard and saw thousands of Jews sitting on the hard ground, terror flooding their eyes, not knowing what would be, all haunted by the horror stories of what would happen when their captors turned them over to the Nazis. Many were crying; some were staring into space blankly; some were quietly conversing with others; most were tearfully praying.

As I looked around from prisoner to prisoner, I was suddenly facing my father standing with the guard only a few feet away. When my father realized that it was me, he began to tremble with terror. He was confronting his worst fear, for he thought that I, too, had been arrested. Mr. Dekner quickly informed my father that this young man was his aide and that we had brought him a meal. I could see the relief in his face. When the guard was out of hearing range, I told my father that I had arranged to have him freed and that with G-d's help he would be released soon.

After we said a very polite goodbye, I turned to leave with Mr. Dekner. As we approached the gate, I learned a new meaning for the word fear. No demonstration of power and influence could guarantee that the door through the gate would open. Even though I was leaving my father and all those poor souls behind, it would be impossible for me to convey the sense of relief I felt as the door opened and we walked out to freedom.

We walked away from the prison with a feigned calmness that neither Mr. Dekner nor I felt. As soon as we were a few blocks away from the gate, I told Mr. Dekner that I trusted him and that I would give him the money for my father's ransom. Mr. Dekner looked at me sternly and warned, "You had better go quickly, it is already 9:30. We have to present the money to the head guard by 10 o'clock."

I dashed to my room, picked up the money I had hidden and set off to Mr. Dekner's house. As I speedily made my way, thoughts of being stopped by the police weighed heavily on my mind. If I were stopped, what would I say? If they found the money I had hidden on my person, what could I possibly tell them? "I am out for my evening walk and I always carry a large sum of money"?

For all my worry, I did not encounter any policemen. I knocked on Mr. Dekner's door and waited for what seemed to be a long time for him to open it. In fact, it was only a few seconds. I was aware of many emotions as I turned the money over to Mr. Dekner: I was relieved, overjoyed, petrified, and completely exhausted.

As he was leaving the house to deliver the bribe money to the guard, he must have noticed that I was still very anxious about my father's fate. "Don't worry," he said. "Your father is going to be released. It will take a day or two, but he will not be taken away with the other prisoners." He reminded me, "Tomorrow morning they are going to empty the camp, but your father is staying behind. They will check his papers carefully to make sure that they are authentic. Then they will let him go because he is a Hungarian citizen."

He spoke with such authority that I felt much more at ease as we went in different directions. However by the time I reached my room, my anxiety had returned; it worsened with each passing minute. I could do only one thing: pray. The whole night, I prayed without stopping, it was not possible for me to sleep. As morning approached, I was overwhelmed by feelings of loss and sadness. I began to cry uncontrollably. I felt so alone and abandoned. I pleaded, "Isn't it enough that I've lost my mother, my sisters and brothers?" With morning's first light, I asked, "Will I now lose my father too? Please, spare him, free him from his captors, and return him to me."

I could not bear the thought that even my father was gone. The brilliant light of the rising sun could not dispel the darkness that had enshrouded my soul.

As I had done a number of times when things became unbearable, I realized that I could not allow myself to be overcome by these feelings of despair. With the help of G-d, my father would be saved. As soon as it was daylight, I dressed and started off to the prison to see my father.

I was about three blocks from the prison when I realized that something was horribly wrong. Yesterday, there had been such a din from the talking, crying, and wailing of the thousands of prisoners that were being held in the camp that I could hear them three or four blocks away. Now, I heard nothing; all was still. I shuddered as I thought, "It is as quiet as a graveyard." My mind raced as I ran the remaining three blocks, throwing all caution to the wind. "What has happened to everyone?" I asked myself.

As I reached the gate, it dawned on me that all the captives were gone. There was not a sound! I thought my heart would stop beating. I looked around frantically. The gate was closed but there were a few solitary souls who were standing forlornly outside the wall of the compound. They were paralyzed by the overwhelming tragedy that had befallen them. They stood there in shocked disbelief, tearfully and helplessly whimpering. I went from person to person, asking, "What happened? Where are the prisoners?"

Two or three people ignored me. Then someone answered me, "The police emptied the prison in the middle of the night. They loaded them all on a train and sent them to be slaughtered. My husband is gone."

Another man interrupted his sobbing to say, "They took them to Majdanek."

It was impossible. My father could not have been taken. I had saved him. I was nearly paralyzed with fright and worry. What could I do to get him off that hateful train? I went along the wall asking each person, "What happened? Where are all the people? Was anyone left in the camp?"

I did not know where to turn. Someone said that a number of policemen had remained inside the camp and that there was still one Jew that they were holding.

Maybe Mr. Dekner had indeed done as he had promised. This man had to be my father. I remembered that Mr. Dekner had told me that my father would not be taken away, that he would not be released for a few days.

Later that day Mr. Dekner confirmed that the single person who remained in the Rumbach detention camp was my father and that he would be moved in a couple of days to a city prison from where he would eventually be released. This is exactly what happened. Within a couple of days he was transferred out of Rumbach. However, the length of his stay in the Budapest prison seemed indefinite.

Chapter 7

A Boy With No Family

With my father incarcerated, I was on my own. At least I had a roof over my head, for I and my friends were still renting a room from the deaf man. When we were alone in our room, my friend and I were able to speak freely without worrying about our foreign accents. Each day, our main concern was not attracting attention as we traveled throughout the city.

One morning after services I remained in the synagogue for there were two men who had just escaped from the Birkenau[1] concentration camp. They were cloaked in dirty,

---

1. Birkenau was built as an extension to Auschwitz and was even called Auschwitz II. Eventually it would be the site of four gas chambers and crematoria. The evacuation of Auschwitz/Birkenau was hasty as the Soviet army neared in late 1944 and did not allow for extensive destruction of the camp, an act which the Nazis perpetrated in other death camps. Today, Auschwitz I and II are part of a museum and research center. Niewyk and Nicosia, *The Columbia Guide to the Holocaust*, New York, 2000, pp. 194-5. For further reading see Gutman and Berenbaum, *Anatomy of the Auschwitz Death Camp*, Washington, D.C., 1994.

torn clothing. They were extremely weak, appearing as if they had risen from the grave, trembling with fear, more dead than alive. I hovered on the edge of the group that converged around these two men.

"The suffering and torture is unimaginable," they claimed. "Every day, Jews are arriving from other camps, where they are greeted with torture and then annihilation.

"Our job in the camp was to assist in the disembarking of people from the trains," they continued breathlessly trying to get their story out as quickly as possible. "We were always stationed at the side of the train, as the men, women and children exited the railway cars. We agreed that each of us would keep an eye on the Nazi guards. As soon as we felt that we were not being watched, we ducked, one at a time, underneath the train and concealed ourselves in the narrow space between the wheels and the floor of the car. When the train pulled out of the camp we escaped unnoticed, not moving until we arrived at the next station. When everything was quiet, we crawled into the woods. Once there, we hid during the day and traveled at night, using the darkness as our protection."

Though amazed at their courage and resourcefulness, I could not help but worry about my mother and young siblings. They had been sent to Majdanek. What of their fate? Were they also being tortured? Were they even alive? I had no idea.

"Where do these Jews on the train come from?" one of the congregants asked.

"The trains come from everywhere. This last train had all the prisoners from Majdanek. As I hid under the train I cried for them because I knew they were all to be murdered."

What happened next I do not remember, for I reeled in shock, my hopes for my family dashed. It seemed my mother, sisters and brothers were gone forever. There was nothing I could do to bring them back. I would never see any of them again. How was this possible? How could such a thing happen?

Somehow, in a daze of sorrow, I lumbered back to my room, collapsed onto my bed, crying myself to sleep. Upon awakening, I forced myself to focus on my father, the only hope I still possessed. He was soon to be released from prison and somehow I had to make sure that nothing went wrong. For the next three or four weeks all my energy and prayer were concentrated on his deliverance. Each day, I stood anxiously outside the prison and waited with great anticipation. As I stood, I remembered my mother, sisters and brothers, while fighting back the tears that would very often cascade down my cheeks. Each evening I would return, disappointed, to my apartment, to rest for the next day.

One evening, upon entering my room I found my friend crying. Before he could say anything to me, I realized that our landlord's son, a well-dressed businessman in his 30's, was there. He approached me menacingly, and without any greeting, demanded my identification papers. He made a show of it as he inspected them with meticulous care.

"Both of you are refugees," he said with fearful anger. "You are putting my poor father's life into great jeopardy. Take your belongings and leave the premises immediately before you bring the police upon us!"

"Please let us stay, even if it is just for the night," I begged desperately. "The police are everywhere," I continued, "if we are out after dark, they will definitely apprehend us."

The landlord's son knew as well as we did that at night the city streets were extremely dangerous. The police, posted at every corner, constantly scoured the streets for Jewish refugees. If we were forced to leave now, there was no doubt we would be detained and questioned. It would not take them long to conclude that my papers were counterfeit. We would be arrested, held at the Rumbach collecting camp and sent to Majdanek, and then on to the death camps at Birkenau. The police had intensified their already diligent searching, round-ing up even more refugees the day after the Majdanek camp had been emptied. The police, we would soon learn, were so aggressive and efficient that it took them only two weeks to refill the camp.

It was clear that beneath his adamant visage our landlord's son was very frightened, and understandably so. Like so many Hungarian Jews, he was afraid that foreign Jews would provoke the authorities. It was against the law and unpatriotic to assist foreigners. Above all, such illegal activities were severely punished. Everyone knew that the Fascists were looking for any excuse to persecute the Jews and that they would attack anyone who interfered with their plan. The Hungarian government knew this well, hunting and deporting Jewish refugees as part of their effort to appease the Germans. They felt it was prudent to return all foreign Jews to their own country hoping that in return for their aggressive cooperation, the Germans would leave them in peace.

The landlord's son responded callously to my pleading and begging, "I am not interested in your problems or anything that you have to say. You are to leave this house immediately!"

I fell to his feet crying and pleading to be allowed to stay until morning. Like a stone, he remained unmoved and refused to listen. In desperation, I ran to the kitchen, grabbed a large knife and offered it to him.

With tears in my eyes, I screamed at him, "Here's the knife. If you are so interested in my death, go ahead and kill me! Do it right now, in your father's house, in front of him, before his very eyes. But don't deliver us to the Nazis and have them kill us. Better to die by the hands of a Jew and not by the hands of our Nazi persecutors. I will not be led to slaughter by those monsters!"

I shocked the son with the ferocity of my emotions, and at that point G-d softened his heart. For the first time he recognized the absolute desperation of our dilemma. He was visibly shaken, and made an effort to proffer his sympathy for our plight. He finally relented, agreeing to let us stay until the morning despite the danger to himself and his father. This act of compassion would save us for another day.

The next morning, as we quickly and silently dressed, our benefactors were up and waiting impatiently for us to leave. At this hour there would be no police walking the streets. No one would stop us and no one would ever know we had been hidden in this house.

My friend and I searched for a place to stay together, but after a few hours we decided that it would probably be easier to find a place as individuals than as a pair. We separated, agreeing to meet later in the afternoon. I wandered the rest of the day throughout the city looking for any place where I could safely stay. My efforts were futile; no one was willing to provide a room for me.

My first thought was to go to the synagogue to find help. However, when I entered, I realized that even here finding a place would be difficult. How could I approach anyone with a request that they hide a foreign Jew? I went into the study hall and listened to the lectures and discussions with the intention of spending the night.

When the lectures ended and everyone left, I had the hall to myself. I was already lying on a study bench when the caretaker entered to make his final check for the night. He spied me immediately and brusquely informed me that I would have to leave.

I told him I was visiting from another city and that I had nowhere to stay. I pleaded, "Please let me sleep here. If I'm on the street, the police will arrest me."

"But if I let you stay they will arrest me!" As he went on, I began to cry and beg frantically. At night, not only was there the ever-present danger of the police, but also the weather was frigid — the lashing wind put the temperature well below zero. Even if I could avoid the police, the cold made sleeping on the street impossible.

The caretaker, an émigré from Poland, had to know what was happening in Birkenau. I am sure he recognized that I was also a refugee and he was aware that the concentration camps would be my fate if the police caught me. After listening to my pleas, the caretaker relented and agreed to let me stay in the synagogue's drafty attic, but only on condition that I was gone before anyone returned to the synagogue for prayers or studies the next morning. He did not want anyone to find out that he had allowed me to spend the night. He locked me in the attic. He understood that even this small kindness could have severe repercussions for him.

For the moment, with the door locked, I was safe. However, the attic was extremely cold. With no blanket, I curled up inside my coat and tried to stay as warm as possible. Unable to sleep, I spent the night listening to the howling wind and my chattering teeth. At least I was not out on the street with the police.

At dawn, as he had promised, the caretaker unlocked the door and told me to leave the synagogue. If it had been cold in the attic, it was no warmer on the street. I went directly to a nearby *mikveh*,[2] the only place that was open so early in the morning. Here, I was able to warm up a little before I renewed my search for a place to live. In this manner, I moved around the city; staying in one place for one night, moving on the next day to a new place.

With each passing day, it was becoming more obvious that it would take longer than I expected for my father to be released and that I would have to care for myself. Almost every day, I encountered other Jewish refugees, living the same unpredictable, transient life as I was. These people

---

2. A *mikveh* is a Biblically prescribed body of water that is used for ritual and spiritual cleansing.

became an important part of my day-to-day existence. Each day we would meet at some preset location where we talked, planned, and helped each other survive. During one of these discussions, I mentioned that I had family in a small city outside Budapest. One of my friends urged me to leave and stay with these relatives. In a small town, a visiting relative might not attract that much attention. Perhaps with the papers that I had, I could even enroll in a yeshiva and study. For Hungarian Jews, life had not yet been disrupted; they retained their basic rights as citizens, and Jewish children still attended yeshiva.

I decided to seek shelter with my mother's cousins, a family by the name of Breuer. The Breuer family was well to do. They owned a successful printing and paper business. They resided in Shafran, a small prosperous city west of Budapest with a population of 60,000. The Jews there enjoyed good relations with the local officials and police. Furthermore, the police chief was purported to be a fine person who usually set free any foreign Jews brought to his station. If I should be caught and identified as a refugee, my relatives would be able to help. I made the trip by train. As always, there were police lurking about on the lookout for refugees. Though I was petrified the entire trip, I attempted to appear as inconspicuous as possible. I sat between two groups of Jews hoping that the police would assume I was with one of them. I was constantly looking toward the front of the car and then behind me to see if anyone was checking the passengers. I was determined not to be captured; I was even prepared to jump from the moving train. Thank G-d, no policeman thought it necessary to question me.

We reached the city by dusk. I disembarked with the same group I had been sitting with, trying to appear as if I belonged to them, and went directly to my relative's home. In the town, I was greeted as a Hungarian Jew visiting relatives in Shafran. No one suspected that I was a foreign refugee. All assumed that I was a citizen just like everyone else.

The Breuers made me feel welcome in their home and helped me to procure papers that belonged to another cousin who was a Hungarian citizen. They immediately registered me in yeshiva as their cousin with the family name of "Gandel." Since Yiddish was the only language spoken in yeshiva, my inability to converse in Hungarian was not a problem.

After everything that had happened to me and to my family, my time living with the Breuers — studying and praying in the yeshiva — provided the semblance of normalcy and stability that I desperately needed. Though I was still terribly saddened over my mother, my siblings, and my father, I could feel myself gaining strength and determination. My relative well being would prove short-lived.

Each day in yeshiva, we would listen to a two-hour lecture by a distinguished scholar. We were given the topic in advance and were expected to prepare for each class. I always studied with more advanced students in the hope that I would understand the lesson more clearly. Three weeks into my schooling at this yeshiva, we had to prepare for a lecture to be given by the dean of the yeshiva himself on a topic so complex that not even the best students were able to prepare properly.

The dean began his lecture and, upon reaching the most confusing point, stopped his discourse, called out my name and demanded, "Gandel, please explain this problem for us." Being the youngest student in the yeshiva and very shy, I was startled that I had been singled out; even if I had known the answer, I would not have been able to give it.

I stood paralyzed and in a panic. In front of the entire student body, the dean addressed me: "Young man, do not come here and waste our time. A person like you is not needed in our yeshiva. You are to collect your things and leave by tomorrow!"

I had been completely humiliated in front of all the students, and totally stunned at the unexpected turn of events. To be expelled from a yeshiva is the greatest shame; it is a black mark on a person's record that he carries with him and suffers from the rest of his life. After the lecture, many students were distressed and expressed their sympathy, for no one knew the answer to the dean's question. I related the story to my cousins in hopes that they would intercede on my behalf, but they were unable to sway the dean's decision.

Many thoughts ran through my mind: Why did he do this to me? What do I do now? I was a refugee, my mother and siblings had been sent to death camps. Who knew when or if my father would ever be freed from prison. Finally I had a place of refuge in Shafran, and then this happened!

The next day I dejectedly went to the yeshiva to collect my books and say goodbye to my friends. Naively, I went to the dean's office to pay my respects. I was allowed into his office where I found him sitting at his desk. He looked at me and spoke with great anger. "You misled me. I have been informed that you are an imposter, that you are an illegal refugee." With great seriousness, he continued, "I cannot keep you here because it is against the law to harbor refugees. Your presence endangers the entire school. You must leave immediately."

Now I understood. Dismissing me from school for my lack of scholarship was only a ruse. The dean had discovered that my papers were counterfeit. He publicly dismissed me over my inability to answer a question so that no one would suspect that I was being dismissed because I was a foreign Jew.

The dean, like so many other Hungarian Jews, did not want the police to discover that he was hiding a refugee. To save one Jew meant endangering the lives of all the Jews in the entire city. The entire world was going insane. They did not want to bring this trouble into their homes.

Expelled from the yeshiva, I had to find a new place to study. The Breuers pointed out that since the dean knew my true identity, it was no longer safe for me in Shafran. I mentioned that I had friends from Pressburg who were safely

This picture of me was taken in 1942 when I was a student in the Yeshiva of Pupa.

residing in the city of Pupa. I might find a safe haven with them. At least I knew people there. One of my cousins suggested that I study at the highly respected yeshiva of the city of Pupa, led by the great Rabbi Yosef Greenwald.

Outside of the Great Yeshiva of Pressburg, The Yeshiva of Pupa was the most organized and biggest yeshiva in all of Europe. However, since the Nazis had closed the yeshivas in Czechoslovakia, there was an overflow of boys on a waiting list for this school. The yeshiva was already severely overcrowded; about 350 students were occupying rooms intended for 250, making it impossible to find dormitory space. Even if I was admitted, the semester had already begun, and I would have an extremely difficult time catching up with the other students. The Pupa approach to the study of Torah was significantly different than the approach I learned as a student in Pressburg. Furthermore, I was concerned that the students were all 18 years or older; many were very advanced in their knowledge and training. I was much younger and much less experienced. I was also afraid that they would discover my real identity and again I would have to flee. I dreaded having to endure the same embarrassment as in the yeshiva at Shafran.

I tried to think my way through this, but realized that I had very little choice. I could no longer stay in Shafran and I needed to have a yeshiva where I could continue my studies and training. I had nowhere else to go, and I did have friends from Pressburg living in Pupa. So, I set out for Pupa and my new life.

Once again I made a perilous trip by train. I had become quite good at camouflaging myself. This time I pretended to be one of the children of a traveling Jewish family. No one questioned me and I arrived safely. The first thing I did was to go to the yeshiva, where I was greeted warmly by the students and teachers. They were quick to point out, however, that I could not stay there because it was already extremely crowd-

Grand Rabbi Yosef Grunwald, the Pupa Rav

ed. Also, in order to be admitted, I would have to pass an entrance exam, and even if I passed the difficult test, I would have to wait for someone to leave so I could take his place. It seemed clear that I would not be allowed to attend this yeshiva. Nevertheless, I went directly to Rabbi Yosef Greenwald, the head of the yeshiva, to plead my case. When I met him, I felt compelled to tell the truth about myself, unlike my conduct at Shafran.

As I finished, I expected the rabbi to send me on my way, as so many others had before. To my amazement and great relief, in this man's eyes I saw only compassion. The rabbi comforted me, saying, "Do not be afraid, Avrohom. I will protect you. You will stay with me."

He was true to his word. He kept a special eye out for my welfare. He became like a father to me, providing for my physical, intellectual, and spiritual well-being. In his shelter I found refuge. Thus life in Pupa provided a measure of safety and calm. From Rabbi Yosef Greenwald, I was privileged to learn

Torah, morals and ethics, love of mankind and, above all, love of G-d. I shall forever be grateful to him, my mentor.

When I arrived in Pupa, my father was still being detained in prison. To my great relief, he was released two weeks later. He remained in Budapest, and our only contact was through the mail. We wrote to each other every day. He was able to obtain money through a banker he knew and managed to send me enough to provide for my needs. Though he was out of jail, I worried constantly for his safety. I knew too well that his "perfect papers" did not guarantee it.

The opportunity to study in the Yeshiva of Pupa was a landmark in my personal development. The knowledge that I acquired there was one of the great blessings of my life. I received much from the students, learning by the examples they provided. They were totally disciplined in their studies, working mightily in Torah. The faculty of the yeshiva made every effort to impart the finest traits of character, intellect, scholarship and community. As a result, the students of this yeshiva were a magnificent example of mutual respect, cooperation and support. I came to understand that all these traits were a reflection of the character, holiness, example and dedicated labor of Rabbi Yosef Greenwald, the Pupa Rov.

Chapter 8

The Beast Comes for the Hungarian Jews

On March 19, 1944, the German army invaded Hungary.[1] I had been studying in Pupa for a year and a half and during this time, the war arena had changed dramatically. Germany was being defeated in ever-increasing frequency. England, Russia and the United States were dumping hundreds of thousands of tons of bombs on Germany itself. With D-Day less than three months away, the Nazis were stepping up their war against the Jews for now it was obvious that they were losing their war against the world.

If there was ever any doubt that the persecution of the Jews in Pressburg had been a carefully choreographed pro-

---

1. Though the Hungarian government officially allied itself with Germany in signing the Triparite Pact in October 1940, their Prime Minister, Miklos Kallay, did what he could to disentangle his country's involvement with the Reich. As a result of Hungary's unwillingness to wholeheartedly do Germany's bidding, Hitler invaded it in March 1944.

gram, the invasion of Hungary[2] proved it. When the Germans came to Hungary, we experienced again the same terrors we had endured in Pressburg. Jews were deprived of their livelihoods as their businesses and property was confiscated; their houses were expropriated and given to the Nazis; their daughters and sons were forcibly taken to work camps. The Nazis misled us for in reality, the work camps were really death camps. Jews who had not yet been taken were herded into ghettos; their money and their personal property were declared free for the taking. All of this was done behind the facade of the law.

As in Pressburg, and throughout Europe, the Nazis achieved their ends in incremental steps, but in Hungary the process transpired more rapidly. The violence directed toward the Jews increased dramatically and diabolically each day, until no Jew was free from their brutality, whether they be adults, the elderly or children. Babies in front of their mothers, and wives in front of their husbands were beaten and killed joyfully in the streets.

The Nazis implemented their policies shrewdly, efficiently and viciously, overwhelming the Hungarian Jews who scarcely understood what was happening to them. They believed that the new persecution was only a passing phase and trusted that they would be safe under the protection of the long-standing laws of Hungary. They never believed that their beloved Hungarian government would cooperate with the Nazis in carrying out the same horrors that they had perpetrated in other countries.

---

2. In January 1943 a committee of Zionists, headed by Dr. Rudolf Kastner, negotiated with Eichmann to trade Jewish lives for money and goods. Kastner and the Zionists wanted young Jewish people to help build up Zionism in Israel. "According to Kastner, the SS man promised that for 6.5 million pengo, 600 Jews would be permitted to leave for Palestine ... Eichmann stated in his memoirs that Kastner 'agreed to keep the Jews from resisting deportation ... if I would close my eyes and let a few hundred young Jews emigrate illegally to Palestine.' These Zionist co-conspirators then set about to lull 750,000 doomed Hungarians to order to save 600 Zionists for themselves. Hilberg, *The Destruction of the European Jews*, New York 1985, vol. II pp. 842-7.

It was understandable to the loyal Jewish populace that refugee non-Hungarian Jews could be arrested and sent back to the Nazis in their native countries to be dealt with according to the laws of their own land. However, the Hungarian Jews thought they were protected by their laws and legal traditions. The government might be antagonistic, but it would never give them up to the Nazis. They had only to wait out this phase, and things would return to normal. However, by May 15, 1944, the Nazis were deporting Hungarian Jews to Auschwitz,[3] the most diabolical of all the death camps.[4]

There is a saying, "There is no man as wise as the man of experience." My father and I had seen the Nazis in action in Pressburg. We had lived through the nightmare of persecution that followed each act of terror. We had seen firsthand how the common citizens, people who knew and lived with us, would look the other way as each new terror was inflicted on their Jewish neighbors. It was clear to my father that Hungarian Jewry was doomed the instant the Germans crossed the Hungarian border.

The Nazi policy was to establish a ghetto or "Jewish Quarter" in each of the key cities. All the Jews from the surrounding area were required to leave their homes and move into the ghetto. Each ghetto was surrounded by barbed wire or walls and was characterized by overcrowding, starvation and slave labor. Eventually, all the ghettos were sealed and the Jews were deported to the death camps.

Within just a few weeks, the situation for the Hungarian Jews had deteriorated seriously. The government, under the direction of the Nazis, had issued a directive establishing that Jews were to move into designated ghetto areas in many of

---

3. By July 7 of that year over 437,000 Jews, 50,000 of them from Budapest, had been taken to Auschwitz. Dawidowicz, *The War Against the Jews*, New York, 1975, p. 381.
4. Over 2,300,000 Jews were murdered in Auschwitz. Levin, *The Holocaust*, New York, 1973, p. 316.

the larger cities. Within two weeks, they announced that the ghettos would be closed. Any Jew that was outside when the ghetto was closed would be arrested and sent to a work camp.

As these changes were occurring, a man I did not know visited me at the Pupa Yeshiva with a message. He related that my father was instructing me to leave Pupa immediately and return to Budapest. The messenger handed me a new set of false papers with a new identity.

My name was to be Jan Kovic. I was to become a non-Jew.

However, I resembled a young Jewish boy from the yeshiva. If I were to pass as a non-Jew, I would have to change my appearance drastically. I needed to remove my *peyos*, a clear sign of my ancestry.[5] I went directly to a barber who was patronized by most of the yeshiva students. I asked him to style my hair to make me look like the non-Jewish boys in the neighborhood. He understood instantly that I was planning to leave the city; that I had no intention of being relocated. He went into a rage, yelling at me that I had no right to flee.

"I know what you are trying to do. You are trying to escape! You will be breaking the law. I will have no part of it." He screamed at me, "*Dina d'malchusa dina*," he railed. "The law of the land is the law."

I returned to the yeshiva and convinced one of the students who knew how to cut hair to do me the favor. Even with my haircut, my clothing still branded me a yeshiva student. My long coat was very different from the short standard waist-length coat worn by the local boys. I asked a Jewish tailor to alter my coat. He reacted exactly as the barber had, railing on and on about the law and how he would not help me break it.

"I know what you are trying to do," he said accusingly, "You are trying to escape the ghetto, and I will not help you!"

5. Based on the verse from the Torah, "You shall not round the corners of your head" (*Leviticus* 19:27), Jewish men and boys allow the hair behind their ears to grow long. This hair is called "*peyos*."

I found another tailor to alter the coat. I purchased a cap similar to the military hat that was worn by the non-Jewish boys. Cloaked in my new disguise, I purchased a train ticket and set off for Budapest, looking like a young Christian citizen with the papers to prove it.

My return trip to Budapest was uneventful. My relief upon reaching my destination alive was nothing compared to my joy upon seeing my father for the first time in two years. We embraced wordlessly for a long time. I could see tears in my father's eyes.

As it turned out, my father's timely directive saved my life, for a few days later, the Pupa ghetto was sealed, as was the fate of the Jews within. Next would come the trains to take "selected" individuals to work camps and then to their deaths. Eventually, the trains would come for all.

This reality tempered the joy of our reunion. We both knew that Budapest was, at best, only a temporary refuge for us. The Jews of Budapest would share the same fate that befell Jews whenever or wherever the Nazis gained power.

The entire time after his release from prison, my father had been able to stay in contact with friends who had survived back in Pressburg, for it was still possible to transport letters across the border. From these friends we learned that the situation in Pressburg was actually better than the conditions in Hungary.

By the end of 1942, the deportations of Jews from Slovakia had decreased greatly. The main wave of murder and destruction had passed over Pressburg, and the searches and arrests had dramatically diminished. Though there had been no official change in policy, this seemed to be a response by the Slovak officials to the efforts of underground Jewish leaders,[6] and also

6. This was due mainly to the efforts of Rabbi Michoel Dov Weissmandl, by means of a $50,000 bribe to Dieter Wislicency, the Nazi representative in Slovakia in the summer of 1942, which staved off any continued deportations of the Jews of Slovakia for two entire years. Abraham Fuchs, "The Unheeded Cry," Brooklyn, 1984, p. xii.

to the bureaucratic chaos that had been caused by the loss of so many Jews from important positions. Only a minute remnant of the original Jewish population of the city was left. Ninety percent of the Jews of Slovakia had been deported. There remained a tiny minority who were so important to the functioning either of the government or the economy that they still had permits that protected them from deportation.

There were also a few Jews hiding under assumed identities or being hidden by Christians. Though the Nazis were certainly aware of their existence, they were not bothering to hunt them down — at least not for the time being.

Knowing all this, we agonized over our choices and finally decided that the wisest and safest thing to do was to return to Pressburg. Ironically, the only way to go back was to cross the border secretly. Even with the best counterfeit identification papers, it was not possible for us to walk back through the guarded border checkpoint. It was simply too dangerous. On the other hand, the frontier was guarded even more heavily now and crossing back would be more dangerous than when we had escaped from Slovakia.

With much prayer and G-d's help, my father found a smuggler who was willing to take us across the border to safety. The man demanded the equivalent of about $5,000 for each of us. Half was to be paid in advance, half after we reached the other side. At the time, this was a huge sum of money. However, as I was to learn, the risks were even greater.

The prospect of signing on with this smuggler was very frightening. The man had no reputation as a successful guide for refugees. He had never taken anyone across the border. The route that he proposed had only been used to transport smuggled goods; he had never taken people over this trail. Moreover, we could not even be certain of a minimal level of honesty in the smuggler. He could easily take our money and then report us to the authorities. In addition, the train trip to get close to the border would also be extremely dangerous. In Hungary, anyone traveling toward the border immediately attracted the attention of the authorities. Even if our papers were checked and approved, we would be watched very closely.

My father decided that I should go first. He found it impossible to leave me behind. He was convinced that no one could be safe in Hungary and that the dangers were increasing by the minute. He reasoned that, if I were captured, he might be able to secure my release. There was a chance that I could be freed because I was so young and traveling alone.

Our parting was extremely difficult. We had known so much fear and pain already, and we were about to cross the very same border that had already claimed my mother, brothers and sisters. Yet, our parting was also an act of faith. If the trials that we had endured at the hands of our persecutors had taught us anything, it was that we had to place ourselves in the hands of G-d and then do what we had to do to survive.

My heart was heavy and my legs felt like lead as I set out. It took all my strength to walk away from my father again. As I boarded the train, I was alone. The trip from Budapest to the border was several hundred miles, and it took a full day of travel. To my total surprise, the day on the train passed without incident.

Whenever the train stopped at a station, all boarding passengers were questioned and scrutinized. Those who appeared Jewish were detained. Many passengers were taken off the train. Some were entire families, including women and children. Watching them being escorted away from the locomotive under guard was particularly heartbreaking for me. As the train began to move out of the station, I could not take my eyes away from these poor families; I could only see my mother and my young siblings.

I disembarked from the train about thirty miles from the border and walked to where I was to rendezvous with the smuggler. During my stay in Hungary, I had walked many miles, but these few were among the most difficult. My knees were literally shaking. As I walked toward the frontier, I felt like a rabbit who could only reach the safety of his burrow by scooting through a thicket where he knew a fox lay in wait to devour him. Like the rabbit, my only hope was to be quicker and smarter than the fox.

I arrived at the meeting place before the smuggler. I was to identify him by a long yellow feather he was wearing in his hatband. I stood off to the side of the road near the high bushes trying to be inconspicuous, prepared to escape into the woods if need be. As I observed the people passing by, I noticed that some men and women had begun to congregate at an intersection a short way down the road. They were all dressed like the local peasants.

As the group increased in number, I scrutinized them carefully. My heart sank. I realized that these people were all Jews. There were about twenty men and women. How could such a large group hope to get across a heavily patrolled border without being detected and caught? Most likely, this group was doomed. Local gentiles walking by stopped and spied this conspicuous group and went off. I knew for a fact they were on their way to police headquarters to inform on them.

I was presented with a horrible dilemma. I had no sense of how to get across the border on my own. I knew the general direction, but knew nothing of the traps or dangers that I would encounter. I decided to stay a significant distance from the group, close enough to be able to observe their movements, but not so close that I would be seen if this group was apprehended. I hid in a sewer culvert near the intersection. The reeds were thick and high enough that I could hide but still peek out to see if the guide had arrived.

At the appointed hour, a man appeared wearing a hunting hat that sported a long conspicuous yellow feather. The entire group, by now numbering more than 20, surrounded the guide. After a few minutes of instruction, with the smuggler in the lead, they trudged off toward the border. As they moved off into the gathering darkness of early evening, I watched from my hiding place. I fully expected that at any instant a platoon of Nazi soldiers would burst from the cover of the fields to capture this wretched band.

I noted the direction they took and the route they traversed through the fields. When I could no longer see them, I scanned the area carefully, crawled out of hiding and followed along the path that the group had taken. I was very careful to keep a good distance away because I knew they would be captured. As darkness fell, the smuggler led the group across fields and orchards, between stables and farmhouses, into and out of the forest. The group walked in the darkness for at least two hours. The entire time I am certain that my own fear and trembling must have mirrored the terror of each member of the group. It was about midnight when we suddenly heard a voice bark out in German, "Halt!"

I dropped to the ground. The Nazis had discovered the group. Quickly, I scampered into a field of thick cornstalks. The corn was taller than I by half a meter so that I could safely stand up. I ran with my head lowered, as fast as my legs could go, driven by the total terror that I felt. All the while I was certain that the Nazis were aiming their rifles in my direction. As I ran, I listened for gunfire for I expected the bullets to hit my body at any moment.

I was carrying all my worldly possessions in two knapsacks which were very heavy, causing my legs to tire quickly. When I thought it was safe, I hid under some bushes to rest and catch my breath. As I cowered under them, I heard footsteps coming toward me and realized that the Nazi soldiers were looking for individuals who ran when the group was stopped. To lighten my load, I hid one of the knapsacks under the bushes and started running again. I ran like a greyhound for a few hundred meters, dashing from one field to the next. It was very dark so they could not see me, but the Nazis heard me and the soldiers kept closely on my trail. Bullets whistled over my head as the Nazis shot in my direction. I was sure that they knew where I was as the bullets screamed by me closer and closer. I ran even faster and heard even more shots. Again, I became very tired; my legs almost refused to move but I forced myself to go on. As my legs began to cave in, I threw off the second knapsack and my overcoat. The voices of the Nazis were closing in on me. There were more shots but by now I realized that they were shooting into the field randomly, hoping to hit one of the refugees. I put my entire trust in G-d and started moving again. I was completely exhausted. I ran a few meters and then crawled for a few meters hoping to regain some strength. After a few hundred meters more I collapsed, terrified and exhausted; I could go no further. I lay there hiding among the cornstalks with the Nazis running through the fields on either side of me. I lay perfectly still, not moving a single muscle, scarcely breathing for fear that I would make a noise and give away my hiding place. After some time, I sat up listening for the sounds of the men who were hunting me. As I tried to clear my thoughts, I was surprised to hear voices speaking German. I realized that while I was lying on the ground, I had fallen soundly asleep. I did not know if minutes or hours had passed. The voices I heard were the Nazis interrogating the people they had captured from the group. They must have had the group walk in my direction while I was asleep. From the sound of the voices, they were now extremely close.

"What is your name? Where are you from? Where are you going? Who is helping you?" The Nazi soldiers were barking questions one after another at their prisoners. As I listened to the prisoners, it was clear from their accents and names that all of them were Jewish. It sounded like many were crying, pleading and begging the Nazis to release them. Many of the Jews were praying. I could hear the soldiers screaming at the prisoners,

"You are all Jews. You are all under arrest. Get in line!"

I heard the order given by the Germans: "March!" I heard the cries and pain of the prisoners as the Nazi gun butts ushered them along. I could hear weeping and the desolate shuffling of feet. I knew that these were dead people.

I was curled up among the cornstalks like a baby in a crib. Desperately, I prayed that some lone soldier was not lurking in the night, waiting for me to move so that I could be added to the group of Jews captured that night. The sounds of footsteps and voices grew distant, until all was quiet.

I stayed perfectly still, frozen in terror. With the wild chase over, new worries raced through my mind, for I had lost all sense of direction, "Which way should I go?" I lifted my head up barely enough to look around the field. I knew that the Nazis had marched their prisoners back the way I had fled. Probably they were marching them toward the nearest town. If I remained here till morning, my fate would be sealed. Once the sun rose, I would be easily detected. In desperation, I scanned the field from my hiding place. I could detect nothing that indicated which way to the border.

"I lifted my eyes unto the mountains, from whence would come my help? My help is from G-d" (*Psalms* 121:1). I prayed desperately to G-d for help. Terror flooded my heart, as I was startled by a sudden sound of cornstalks snapping underfoot. My worst fear had come true. One of the Nazis had remained behind to ambush me.

Every muscle in my body froze. I did not breathe for fear that making even the slightest noise might give away my position. I stayed perfectly still. For what seemed like nearly half an hour, the noise was repeated every few minutes. Again and again I heard footsteps on the cornstalks and grass. The sounds were getting louder; whoever was there was coming toward me! I listened more intently to determine how far away the noises were. Maybe it was just my imagination, I told myself. Maybe I was hearing things and it was only the sound of the wind rustling the cornstalks and the brush. Then I heard it again and this time I knew I could not be mistaken. Someone was walking very slowly through the cornfield.

Yet it suddenly occurred to me that perhaps this person was someone from the group who had escaped. It was possible that he was just as frightened as I was. Maybe I could find a way to approach him and together we could find a way out of this predicament. However, the thought recurred that the footsteps could be those of a Nazi soldier searching for any Jews that had escaped. If I gave my position away, he would kill me.

At that moment, G-d gave me the insight to test whether the sound was coming from friend or foe. I waited until I heard the sound of another footstep. When I did, I carefully shook some of the cornstalks near me, ever so slightly, to make the slightest of sounds. I reasoned that if the person who was moving about was a Nazi soldier he would not notice such a slight sound. He would simply assume it was a normal sound of the night, perhaps a small animal running through the field. But if it was one of the refugees, gripped by the fear of possible capture, he would stop in his tracks and lie quietly, afraid to make another sound.

The instant I rattled the brush, the field became totally quiet. After about five minutes, I heard another slight sound. I shook the cornstalks again. Again, all was silent for a few minutes. When I heard the next noise, I repeated my noise. Again, all became quiet for a little while. In this way we conversed, using secret sounds of the underbrush, deep in the darkness of the night. I was now certain that I was dealing with another person as afraid of death as I was. The other person hiding in my field was as afraid of me as I was of him.

It was clear that I had to find a way to approach the person communicating with me. It was possible that he knew the way better than I did and I did not want to lose this opportunity to save my life.

I had not moved at all during this entire time except to shake the cornstalks. I was sure that the other person did not know exactly where I was. I waited for him to start walking again, but this time I did not scare him. Instead, I listened carefully to determine where the footsteps were coming from and where they were heading. When I was sure of his direction, I leaped up from my hiding place and charged toward him. I wanted the element of surprise on my side. When he realized that someone was approaching him, he ran off in the opposite direction. I ran after him with all the strength I could muster. Finally, after about 100 meters, he tired for I was rapidly closing the gap between us.

When I got within 15 meters of him, the man stopped in his tracks and turned to face me. Though I too was extremely tired, I did not let up my pursuit of him. As I got closer, he straightened up and like a cornered animal prepared to defend itself. I could see him well enough to make out something in his right hand gleaming as he raised it over his head. With the little bit of light provided by the stars, I could see the glint of the blade of a large knife. He must have thought that I was one of the Nazi soldiers and he was ready to kill to survive. I stopped the instant I realized that he intended to stab me on the spot. By now, we were about three meters apart. He approached me with the knife still menacingly raised. We were close enough that I could see a surprised look on the man's face as he realized he was about to murder a young boy. He froze in his attack posture, the knife raised over his head. After a moment, relief cascaded across his visage, he lowered his arm and he returned the knife to the sheath at his belt.

He had the look of a local farmer or peasant, not that of a killer. His dress was the typical traveling attire for the local gentile population. I noticed that he had a large yellow feather inserted in his hatband, the signal by which we were to identify our guide.

I asked him if he was our guide. He responded that he did not remember seeing me earlier. I explained that I had remained at a distance for I had expected the large group to attract attention. He told me that I had made a good choice and that I was a smart young man. With great sadness, he confirmed what I already knew. The group had been betrayed and the Nazis had apprehended everyone. Our guide was the only one who escaped. He was at the head of the line, and when the Nazis pounced, he escaped into the cornfield as I had done.

Again, I had to reconcile my joy and relief at having eluded the Nazi killers with the unbearable sorrow that I felt over the certain fate of another group of Jews. Further, I know and I can testify that it was decreed from Heaven that this gentile was spared in order to save me from death at the hands of our Nazi tormentors.

The guide agreed to bring me over the border, but we needed to make new plans quickly. Many hours had passed. To cross the border would require another four hours of traveling under the cover of darkness; however, sunrise would be in an hour. We would have to spend the daylight hours hiding. The guide told me that his farmhouse was just outside of a nearby village. He could hide me there for the day. It was a short walk and we could reach it before daybreak.

We traveled mostly through corn and wheat fields and small forests. Occasionally we happened upon actual roads only to warily cross them. It was clear to me that we were still in danger. The guide was nervously vigilant and methodical as he moved silently through the fields. Whenever we had to traverse a relatively exposed area, he became most careful. We would wait quietly under cover for 10 minutes to see if anyone might be lurking out of sight. Only after he was certain that no one was about did he proceed. At daybreak, the guide grabbed my arm and pointed to a farmhouse in the clearing in front of us. He said, "That is where we will hide you. That is my home."

I was greatly relieved and started to walk toward the farmhouse. The guide pulled me down to the ground and whispered that we had to wait for a signal that it was safe to approach the house. The guide instructed, "The signal will be hung out with the morning laundry. A dark blanket will signal danger and a light-colored blanket will signal that all is clear."

We waited, the guide patiently, while I continuously looked about in every direction for some sign of impending danger. As promised, 10 or 15 minutes after the sun came up a woman came out of the farmhouse with a basket under her arm. She proceeded to hang up a series of common laundry items and finally a yellow blanket.

We quickly walked across the field. As we approached the farmhouse, the guide whistled loudly. This must have been a prearranged signal because the woman quickly emerged from the building. The guide introduced the woman as his wife. After he explained the situation to her, they decided to hide me in an old unused oven. I spent almost the entire day in that oven feeling some safety for the first time in days; most of the time I was asleep.

As soon as it was dark, we were on our way and I was back in that now familiar state of unrelenting fear. Though I was so terrified that I could hardly breathe, I managed to keep up with the guide and follow his every direction and warning. True to his promise to me, and with G-d's help and protection, we made it past all the guards. We crossed the border into Slovakia. I was the only Jew to make it of the more than 20 who tried.

Chapter 9

Alone Again

Once in Slovakia, I went immediately to the Yeshiva of Nitra, about 100 kilometers east of Pressburg. It was the end of the summer of 1944, and Germany was suffering continued defeats. There were uprisings in Poland, Slovak and Paris, with Paris being liberated in six days. The Germans surrendered in the Crimea. The Soviet Union liberated the first death camp, Majdanek, and the Allies had Germany surrounded.[1] The Nazis themselves attempted to assassinate Hitler.

Despite the state of the Jews in Slovakia — what remained of them the Yeshiva of Nitra continued to serve as a haven for the Jewish community. Rabbi Michoel Ber Weissmandl, the son-in-law of the Nitra Rav, was one of the great heroes of the Holocaust era. When the Germans

---

1. In the face of the Red Army's advance, Majdanek was liquidated; Gutman *Encyclopedia of the Holocaust* (New York, 1990), p. 940.

Map indicating locations of Pressburg (Bratislava), Nitra, Budapest, Vienna

invaded Slovakia, Rabbi Weissmandl was instrumental in arranging for Jews to live in and around Nitra in some safety. His efforts were truly heroic, just as they had been earlier in Hungary, where he had devised and implemented plans for saving Hungarian Jews after the German invasion of that country. (This story is thoroughly documented in his autobiographical account, *Min HaMeitzer.*) When the Germans invaded Slovakia, Rabbi Weissmandl came to Nitra to bargain directly with the top Nazis, including Eichmann and Himmler, to buy Jewish lives. His negotiating skill and his leadership of the surviving Jewish community produced the special situation that existed in Nitra. He was able to establish ongoing negotiations with the Slovak and German Nazis to procure an agreement with the local authorities to let Jews stay in the Rav's house, within the walls of the yeshiva complex, and in the courtyards of the houses in the area. They would not be arrested and sent to

The courtyard of the Nitra Yeshiva with Rabbi Ungar (second from right) and Rabbi Weissmandl behind him.

the slaughter as so many Jews had. Nowhere else in Slovakia could Jews be safe from the violence of the Germans. Consequently, Jews from all over had congregated in and around the Yeshiva of Nitra and were living in relative peace and security in an enclave that came to be referred to as the "Jewish Vatican." Often a deal would be negotiated allowing a new refugee to enter the complex and every day Rabbi Weissmandl would win assurances that a raid on the complex would not be carried out by the Nazis that night.

His success in dealing with our persecutors did not lull Rabbi Weissmandl into a false sense of security. He admonished every student to be prepared. He required that every student must have a compartment hollowed out in his shoe to hide a hacksaw blade. If a student were captured and loaded onto a train, he could use the blade to cut through the bars on a window or through a latch or lock of a door. If one managed to saw through a lock, it was critical that he could escape by jumping from the moving train. Hence, every able-bodied student was taught how to jump from a moving vehicle. Later in the war, Rabbi Weissmandl himself, while being transported in a cattle car to the death camps, used his hacksaw to cut through the bars of his car's window, leaping from the speeding train to safety.

My arrival at the Yeshiva of Nitra marked another dramatic change in my life. The renowned rabbi, Shmuel David Ungar, was the Nitra Rav and was also head of the Yeshiva of Nitra. He was a close childhood friend of my grandfather, the esteemed scholar Reb Avrohom Streicher. Rabbi Ungar showed me special love and treated me with particular kindness and compassion. He also went out of his way to assist in my acceptance by the students and faculty of the yeshiva. "Avrohom is a student of the Pupa Rav," he told them, "and a student of the Pupa Rav must be treated with respect." My status was elevated accordingly and I began to enjoy the prospect of resuming my studies.

I was settled in a room the first day in Nitra. The first thing I did was to send a message to my father about my experiences crossing the border and about conditions in Nitra. It was not possible to send letters across the border by postal service, but for a substantial price, it was

Rabbi Chaim Michael Dov Weissmandl prior to the war.

possible to get gentiles to transport our letters. Once on the Hungarian side of the border, these letters could be delivered by the regular postal service.

I expected my father to immediately join me. When I received no response from him, I became very worried. We all knew that people disappeared suddenly and without a trace. You could only be confident about the safety of the people you could see on a daily basis. Anytime you lost contact with someone, you could not be sure he was still free or safe. One of the most unbearable realities of the Nazi presence was that people vanished.

With each passing day, I grew more and more worried. If something had happened to my father, each day that passed made it more difficult to undo the situation. If he had been captured, the only real hope I had for his freedom was that he was still in the hands of the local Nazi authorities. They could be influenced with offers of money or jewels. Once my father was turned over to the Germans, it would be difficult to alter the situation. The Germans were much harder to bribe.

After several weeks, I received the news I had dreaded. I learned, to my great anguish, that my father had been captured as he tried to cross the border. It had been necessary for him to hire a different smuggler, for my smuggler had given up the profession after my harrowing trip. The new guide was dishonest. He had taken my father's payment but he did not show up at the rendezvous. Instead of the guide, the local authorities greeted my father. This was the bitter fate of many Jews who turned to smugglers in the hope of finding their way to freedom. I was told that my father had been taken directly to a local prison. Though I was terrified that he would be killed, I could not have imagined the brutality that was actually to be visited upon him.

When my father had been captured in Budapest during Succos of 1942, I was in the same city and could appeal to family and to local people to help me arrange my father's release. Now, I was in a different country and I could do nothing to influence my father's situation.

Yet, I could not accept that there was nothing that could be done. I sought out every influential person in the Nitra complex, but they all responded in the same way. Conditions in Hungary had deteriorated so rapidly that it was too dangerous for any official to meet with a Jew, either directly or through some intermediary. It was impossible to contact the government functionaries who had always helped in one way or another in the past. Raising enough money was not the problem. Rather, it was impossible to get to the authorities to make the request and deliver the money.

I became more and more frantic. Finally, I appealed to Rabbi Weissmandl. "Please, you have to do something. The Nazis in Hungary have captured my father. Please help me!" Rabbi Weissmandl explained that there was nothing that he could do. "You have to do something," I persisted.

Rabbi Weissmandl explained with great patience that the problem was that my father had been captured in Hungary not in Slovakia. If he had been in Slovakia, all that would have been needed to have him released was a large sum of money, but he was imprisoned in Hungary and nothing could be done from Nitra.

I angrily accused the rabbi of not doing all that he could to save a Jew, of being indifferent to my father's fate. I spoke impolitely and Rabbi Weissmandl grew agitated and upset. However, he reiterated in a voice of great authority that he could not secure my father's freedom.

I knew that I was being rude and disrespectful. I eventually came to understand that under the circumstances, there was nothing he could do to help my father. I remember that day and Rabbi Weissmandl[2] very well, especially the strength in his expression and the sadness in his eyes. Soon the war would separate us. The rabbi would die before I ever had an opportunity to apologize for my behavior.[3]

---

2. Rabbi Michoel Dov Weissmandl was one of the Working Group, a Jewish underground organization in Slovakia that became the central agency for rescuing Jews and establishing links to Jewish and non-Jewish organizations abroad. He repeatedly demanded the Allies bomb the railway lines, bridges and tunnels leading to Auschwitz. "One of the Working Group's most important activities was the 'Europa Plan' – the scheme for the rescue by ransom of the remnants of European Jewry." This was the first of the rescue operations known as "blood for wares" for the rescue of Hungarian Jewry in the spring of 1944. Livia Rothkirchen, *Rescue Attempts During the Holocaust: Proceedings of the Second Yad Vashem International Historical Conference*, Jerusalem, 1977, pp. 423-35.

3. Rabbi Weissmandl saved tens of thousands of Jews, even though he met with overwhelming resistance to his unrelenting efforts to procure funds to save European Jewry from destruction. Rabbi Weissmandl even had delivered directly to President Roosevelt maps showing in detail the Auschwitz death camp, but America refused to bomb them knowing full well that tens of thousands of lives were being lost every day. They bombed sites a few miles away from Auschwitz, but the train tracks, crematoriums and gas chambers they left untouched. All of this proved too much for Rabbi Weissmandl, and he died, in America, after the war.

Chapter 10

The Beast Srikes Our Sanctuary

While I was attending the yeshiva and looking for a way to free my father, partisan resistance[1] began to play an important role in Slovak life. As the Slovak government had come increasingly under the influence of Nazi propaganda, support for the resistance movement began to grow.

At first, the partisans spent most of their time hiding and organizing in the mountains and forests, presenting little problem for the government or its Nazi friends. By the late summer of 1944 though, this situation changed dramatical-

---

1. During World War II, partisans were rebel fighters who fought primarily in Eastern Europe and the Balkan states against the Nazis in German-occupied countries. These guerrilla fighting units grew out of a frustration with the occupier – with having to obey their orders and surrender their property or money to them. Though some partisans may have been motivated by a distaste for Nazi ideology, this was not necessarily their primary reason for taking part in the resistance. Indeed, many if not most partisans, large number were virulently anti-Semitic. Isaac Kowalski *Anthology of Armed Jewish Resistance*, Brooklyn, 1985, pp. 110-22.

ly. More and more, the partisans were coming out of their hiding places to harass the forces of the Slovak regime and were beginning to cause serious disruptions. They attacked supply lines, weapons depots, communications and small army units. The Slovak uprising was so successful that the rebels established a dissident government in the middle of Slovakia in the city of Banska Bistrica.[2] Until this happened, the Germans had been satisfied to let Slovakia remain a protectorate. We knew that they would not tolerate a rebellious government in Slovakia. Our days as an "independent state" were numbered.

In September 1944, the German Army invaded Slovakia for the first time.[3] Before the invasion, Slovakia existed as a sovereign country, a faithful ally of the Hitler regime, under the protection of the German Third Reich. The Slovak government, with the support of many Slovak citizens, was pro-German and enacted most of the German program, especially with regard to the Jews. However, as the partisans became

A unit of the Slovak army preparing to defect to the Partisan cause, October, 1944.

2.Gutman, *Encyclopedia of the Holocaust* (New York, 1990), pp. 1370-1372.
3. In desperation, the Jewish leaders in Bratislava tried to bribe the Germans for Jewish freedom. They proposed that their overseas relatives turn over money in exchange for the safety of the remaining Jewish community. The Germans turned down the proposal. Hilberg, *The Destruction of the European Jews*, New York, 1985, vol. II, p. 741.

emboldened by their own ability to disrupt the Nazi efforts, the government reacted by punishing the people who helped the partisans. The end result was that an open rebellion erupted in the Slovak army.

Nazi Germany responded by invading Slovakia, under the guise of helping the loyal army suppress the rebellion and to eliminate the partisan threat. However, this was not the actual reason. By now, it was clear to the German Reich that they were losing their war against the Allies. Despite this, they did not desist in their satanic war against the Jews. Rather than gathering all of their resources for a concentrated war effort, they siphoned off their resources and men from the front in an effort to escalate their war against the Jews. The war against the world was only a pretext; it was the war against the Jews which was their primary obsession. They were desperate to finish their war against the Jews before the war with the world finished them.

In Slovakia the German invasion increased the activity of the partisan rebellion. The invading Germans reacted by renewing the worst of the abuses previously heaped upon the Slovak Jews. The German Nazis hunted Jews. When captured, they were either shot on the spot or briefly held in local concentration camps before being deported to death camps. For most of the surviving Jews of Slovakia, this meant death in Auschwitz.

As the Germans entered Slovakia, we all knew that the brief respite that we had found in Nitra would soon end. Again, I needed a plan if I were to survive. Clearly I could not stay in the yeshiva and wait for the Germans to come for me. I decided to travel to Pressburg to obtain false Slovak papers that would let me resume my gentile identity.

About two weeks before Rosh Hashanah, I visited the Nitra Rav in his room to take my leave and ask his blessing for my trip. He was not sympathetic to my going to Pressburg. He wanted me to stay to complete my studies and take the final exams which were to be given in a few days.

Instead of a blessing, he said to me: "How can you leave now? We are just about to have the big examination on *Meseches Beitzah*[4] and the laws of *mikvaos* in *Yoreh Deah!*[5] Stay, and when you pass the test and when you know *Meseches Beitzah* word for word, then you can travel to Pressburg with my blessing."

Even though I felt that it was urgent to get my papers and a new identity, I followed the Rav's instructions. I stayed in the yeshiva and prepared for the test. It was difficult to concentrate on the work I had to do. There were daily reports of atrocities in other cities, rumors were being spread by everyone, and we all were certain that the Nazis were coming to Nitra soon. I was also distracted by the reports of the activities of the partisans. The rebel group was beginning to be an effective resistance to the Nazi persecutors and their actions gave me a feeling that there might be an alternative to running and hiding. Despite all of these things pulling at me, I managed to study diligently for several days.

I was still very anxious to get to Pressburg. With each passing minute I could feel the Nazi presence closing in around me. I was more convinced than ever that a new gentile identity was my best chance for surviving the Nazi invasion.

Early the next day after my exam, I went to visit my rebbi[6] to arrange my departure. He was very happy to tell me that I had done very well on the test. He gave me a warm farewell blessing. He also warned me not to stay more than two or three days in Pressburg; as soon as I received my new papers, I must leave. It was very dangerous in the cities; there were stories of Jews being stopped and murdered on the spot by soldiers. He urged me to return to the yeshiva so that I could continue my studies. He expected

---

4. The section of the Oral Law which deals mostly with the laws of the holidays.
5. The complex laws of the construction of ritual baths.
6. Rebbi is how a student refers to his Torah teacher; literally, "my master."

that everyone would be safe there under the protection of Rabbi Weissmandl.

I left for Pressburg immediately. The trip took only a few hours and to my surprise I completed it without incident. Once there I made contact with an individual who agreed to provide me with the papers I sought.

On my second day of hiding in Pressburg, I received horrible and tragic news. To this day, the memory of that moment sends a shudder of agony through me. The day after I left the city, the German Nazis marched into Nitra killing or capturing nearly every Jew. Those captured were immediately sent off to the death camps. Only a very few Jews had managed to hide and elude the grasp of the murderers.

Rabbi Yonah HaLevi Forst, for whom I had come to have great respect and affection, was one of the few who had escaped the Nazi attack on the yeshiva. He had looked after me while I was in the Yeshiva of Nitra, helping me with both my spiritual and material needs. With all the horrors I had survived and with so much evil visited upon the Jewish people, the rabbi helped me to approach my studies as a source of faith that made it possible for me to endure. In addition, the rabbi enabled me to have access to the financial resources that my family had in bank accounts, money that enabled me to outwit the Nazi efforts to capture and kill me.

For the Jews who were able to survive in Slovakia during the period before the Nazi invasion, money for day-to-day needs was a continuous problem. Every Jew had to work out ways to buy at least some essentials on the black market. Often this meant selling jewels and gold for currency or rations. Many gentile Slovaks who were in the financial community, usually those sympathetic to the plight of the Jews, helped Jews, often at great risk to themselves. Rabbi Yonah Forst had arranged for me to get money through a gentile banker who was a friend of my father. My father's own banker had access to all of our accounts, but was not able to take money out of those accounts for fear of attracting attention to us. This gentile banker was willing to provide us with money on an IOU. After the invasion, I was able to go to this banker and obtain money in this manner. With my Christian identity I was able to use the money to help other Jews.

A few days later, I learned further details of the barbarity of the German army. The yeshiva consisted only of students and their teachers, none of whom were in any way a threat to the Germans. However, when the soldiers broke into the yeshiva grounds, they acted as if they were conducting a military operation against an armed force. When the Nazis reached the courtyard, they had their guns ready to shoot anyone who resisted. None did. Many were praying and some were crying but no one raised a hand or a weapon against the Germans. Everyone in the courtyard knew his fate. One of those in the courtyard was a close friend from my childhood in Pressburg, Rabbi Yaakov Lowy. As the Nazis were collecting the Jews in the courtyard, he tried to flee by climbing the fence. No order was given to stop him. The Nazis shot him in the back as he tried to scale the fence, killing him instantly. They would let no one minister to his body which they left hanging there for many days.

The body of this exceptional young rabbi, cut down so mercilessly in the prime of his youth, abandoned to die on that fence, separated from all that mattered to him, became for me a symbol of the cruelty perpetrated on the Jews by the Nazis. May G-d avenge his blood.[7]

"O, that my head were waters, and my eyes a fountain of tears, that I could cry day and night for the dead of the daughter of my people!" (*Jeremiah* 8:23).

---

7. Reb Yaakov Lowy was eventually taken down from the fence by a non-Jew who buried him in a gentile cemetery. After burial this gentile was besieged nightly by the same dream, of Reb Yaakov Lowy visiting him from the next world insisting that he be buried in a Jewish cemetery. Finally, the gentile relented and buried him a second time in a Jewish cemetery. After this, the nightmares ended. I heard this story, after the war, from this gentile himself.

Chapter 11

My Return to Pressburg

Because Nitra no longer offered a safe haven, I was determined to find a way to survive in Pressburg. With papers attesting to my gentile identity, I was able to move about quite freely. There were very few Jews left in Pressburg, but there were some who were living openly as gentiles like myself, and a significant number who were in hiding. And even at this late date, there remained a few "essential Jews" protected by permits from the Slovak government.

In October 1944, Soviet troops occupied Estonia and captured Riga, the Allies liberated Athens and the gas chambers in Auschwitz were used for the last time. I, meanwhile, spent Rosh Hashanah and Yom Kippur dressed like a gentile. Even as a Christian, I needed a haven where I could sleep without fear of a Nazi raid. Within a few days I was able to contact a gentile businessman who was an acquaintance of my father. This man was greatly saddened by what had happened to my father and the rest of my family. He offered me a place to stay where he thought I might be safe, a house in the country where a Christian could live without being noticed by the Germans.

The house was a weekend cottage at a resort area for wealthy Slovakians situated at the edge of a forest and hiking area. There were twenty log-cabin cottages. I was known by The other vacationers, who happily hiked all around the surrounding area, never suspected that I was a Jew. My bungalow contained four bunk beds, a fireplace, dishes and even musical instruments, as the owner was musically inclined.

During the days, my life was closer to normal. I spent most of my time with the few Jews that remained in the city, either on the streets with a group of disguised refugees I had come to know, or in the home of Shlomo Stern, a friend of my father's family. Reb Shlomo's son was my boyhood friend, Yisroel Stern (he and I have maintained a close friendship to this day). Reb Shlomo was a most exceptional man, a true servant of his people, who disregarded all danger to himself and saved thousands of Jews. He was slim and tall, stately and distinguished with gold rimless glasses. As a businessman and a banker in foreign exchange, his home was the meeting place where the surviving leaders of the Jewish community would come together each day to plan their dealings with the Nazis. These men, all known by the Germans, were free because they were of some worth to the Nazis. They used their influence and extensive financial resources to implement plans for rescuing Jews who had been captured or who were in hiding. Almost every day he was involved in secret negotiations with Himmler and his deputies to order to stop or delay the Hungarian deportations.

On one of my visits to Reb Shlomo's home, I found a large group of religious leaders who had already convened their daily meeting. I looked around, noting each of the distinguished men assembled in the living room. To my delight, I realized that one of these men was Rabbi Weissmandl from the Nitra Yeshiva. When the Germans stormed it, he eluded capture and fled to Pressburg.

As I observed their discussions, it was clear that Rabbi Weissmandl was greatly respected by all the leaders as a renowned negotiator whose wisdom in dealing with the Nazis had saved many lives. As he led the discussion, he pointed out that the situation had become so desperate that they had to act quickly to rescue even one or two Jews at a time. This would have to be the strategy for saving what was left of Slovak Jewry.

I was greatly impressed by the exchange of ideas as the men discussed alternatives. I timidly moved closer to the group in order to hear better. I had been listening for a while when Rabbi Weissmandl noticed me and focused on me intensely. He leaped from his chair, took three or four quick strides and stopped directly in front of me with an accusing look. I was perplexed as to what I had done wrong. He reached out and grabbed the *tallis katan*[1] that was visible under my gentile shirt. With one dramatic sweep of his arm he pulled the garment from under my shirt and held the *tallis katan* in his outstretched hand. The great rabbi rebuked me for being careless with the *mitzvah* of protecting one's life.

I can still hear the clear tone of authority in his angry voice: "Don't you know that the priority of saving your own life pushes aside all the *mitzvos* of the *Torah*? You can do nothing that might identify you as a Jew!" He spoke directly to me, but every person in the room understood his message. The passion in his voice made it clear to everyone that saving Jews had first priority. And as he returned to his seat to continue the meeting, the planning began with renewed urgency.

---

1. A Jewish man is commanded by G-d that when he wears a four-cornered garment, every corner has to have symbolically knotted fringes attached to it called tzitzis (see *Numbers* 15:37-41).

Interior of the Schierstube

I spent my days talking with the group of friends I had made among the refugees who were hiding about the city or listening to the talk in Rabbi Shlomo's house. For both groups the topic was identical, "Will today be the day the Nazis come for the last of us?" Everyone expected the Germans to conduct a coordinated operation that would sweep through the city to seize the last of the city's Jews. They all had plans to either hide in some secret place or disguise themselves as Christians or pay a non-Jew to shelter them.

On Yom Kippur, we prayed in the "Schierstube" — the famous synagogue where the most renowned rabbis of Pressburg had not too long before delivered their lectures to the students of the *yeshiva gedolah*. It is impossible to describe the intensity and range of emotions that fired our prayers that day. We mourned the destruction of our people and poured out our hearts. Every person bore a personal burden of sorrow and suffering. Many had been beaten and tortured; everyone had lost friends or relatives. Some had lost everyone. As we prayed, we pleaded for ourselves, that we, the last remnants of our community, be spared. Although no one verbalized it, I am sure that we all shared one thought: that this could well be the last Yom Kippur for each of us. Though we had endured horrors beyond human comprehension and we would greet each new day expecting even worse, our faith in G-d did not waver. We did not turn away from our G-d. Rather, through it all, we came to better understand that G-d was our only true refuge. The Nazis could take everything away from me but my faith in G-d was untouchable.

At the conclusion of the fast, I was invited by Rabbi Moshe Cohn, a trusted friend of my father, to his home for dinner. Rabbi Cohn had achieved great stature as a *Torah* scholar and was serving as a *bochen*, a man who conducted the formal tests for the *yeshiva ketanah*[2]. I truly enjoyed the opportunity to share this meal; the evening rekindled memories of a time when life was normal. After dinner, Rabbi Cohn urged me to remain overnight. The hour was late and we were all exhausted. "Why do you need to travel out of the city so late at night?" he said. "It's so dangerous after dark. Stay until daybreak, and then you can leave." I dismissed his concern, saying that I felt I should leave for my bungalow. Reb Cohn begged me to stay for the night. In spite of all his pleas, I returned to my bungalow.

I slept that night in the safety of my own "home." As usual, I awoke before sunrise and I prayed. It was my first act of the day, to acknowledge my faith and to reestablish my connection with my G-d. When I finished, I put on my Christian disguise and set off for the city.

While I was waiting for the train, I listened to the conversations of two peasant women standing next to me on the station platform. Eavesdropping was a valuable source of information about what was actually happening in the city. Too

---

2. A yeshiva for younger children.

often what I overheard were rumors of impending disaster, but nothing could have prepared me for what I was to discover this time.

Some time around midnight, Nazi soldiers had descended upon the city, raided the Jewish neighborhoods and gathered up all the Jews they could find — men, women, and children. One of the women said, "By now the Germans have those Jews loaded onto cattle cars, and are taking them to the camps." I had to force myself to appear calm, for inside I was devastated. For a long moment I could not move. One question tore at my heart amid all my raging emotions. I wanted to yell at them: "Why didn't you say 'death camps'? That's what they are!"

Instead I nonchalantly walked off the train platform back to my bungalow. I knew the Nazi soldiers were well practiced in this exercise. Most, if not all, of the people with whom I had spent the evening were probably gone. I feared that the families I had met, the leaders in Reb Shlomo's house including Rabbi Weissmandl, had all been taken.

I was to learn that my worst fears had been realized; all of them had been captured by the Nazis, even Rabbi Moshe Cohn and his entire family. Had I accepted his invitation, I too would have been doomed to the death camps.

Once back inside the isolated world of my little bungalow, I broke down totally. I sat there and shed bitter tears. Now I was totally on my own. Where would I turn? There was no one to whom I could go. From the time I was 9 years old, I had witnessed the destruction of my world. For nearly five years, I had been running from place to place and city to city, always one step away from being captured by the Nazis. Pressburg had represented normalcy to me and when I had returned I thought I would be able to enjoy some rest and peace. For a little while, I had managed to convince myself that I had found it. Now, all that I had held onto for stability had disappeared like a wisp of smoke.

Despite my despondency, in this nightmare of pain and suffering, G-d's providence had spared me. Why me? Why was I guided to act in ways that saved me from the Nazis? There had to be a reason why I was spared. What was it?

For days I remained in the bungalow. The holiday of Succos arrived, and I had nothing to prepare and no one with whom to prepare: no *lulav* and *esrog*, no *succah*, no festive meal.[3] I had to do something, to make some positive assertion of my faith. There must be some way that I could feel the holiness of this day. I searched the bungalow looking into every corner and in every space. Finally, I found two candles, which I lit in honor of the holiday. The light and warmth of those two candles helped and I sat there feeling somewhat comforted for the first time in days.

Later that night, as I was preparing for sleep, there was a sudden banging on the door. I was seized with fear that the Nazis had finally come for me. Before I could even consider a plan of action, a hand pushed a side window open and someone was climbing into my room. Immediately, I recognized the intruder as a fellow refugee, Yoni Rosenberg, a teenager like myself. I had met him in Pressburg, and we had befriended each other. I had hidden him in my bungalow for a few days before Yom Kippur. Though he had been in the city, he had managed to elude the Nazi roundup. As soon as he got to his feet, he walked over to the candles and extinguished them.

Yoni reprimanded me, "How could you be so careless with the *mitzvah* of saving your own life?" This was the exact question with which Rabbi Weissmandl had confronted me. I had been in such need of some solace, of the familiar comfort of the holiday, that I never once considered that the candles would put me in danger. In the darkness, it would be possible to see their light from a long distance, a light that might bring

---

3. Integral elements the Succos holiday. See *Leviticus* 23:39-43.

someone to investigate. Such were the facts of our plight. Anything that identified me as a Jew endangered my life; even the tiniest external display of faith could be lethal.

My friend had witnessed the attack of the Nazis firsthand and had spoken to others who had provided their own accounts. By now the pattern was all too familiar. The Nazis swept through each neighborhood, going from house to house and room to room. Dogs were used to find those who were hiding. People were shot where they stood in front of their children and spouses; babies were killed in front of their parents with no more concern than one might have for killing a mosquito. And all the while they laughed as if killing, torturing, breaking us was their greatest amusement. Those who were still alive were taken to detention camps and deported to death camps within a day. By now, all those captured were gone. There would be no rescues for these Jews. The only good news that my friend could offer was that my father's dear friend, Reb Shlomo Stern, was one of the few who had managed to evade the Nazis. Yoni and I spent most of the night talking. Exhausted, we finally fell asleep a few hours before dawn.

After Succos, we could no longer remain in the bungalow. As winter approached, the vacationers returned to their homes. We were worried that the Nazis would not discontinue their patrols of the farm areas to look for the few Jews who might still be in hiding. These vacant cottages were an obvious hiding place. If the Nazis observed any activity on the bungalow grounds, they would certainly investigate. So, with all our worldly possessions in our respective knapsacks, we embraced and said our good-byes, knowing that we would probably never see each other again. My friend set off for Pest and I, once more, to Pressburg.

Disguised as a non-Jew, I was able to travel into the city without incident. I managed to rent a room from a gentile family who did not ask if I was a Jew or why one so young might be alone and in need of a room. I told them that I was a student, and every morning I would rise early and allegedly leave for school. They did not feel compelled to question me, as I was able to speak the Slovak language as if it were my native tongue. Because of my fluency, no one suspected that I was Jewish, so I could move around the city freely and make contact with the few Jews that were left.

Though I was relatively safe, the Gestapo continued to mount an unrelenting effort to root out the few Jews who remained in Pressburg. They did not spare any effort or overlook any possible strategy to catch us. They were possessed by the lust to murder Jews and to wipe the earth clean of any trace of G-d's chosen people. As the number of surviving Jews decreased, the number of Nazis employed in the effort increased.

The traps they devised were as horrible as their treatment of the Jews once they apprehended them. Torture was a mainstay of their strategy. When they managed to capture a Jew, through a trap or through an informer, they assumed that he knew the identity of others. They would torture their captives barbarously to elicit details about other Jews in hiding. They would hold members of a family hostage. If one did not agree to help in the effort by pointing out other Jews, the Gestapo would murder a son or a daughter or a wife. When faced with the unimaginable and unending pain that the Nazis expertly inflicted, many could not withstand the torment and provided them the information they wanted.

Once they had broken someone, the Nazis had another particularly malicious technique for using that individual as bait to capture others. They would have that person walk through the streets in non-Jewish disguise with the Gestapo in street clothes following closely behind. When other disguised Jews recognized him they would walk over to exchange greetings, and then the Gestapo would pounce upon these unsuspecting Jews.

Consequently, whenever I walked down a street, I never spoke to anyone. I was careful to walk by each person I passed on the street without any hint of recognition. When I saw another Jew, I rejoiced inwardly that he, too, had escaped. But there were no shared greetings as we passed each other. I acknowledged other Jews only in hidden alleys or behind closed doors after taking many precautions to guarantee that no one was watching. I trusted no one.

During those years of fury, we would again see the prescience of the words of our sages, even in the interpretation of a verse in *Psalms*: "Every day we have been killed for Your sake" (44:23). This refers to circumcision. The commentators had puzzled over this remark. Does any child ever die from a *bris*?[4] How do our rabbis tie this verse to circumcision? During the years of the Holocaust, tragically, we discovered an answer. Thousands of Jews hid under non-Jewish identities. When a male was suspected of being a Jew, there was a simple way of checking. When it was determined that he had been circumcised, he was murdered with exceptional brutality. Among those identified in this way and then killed were some of my closest friends and other acquaintances from the Jewish community of Pressburg. Thus, many, many Jews were killed for "His sake."

---

4. Circumcision. Literally, *covenant*.

Chapter 12

I Join the Resistance

One day as I was walking, I spied a man dressed like a non-Jew who looked very familiar. As he got closer, I realized that the man was Reb Meir, a family friend from our community in Pressburg. I almost yelled with joy, for I had reconciled myself to the idea that I would never see the people from my past again. Seeing him was like having a miraculous vision.

With all my might, I controlled the urge to call out to him. Fortunately, he had not recognized me for he might have called out to me, and after I had walked past him for five or six paces I turned around and followed him. I noted everyone in the area, careful that no one was following him. After three or four blocks, I was satisfied that the Gestapo was not using him as bait. I caught up with him and as I walked alongside, I suggested that he follow me into the next alleyway. I hoped that he would reason that if I were pointing him out to the Nazis, I would not need to invite him into a hidden alley.

Thankfully, he came to this conclusion. When we were out of sight, Reb Meir could get a clear view of my face and he recognized me instantly. For each of us, finding a survivor from our past life was an intensely joyous experience. Those of us who survived and retained our faith had to learn to cope with despair in many forms. One of the worst expressions that the loss of hope takes is that it disconnects a person from his past. Because we had all lost so many of the people that connected us with our history, it was difficult to muster the strength to endure. Consequently, meetings like this back-alley reunion had a much greater significance than the meeting of a young man and a respected family friend otherwise would have. For me, this meeting was a reaffirmation of my membership in a community, the Jewish community.

We exchanged stories of our friends and families. He was saddened by the fate of so many of my relatives. He told me that his entire family had escaped the Nazis and were still safe. They had found shelter in the home of a gentile.

However, Reb Meir explained, he was in terrible trouble. His "landlord" had stolen all their money and, eventually, all their gold, silver, and jewelry. It was not likely that the landlord would turn them over to the Nazis for he would have to answer for having hidden the family in the first place. However, once he realized that no further payment could be extracted from this Jewish family, he would put them out of his home. If Reb Meir could not put together a week's rent soon, he and his family would be out on the street where they would quickly be picked up by the Gestapo and carted off to the death camps.

I had money with me and gave him all that I had. Reb Meir thanked me profusely, but he pointed out that it was enough for only one week's rent. His family would need much more for the long term and he would have to find a way to raise the additional money. He was very upset over the grim prospects of finding such a large sum. I told him he had no need to worry; I could bring him the money he needed. There was disbelief in his eyes. I told him I would meet him in one week with the money. I explained where we would meet and I gave him a series of precautions to follow so that no one would be able to find out about our meeting place. He was reassured by my confidence, and agreed to meet me.

We parted, leaving the alley separately and going in opposite directions. I always tried to look "normal," was ever vigilant on the lookout for people moving together (even people separated by some distance) or for people in civilian clothing who seemed to be observing others. The Gestapo, the most aggressive persecutors of the Jews, often patrolled the streets dressed as civilians. I was always on the lookout for uniforms of any kind. I had become quite skilled at switching directions midstride, as if I had seen something in a store window or recognized a friend on the other side of the street.

One week later, I waited for Reb Meir at the agreed-upon site. I was always very nervous before a meeting. This was a most dangerous time. If the person with whom I had agreed to meet had been captured since our last meeting, I could not expect him to keep our secret. No one could be counted on to resist the torture of the Gestapo. This is what they did best. Often, informing on another Jew was the only faint hope the interrogators teased a prisoner with as the only way to save his own life or the lives of his family.

Therefore, as I waited I knew that I might be waiting for the Gestapo. I tried to give myself a chance at survival by picking meeting places that had multiple exits that led to escape routes through back alleys. I had made a decision that I would not surrender meekly if the Gestapo accompanied my contact. I would make a run for my freedom. I might escape but, if not, it was far better to be shot in the back than to be captured and tortured.

Reb Meir arrived exactly on time but to my horror he had someone with him. When he saw how upset I was, Reb Meir assured me that his friend was dependable and also greatly in need of my help. He introduced this new man as a Pressburg Jew by the name of Yosef who had exactly the same problem that Reb Meir had. Yosef had run out of money and expected to be thrown out by the gentile family that was hiding him and his family. I did not have enough money to take care of both of them, but I gave them all that I had. I assured them both that I could get the money that they needed and we agreed to meet again the following week.

I had made a promise I was not certain I could fulfill. I needed to solve two major problems. First, I would need to work out a dependable way to secure money on a regular basis. Second, I would have to devise a safe way to meet these people to give them the money they needed.

The next morning, as I walked along a street in Pressburg grappling with these problems, a woman in her late-50's who looked very familiar caught my attention. I observed her for a few minutes before I realized it was Helena, the Polish gentile woman who worked as a maid in the home of Reb Shlomo Stern. Helena had been very devoted and loyal to Reb Shlomo. Beneath her ordinary demeanor, she was a committed anti-Fascist who assisted Reb Stern in his underground efforts to save as many Jews as possible.[1] Many times she helped by being a courier, transporting information and funds

---

1. By the end of 1942, European resistance movements were growing. Resistance to the occupying power was found in every occupied country in Europe. Not all the members of the resistance were Jewish, but they were all anti-German. Many were motivated by patriotism and the hatred of Fascism. The resistance lacked money, weapons and trained personnel. "All it could do was to produce as many 'pinpricks' as possible, without expecting to gain any real victory." Henri Michel, *The Second World War*, New York 1975, pp. 293-306.

from one contact to another. Helena was able to move freely through the city streets because she appeared like the ordinary gentile citizen that she was. Since she too had survived, my first thought was that Helena might be able to get a message to Reb Shlomo for me.

I watched her for about five minutes to make sure that no one was watching or following her. I approached Helena and asked her to follow me into the next alley. I hoped that she would remember me and trust me. She must have realized that if I were pointing out Jews for the Gestapo they would have grabbed her without a word. In the alley we exchanged an emotional greeting like the reunion of family members spared by the angel of death.

Helena was overjoyed to see me alive and safe. For me, the woman was heaven sent. I explained the situation — that there were two Jewish families in hiding who needed money to pay their non-Jewish landlords who were threatening them with immediate eviction. I told her that I was willing to be the person who arranged the meetings, but I needed someone to provide the money. I asked her to take a message to Reb Shlomo. Could he send money to cover the needs of these poor Jews I had met? Helena said that this would be a difficult undertaking, but she would do her best. She agreed to meet me the next day.

The next morning, Helena appeared at the meeting place exactly on time. As she handed me an envelope, she told me that Reb Shlomo had sent the money I requested. Further, she said he had instructed that we were to set up a procedure so that we could meet regularly to provide money for my families.

I could not have been happier. My two families would be safe for the time being, and I was doing something active, fighting back, frustrating the Nazis. This gave me a wonderful feeling of satisfaction.

The money to the two families was delivered and both men showered me with gratitude. The relief that they felt was overwhelming. After they had thanked me and we had arranged our next meeting, they asked to discuss another matter. Each knew of another family that shared their plight. These were families who had made the mistake of giving all their money to the landlord up front and now had to pay a weekly ransom to stay sheltered and alive. They both made the same request. They looked directly into my eyes and asked, "Can you help these people?"

I thought for a minute. This was a daunting undertaking. Was it possible? Could I get all the money that this would require? Could I get the money to all the people who needed it without being discovered by the Nazis? I knew that I had to try.

I agreed to help. Through Helena I received a commitment from Reb Shlomo for as much money we would need. As it turned out, each of these families was in touch with others and these in turn were in touch with still others and so on. In no time, I had a network of fifty-eight families to take care of, all with the same problem. They were hiding in gentile homes and needed money to pay for their hiding places.

We were able to help them all because there were Jews willing to give all their worldly goods, and because there were men like Reb Shlomo, who had the respect and good will of the banking community. This made it possible to get access to money even while the Nazis and the Gestapo had made laws that prohibited Jews from taking money out of their own bank accounts. While the Nazis and the Gestapo spared no effort to find and kill us, there were those who risked everything to help.

My families were able to be aided, but because of the widespread net that the Gestapo had laid to snare those few hidden Jews, elaborate safeguards had to be established; certain conditions had to be met before making contact with any family.

The first stipulation was that every rendezvous had to take place after nightfall, in dark alleyways out of the view of any potential passersby. The second condition was that no one was to acknowledge me or talk to me on the street unless I spoke to him first. The third rule was that if either the family representative or I did not arrive at the designated time, the rendezvous would be postponed to the next night at the same time and same place. If the person did not come to the appointed location on the second night, we knew that he and his family had been taken by the Nazis.

Even though everyone was disguised as a non-Jew, most did not have identification papers. If a person were caught walking around without papers he would be sent to certain death, but not before being tortured for details about other Jews in hiding. Therefore, our meetings were very dangerous for the people I had to meet and also extremely dangerous for me. I could never be sure that the person I was about to meet had not been captured and tortured. I had to be careful that my clients were not bringing the Nazis. I did this by making sure that no one was being watched or followed. All the meeting sites were situated so that I could watch the person approaching the site from several different positions. I chose meeting places where it would be difficult for someone to sneak up on me.

We could not use the actual homes where people were hiding for our meeting place. It would have been too dangerous for everyone. The biggest worry was that the Gestapo might be following me or might have staked out the house because they had been informed about the family. In any case, the gentile landlords would hardly permit their tenants to reveal to anyone that they were hiding Jews. I made sure I did not know where the Jewish families were staying. I never wrote down any details of my dealings with anyone in these matters. There was no list of names or addresses or meeting places or meeting times. I memorized all 58 names and the times and places of each meeting. In this way, if I were caught and tortured, there would be no chance that their whereabouts could be forced out of me. I bore no delusions about my ability to resist the Nazis if I were caught. This is why I had vowed that I would not allow them to take me if I were trapped; I would die trying to escape.

In order to provide the money that the 58 families needed, I had to be out on the streets constantly. It was essential that I use a number of different meeting places. If each family representative met me in the same place, we would have attracted attention. So I would meet one individual in one alley, give over the money he needed, arrange our next meeting, check to make sure no one was watching us and then rush off to my next meeting place. Before each rendezvous, I had to watch the meeting place from a safe distance to be sure that no one was lurking to ambush me. And after each meeting I had to be sure that no one was following me before I went on to the next. I knew that even though I was disguised as a gentile and had the papers to prove it, I was on the street far more frequently than was safe. Sooner or later I would be stopped and checked.

I became an active participant in other aspects of the resistance, too. I encountered a friend who was involved more deeply in the underground, and based on his good word about me, I was able to play an even greater role. I would be given orders to meet a contact in a certain place at a certain time. Our password was "Amcha" which means "Your Nation" (as Jews, we were part of G-d's nation). I was given a way to detect my contact; he would be wearing a feather in his hat or a blue kerchief in his breast pocket. I was the middleman, picking up one parcel from one contact and passing it to another. I never knew what I was transporting or whom I was delivering it to. Also, I gathered information, which was then relayed to the partisans stationed in the mountains, of any newspaper accounts of troop deployment or activity.

One afternoon while I was walking between meetings my worst fear became a reality: Two Gestapo officers stopped me. They demanded my papers. As casually and calmly as I could, I took them out. As I stretched out my hand to give them over, one of the Gestapo grabbed the papers from me. I knew I was in trouble as I watched him put the papers in his coat pocket without even looking at them. Before I could move a muscle or think of running, they each grabbed one of my arms and ordered me to march.

"What do you want of me? What have I done wrong?" I asked in Slovak. One of the reasons I felt somewhat safe in my gentile disguise was the fact that I spoke the language perfectly. I was taken by surprise, therefore, by their reaction to my questions. "Don't hide behind the Slovak language," one of them answered me as he gave me a sharp shove. As I turned to see my assailant, I was shocked by what I saw. His twisted face reflected pure hatred, as if he had encountered his most despised enemy. I was looking into the face of the devil.

I received another shove and an even more hate-filled glare from the other Gestapo thug. "Speak to us in German, you cursed Jew." He shouted at me.

They had not even looked at my papers when they took them from me. They were not questioning their validity. It seemed as though they already had decided that I was a Jew in disguise. Did they know that I was a Jew, or did they only suspect it because of the way I looked or because of something I did?

I realized that most likely I had been given up by an informer, probably one of the very people whom I had included in my group of families. I also realized that this meant that one of my families had been captured and tortured. If this were true, another Jewish family had already been destroyed.

As we moved forward, me in their iron clutches, I decided that I had to try to escape. I would walk with them without any resistance. Hopefully, they would realize that I was too frightened to escape and would relax their grips. I would wait for the right chance to escape. But I could not make a mistake; I would get only one chance.

There were two main Gestapo stations in Pressburg. One was located in the heart of the city, and was the overall administration center for Gestapo operations. The other station was at the edge of the city and was known as "*Gehinnom*"; simply put, "Purgatory." It was here that they took Jews to be tortured. No Jew came out of *Gehinnom* alive. For many of the Jews who died in this building, the final torture was the realization that the same fate awaited their loved ones. For some, their last desperate act was to give up a name in a futile attempt to save themselves or their families. However they died, no Jew killed in this evil place received a proper burial. The magnitude of the atrocity inflicted in this building is unimaginable. After the war, 200 bodies were found in the station's cellar. Because of the cold, they had not decomposed. The marks of torture were clearly visible, a silent witness for any with the courage to look.

As I waited for my chance to escape, I decided that if they went toward the station at the center of the city, the head-

This is where I was apprehended by the Gestapo. The trees in the middle of the picture are at the critical intersection: If they took me to the right, I still had a chance; if we went to the left, I was doomed.

quarters, it would mean that they were not sure that I was a Jew and they intended to check my records in the office. If, on the other hand, they turned toward the station at the edge of the city, it would mean that they already knew I was a Jew and I was doomed. As we approached the critical intersection, I prepared myself, for if we turned toward *Gehinnom*, I had to act immediately.

When we reached the crossroads, my worst fear was realized. We turned toward *Gehinnom*. From that point on I had nothing to lose. For me, anything less than escape meant certain death. If I allowed myself to be taken into the lions' den, I could expect to be subjected to the most inhuman methods of torture and then to die an unimaginable death. And most frightening of all, I could not know what secrets and information they might squeeze from me that would give them the others. I thought, "Here I am, in my own city, marching toward my doom, both arms held tightly, a Gestapo murderer on each side — better to die right here in the street."

"In Your hand I entrust my soul; You, O G-d, have saved me" (*Psalms* 31:6). With that thought, I decided to break free and make a run for my freedom. I knew that there was only one chance in a thousand that I would not die in a hail of bullets.

My advantage lay in my knowledge of every street and alleyway in the city. Soon we would be passing a house that would provide an opportunity for escape through a series of mazelike alleyways. There was a walkway along the side of the house that led to the backyard. It was just a few meters to a gate that opened to the first short alley. About 20 meters along that alley, there was a right turn into a second alley which after a few meters led to yet another alley and then onto a street that would be crowded with people at that hour. When we passed the house, if I could surprise my captors, I would be close enough to the walkway that I might be able to make it to the back gate.

We encountered a crowd of pedestrians at this intersection, allowing me to escape.

I ran down this street after fleeing the Nazi bullets.

Through the grace of G-d, just as we neared the house, a crowd of people approached from the opposite direction. We were almost even with the house on my right. I waited for an instant while the crowd passed between the house and us. With all my strength, I ripped myself free of the

Gestapo guard holding my left arm and then used my left arm to pull my right arm free from the other officer. In the same motion, I was running at full speed into the crowd of people. There was total confusion as the Gestapo yelled for me to halt. But no one in the crowd had the presence of mind to seize me.

I flew like an arrow toward the gate. The Gestapo fired into the crowd what must have been more than a dozen shots but, through G-d's mercy, I was not touched by one. I have no idea whether those bullets hit any of the people in that crowd.

I did not look back, but with every bit of energy ran like a hunted animal, without thinking. I fled through the alleyways into the street. By the time the Nazis reached the gate, I was already hidden among the crowds of people strolling along the avenue. As I walked along with them, I was moved by the fact that they were going about their usual business as if this was just another day. I wanted to scream at them that the Nazis were trying to kill me because I was a Jew, that I had barely escaped and that my life might end at any second! Instead, I walked along, feigning calmness, as if I was a gentile doing my day's business with all the other citizens.

Even today, more than fifty years after that harrowing ordeal, when I remember those moments when the bullets whistled past me, my entire body shakes. I do not know what merit stood in my favor that allowed me to be saved and I am sure I never will. However, I do know that G-d, in His compassion, caused it to be, "For He will command His angels on your behalf, to protect you in all your paths" (*Psalms* 91:11).

Though I had escaped again, I was in a terrible predicament. I no longer had identification papers. If I were to be stopped, I had no chance. The Gestapo knew my name, albeit a false name. What was more important was that they also had my picture. Most likely, they had some knowledge of my involvement in the assisting of hidden Jews, so they could be expected to use the picture to hunt me down. I had no choice but to don another name and identity.

I had nowhere to stay. I could not go back to the house where I had been staying. Since they seemed to be looking for me, they probably had my address. If so, I could be sure that they were waiting for me at the house. Clearly, I could not even take the chance to get what was left of my worldly possessions. As difficult as all this had been, I was relieved that I had kept no records of my dealings with the families I was helping to hide. When the Gestapo searched my room, all they would find would be a few items of clothing. No Jew would be caught because of me.

As if the process were part of some sacred ritual, I began establishing a new identity for myself. In the course of my deal-

The palace used as Nazi headquarters. It is now a municipal building.

ings on behalf of my Jewish families, I had come to know the identities of a few gentiles who were active opponents of the Nazi regime. These people were members of an underground movement that was working to resist the Nazis in the cities and providing help to the partisans, who were actively fighting the Nazis and the German Army in the countryside. I met one of these gentiles on the street. When I explained my situation, he said, without the slightest hesitation, that he would help me.

He brought me to his home, where I dyed my hair and eyebrows red. With the new clothing he gave me, my entire appearance changed. At the same time, this non-Jew, at great personal risk, obtained new false papers for me with a new name and a different picture. I was a new person.

With new papers and a new face, I was able to go back onto the street in relative safety. The first thing I did was to look for a new place to live. I was totally exhausted and needed to rest my aching bones for a few days. However, finding a suitable room proved to be quite difficult. If I were to resume my role as financier for the Jewish families hiding in Pressburg, I would need a very special apartment with several critical characteristics.

First, I needed a place on an upper floor. This would allow me to escape through a window if the Nazis came into the house looking for Jews. When they searched the ground floor, the Nazis stationed guards at every possible exit, both doors and windows. However, when they searched the upper floors, they usually entered the house and went up the stairway, leaving no guards at the doors or windows. Thus there would at least be a hope that I could get out and get away.

Second, I wanted a room facing the backyard, rather than the front of the house. This was also an important part of my escape plan. Third, as had been the case in my last home, there had to be a walkway leading from the backyard out to other courtyards and alleys, so that I could get to another street. Lastly, I needed a place where the drainpipe that ran down from the roof to the yard was accessible to the window in my room. This would allow me to slide down to the ground, as did the spies of Joshua in Jericho (see *Joshua* 2:15).

With G-d's help, I found a small room that met all my requirements in the home of an elderly gentile woman. I moved into this room immediately and set up specific rules for myself to regulate how and when I could go out and come back. I wanted to ensure that no one would discover where I was living. I did not want to return to my room to find that they had laid a trap for me.

I never entered the house without first making absolutely certain that no one was following me. As I walked along I would try to take note of all the people around me. I noticed something about each person. To my left was a man with a dark-brown fur hat; behind him was a lady with gray hair under a gray scarf; to her left was a man with black leather gloves and a large band on his hat. As I walked along I made a mental picture of the people in the area. When I was a few blocks from my residence, I would stop and wait for a few minutes. To make myself less conspicuous, I would take out some papers and act as if I was following directions or looking for an address. I could expect that all the people near me would continue walking. Anyone who stopped or loitered in the area was a potential problem; he could be someone who was watching me.

When I traveled on the local tram, I always got off one stop before or one stop after my real destination. Also, I never waited for the tram to stop. Rather, I would jump off while it was still moving; so that if anyone was following me, I would be long gone by the time he got off. If someone leapt off the tram immediately after me, I had good reason to believe that he was following me.

When I was safely hidden in my room, I still had to have a list of procedures that would give me a chance to escape if the

Gestapo appeared at my door. I kept a chair propped under the doorknob so that they would have to break down the door to get into my room. I never locked the window. In fact, I opened and closed it each day to make sure I could open it quickly and easily. When I slept, I kept the window open about 15 centimeters. This would allow me hear everything that was going on in the street and then to quickly escape. When soldiers accompanied the Gestapo, one could hear the tramping of their boots blocks away. I slept fully dressed, including my shoes. My coat and gloves were always ready, to be put on, right next to the window. I was prepared to exit my window in an instant. My senses were tuned to any unusual sound. Even while asleep, the slightest noise would awaken me and I would be poised at my window in a heartbeat.

The details of how I was forced to live in order to survive convey only the most superficial sense of what it was like during those times. Every second of every day, I lived in total fear and anxiety. I was fully aware that each minute could be my last. Any person I encountered could be the person who would kill me or turn me over to those who were sworn to kill me. That person could be a Gestapo agent in street clothes, a gentile store owner, a gentile landlord or another Jew in hiding. Every sound could signal a predator stalking me. Only total vigilance could ensure the possibility of survival. Even in sleep, it was not possible to find rest. This had been my life for most of the last five years and would be my way of life for the foreseeable future.

Though I had a new identity, my problems were not over. The Gestapo had issued a new decree requiring that all identification papers be revalidated every two weeks. In order to comply, one had to appear in person in front of a Gestapo officer to have his papers stamped. Without that stamp, the papers were invalid, and if you were stopped and your papers were not revalidated, you were taken in for questioning. Jews in hiding, who had false papers, needed this stamp from the Gestapo. If they were taken in for questioning, they were doomed.

I learned that the head of maintenance in the municipal building where the Gestapo conducted their revalidation program claimed that he could gain access to the Gestapo offices at night and procure their official stamp. For a fee, he agreed to validate any papers that I would present to him. Hence, every other week each of my families gave me their papers and I handed them in to my contact for revalidation. This official also provided me with any other documents that we needed, for instance, travel permits. I worked with this man for some time. Fortunately, I realized that it was becoming too dangerous and decided to stop this contact. A few days later, the Gestapo caught a number of people who were providing their official stamps and permits for money. The head of maintenance was one of them and I would have been another if I had not stopped this contact when I did. Unfortunately, this roundup led the Nazis to some of the people to whom I was supplying money. The Gestapo was able to force them to admit that they were receiving money from me. They also forced my description out of them. The Gestapo concluded that I was not only helping to hide Jews, but that I was also working for the resistance. As a result, they made my capture a high priority. I was extremely fortunate that no one knew where I lived for they could not tell the Gestapo where to look for me.

A few weeks later, in the middle of a cold and gloomy night, as I lay on my bed half-asleep, I was startled by a sudden noise. Instantly, I was wide awake, trying to determine what had awakened me. I heard the sound again and it seemed to be coming from the first floor. I jumped out of bed and ran to the window, listening as I pulled on my coat and gloves. When I heard the landlady talking to someone, I could sense the terror in her voice. I also realized that someone banging on the front door had made the sound. Only Nazi soldiers and the Gestapo pounded on the door of a private house in the middle of the night.

Without hesitation, I climbed out of the window, firmly clutched the drainpipe and let myself down to the ground. I do not think I made even the slightest sound. I ran noiselessly through the yard, through the back gate and into the alley. As I had planned, I followed the maze of alleyways into another street. I thanked G-d that I had escaped their evil clutches once again. As far as I knew, the Gestapo were still trying to convince the landlady to open the door. I was pleased by the thought that when they finally did get into my room, all they would find would be some gentile clothing.

City Hall, occupied by the Gestapo, is where I worked with the head of maintenance to validate papers for desperate Jews.

Chapter 13

Someone Steps Forward: His Kindness Continues

The next day, I wandered through the city with the feeling that the noose was tightening around my neck. In the last few weeks my situation had become dramatically more perilous. It was clear to me that the Gestapo was specifically hunting for me. It was equally clear that I had to leave Pressburg. However, I knew that leaving the city had resulted in a tragic end for many Jews who had tried.

I was also very worried about the safety of my families to whom I had been delivering rent money each week. If I was to leave the city, and they did not receive their regular sum, they would be evicted. I could be certain that within one week hundreds of people would be captured, tortured and murdered.

At first, I did not know what to do. I felt that I would eventually be captured if I were to walk along the streets. But just as surely, something had to be done to find someone who would be willing to take over my job and he must be found soon. I knew that I had no real choice. I would continue my efforts to protect my families. I understood that I would be able to help these people for a short time only. Soon, the Gestapo would capture me.

I needed to find a Jew who could act as a liaison to Reb Shlomo Stern, the good man who was providing the money, and who could act as a conduit to distribute the money. How could I ever expect to find a trustworthy person who would be willing to risk everything, who could keep the details of the entire undertaking in his head without a piece of paper? Where would I find someone who knew every detail of the city and had used this knowledge to outwit the Nazis for years? The more I thought about the situation, the more discouraged I became for the fate of my families.

Looking back on those days, I wonder how I could have become discouraged. I had been delivered by G-d's mercy from totally hopeless situations time after time. Once again, facing this seemingly impending tragedy, I would be a witness to G-d's helping hand.

I was walking along the street, immersed in these thoughts, when a heavenly emissary suddenly appeared in front of me. This vision presented itself in the person of a young man, a dear friend named Shlomo ben Mordechai HaLevi Greenwald. He was standing in the doorway of one of the houses that I was walking past. I stared at him in an effort to make sure that this person was indeed my friend. He was pale as a corpse, trembling from the cold, looking as if he would die at any moment.

As always, my first reaction was to be careful. Before I acknowledged him, I looked about diligently to make sure that we were not being observed or followed. I watched for about five minutes making sure that no one was waiting around. My friend did not move once the entire time. When I was satisfied that I was not being followed, I walked over to him. As I stood in front of him, he made no sign that he recognized me, in fact he hardly blinked. I did not know what to make of his lack of reaction. In a whisper, I told him who I was. He looked at me with a totally surprised expression on his face. It was then that I realized that my disguise was so effective that he had no clue as to my identity. When he realized what I was saying, his puzzled expression turned to an immensely happy smile. He reached out and hugged me silently. Suffice it to say that we were both overjoyed to find a childhood friend alive. But for all our joy, we both knew that it was too dangerous to continue our reunion in public. I suggested that he follow me at a discreet distance to a safe alleyway.

Once we were hidden in our alleyway refuge, we eagerly exchanged the details of our personal condition. I asked him

The arched doorway where I found my friend Shlomo Greenwald standing in the bitter cold

Shlomo Greenwald, 1944

why he was standing in that doorway, out in the bitter cold. With his teeth chattering as he talked, he related the amazing story of how he was contending with his landlord's curiosity. Shlomo also had acceptable gentile papers that had allowed him to rent a room from a non-Jew. However, the landlord had asked him if he was working. "Of course," Shlomo had answered, without telling the landlord where he worked.

To maintain the illusion, Shlomo left the house every morning as if going off to work and would return home from work in the early evening. Throughout the day, he would go from one apartment building to another, staying in the stairwell for a half-hour, then standing in the doorway of another for the next half-hour. In this way, he would pass the entire day. In the late afternoon, when he had finished his "day's work," he would find rest and warmth in his apartment.

For Shlomo, as for all the surviving Jews in Slovakia, survival was totally dependent upon the ability to appear "normal" in the gentile world. Any oversight, no matter how trivial, that caused someone to look more closely was to invite death.

And if hiding meant blending into the gentile society, survival was a minute-to-minute battle to devise strategies to stay alive one more day or even one more hour. In addition to the unimaginable stress of such a lifestyle, hiding in this way imposed a terrible sense of isolation. Each of us had to limit our contact with other Jews for our own survival; there was the ever-present fear of attracting attention. The brutal torture the Nazis employed was diabolical and you could not allow another Jew to know where to find you, not your best friend, not even your brother, because if he is caught it is a good chance that you will also be caught. It was almost certain he would not be able to keep your whereabouts secret.

As Jews we derive much of our strength from our community which defines not only our role but also our moment-to-moment dealings, hence this isolation was another trying hardship. To be alone in a room at night, in a stranger's house, in a neighborhood that hates him, in a city that wants to kill him and everyone like him was in itself a prison sentence, was in itself another torture the Nazis imposed on us.

Shlomo and I had talked for about half an hour when I realized that he was now shivering severely. I felt terrible that I had not understood how frozen he was. Obviously, we had to escape the cold. Shlomo agreed, but he did not know of a place that was warm and safe. I remembered that there was a medical building within a few blocks where we might be able to warm ourselves and not attract attention. The building housed a number of medical offices spread out over four or five floors. There was a waiting room on each floor where patients would sit for hours before they were called in to see the doctor.

I told him, "Go sit in one of the waiting rooms and when your turn approaches, leave and go to one of the doctor's offices on another floor. This way you won't have to stay out in the cold. You should be able to stay indoors for a few hours."

Shlomo agreed but asked if I could show him where the office building was. Usually, I would have given him directions and told him that I would meet him there. Walking together was simply too dangerous. But a fellow Jew was in need and only I could help. Perhaps in the merit of this kindness Hashem would protect me. I agreed to escort him. Maybe it was because he looked so pale and weak that I felt compelled to accompany him.

We had traveled 100 meters and were crossing a street when Shlomo mumbled that he was not feeling well, that his head was spinning. I looked at him and could see that he was about to faint right there in the middle of the street. His eyes were glassy and he was having difficulty walking. I quietly pleaded with him to summon all his will and strength. If he did collapse, I would have no choice but to abandon him. If he fell to the ground, surely a passerby would summon a police officer. I could not place my life in such great danger, I had promised my mother that I would remain alive.

Thank G-d, he made it to the other side of the street. I grabbed hold of him with all my strength, and leaned him against a wall so that he would not fall over. I talked to him and calmed him down. After a few minutes, he said he felt better, so we started walking again. We had to walk only a few blocks and in five minutes we made it to the medical building. He stayed in the building for most of the day and by midafternoon he felt strong enough to walk back to his room. I found out that Shlomo's condition was caused not only by the cold but also by the fact that he had not eaten in days. This was just another accepted fact of our lives, never knowing when we would eat next.

I managed to tell him the details of my situation; about the work I was doing in providing money for my families and about the fact that the Gestapo was close on my trail. Shlomo informed me that I could no longer carry out this task no matter how important it was. I would be captured and there would be no one to help these Jews. He was convinced that someone else should assume the responsibility. With great joy he said that he wanted to take over for me. I tried to make him understand the risks and the precautions he would have to employ to avoid capture. Despite the extreme danger involved, he took full responsibility for more than 50 secret meetings and payments.

His reaction to my story was proof that it was G-d's will that had decreed that Shlomo and I should meet on that day in that place. G-d placed me where I needed to be to help Shlomo survive that day. Shlomo was so cold and sick that I am sure he would have collapsed in the street where he would have been captured. And for myself, when I had given up any hope of finding a way to take care of my families, G-d led me to a doorway. That one doorway held a person who had the courage to risk everything to take care of my families and had the intelligence to outwit the Gestapo to do it.

Shlomo's family had an important place in the Jewish community of Pressburg. His father, Rabbi Mordechai Greenwald, was a teacher at the elementary yeshiva, Yesodei HaTorah. Rabbi Greenwald and his entire family were captured and killed by the Nazis. Only Shlomo survived the war by hiding as a gentile. He passed away in New York City in 1972. Though Shlomo had no children of his own, the merit of risking his life day by day to save hundreds of Jewish souls, so many of them children, will stand as an everlasting tribute to his family and to him.

With the certainty that Shlomo would take care of the families, I was now free to leave the city, and, in fact, I had no choice but to do so. The Gestapo had my picture in my latest disguise and they were posting it in every police station, on the streets and throughout the city. More importantly, it appeared that they had made my capture a high priority. I was a dangerous criminal who had committed the worst of crimes: In my small way, I had thwarted the Nazi effort to annihilate the Jewish people. I would slip out of Pressburg quietly, but this was not enough for me. I had to take revenge against the Nazis.

Chapter 14.

Becoming a Partisan

Joining the partisans would not be easy. If it was dangerous to hide in Pressburg, it was much more perilous to try to leave it. To hide in the city, one had to avoid the Nazis at all costs. To leave the city, one had to place himself in the hands of the Nazis at numerous checkpoints. It was not a matter of simply getting on a train and leaving. You could only buy a train ticket if you had a travel pass. This rule applied to everyone: to travel outside the city limits required a stamped travel permit, and only the Gestapo issued these permits. Every exit route was guarded and you had to show papers — travel permits or travel orders — to pass through these checkpoints. If you had no permit, you were taken back to the Gestapo station for further questioning. In my case, the Gestapo had my picture and they were looking for me. They would identify me immediately, without having to ask a single question.

Fortunately, I had already formulated a plan to leave the city and join the partisans. One key element of the plan was to have a partisan unit to join. My efforts during the preceding months, had enabled me to discover a number of people who were involved in the underground resistance in Pressburg. These people could connect me with the partisans. Once I made my intentions known to the underground, it was only two or three days until I was handed a piece of paper that would be my admission to the partisans. It told me to go to the town of Svetkrisenteronim and travel across the Hron River to a little village called Dornosdena. Once in this village, I would be contacted.

The other crucial element of my plan was to have a way to travel safely. To join the partisans I had to get to the mountains. Therefore, I had taken the precaution of procuring a stamped Gestapo travel order and a travel permit while I could still employ the services of the janitor at the Gestapo offices.

I would never have escaped the city or been able to purchase a train ticket without these permits. The permit would allow me to leave, but it would not allow me to approach the frontier where checkpoints marked the edge of the territory that the Germans controlled. No one passed these checkpoints unless he had a specific travel order. Since the Gestapo had issued my travel order, no one would dare question it. The travel order specifically directed me to go to Svetkrisenteronim, a town next to an area that was known to be in the hands of the partisans.

By this time, the Slovak army, which had joined the revolt earlier, had been defeated and the Nazis had captured most of the soldiers. Some soldiers escaped the Germans and fled to the mountains. Once there, they joined the partisans. The surviving hard-core partisans were holding out in the mountains and were fighting the Nazis. For the most part they were fighting for their survival, but we often heard reports that they had managed to inflict significant damage on the Germans on a hit-and-run basis. I was proud that I was now a young man who was going to be a partisan; I was going to stand side by side with real soldiers to defend myself and my people from the Germans. The thought that I would be able to fight back, that I could kill the Nazis, that I could help stop the Nazi monster, was exhilarating. Visions of valor and heroism filled my naive imagination. I was anxious to get to the partisans and begin my new life as a warrior. Even with all I had seen and experienced, I was still very young and had much to learn about life and war.

When the time came for me to leave, I became increasingly nervous. I understood that, as a partisan, I would be in mortal danger every second. At any instant, a shrill command or an outstretched arm could end my freedom. With no warning, a bullet could end my life.

As I approached the train station's platform, where there should have been hundreds of civilians, I could see only military uniforms. There were mostly regular army uniforms intermixed with uniforms bearing the hated SS insignia. Each soldier carried a gun of one type or another slung over his shoulder and a pack on his back. Military personnel were milling around awaiting transportation to somewhere in the war. By the time I was actually on the platform, I could see that some of the soldiers were standing guard, spaced every three or four meters with their weapons at the ready. Most of those on guard were the SS troopers. As I walked past those soldiers, I was aware of the presence of the most hated of all, the Gestapo. It is impossible, and it would in fact be a lie, to refer to them as men or as people. They were predators and it was possible to pick them out of the crowd, simply by the way they moved and the way they glared at people. As I moved past a Gestapo agent, his eyes followed me, checking every detail, looking for a reason to kill me. It was more than a look of hatred. It was a look that conveyed an intense desire to destroy me. I knew that if he detected one detail that raised any suspicion, he would pounce on me like a hungry cat on a wounded bird.

With all these terrifying visions assaulting my imagination, I walked the entire length of the platform, through all those soldiers, to the ticket window. One slip and I was a dead man. At the window, using all my will to control my panic, I presented my permit and requested a ticket to Svetkrisenteronim. I tried to appear calm even though I was so nervous my legs trembled exceedingly. I expected the ticket agent to yell for the Gestapo and I was ready to run, though, where one Jewish boy surrounded by hundreds of armed Nazis could run, I had no idea.

To my surprise and relief, the ticket agent looked at my permit, pushed a ticket toward me and asked for payment. I handed him the money and asked when the next train would leave. I only had to wait 10 minutes, but it seemed like hours. I had to wait without raising suspicion, without provoking the SS guards or the Gestapo. Within a minute a Gestapo agent stepped in front of me demanding my papers. My heart was pounding so loudly, I was sure he could hear it. It took all of my courage and self-control to stand calmly and hand over my travel order as if I had nothing to fear. This moment was a nightmare; by a supreme act of will I was frozen in a posture of external composure while every nerve and muscle was screaming for me to run. It seemed to take forever, but I am sure only a few seconds passed as he carefully read my travel order. As he began to raise his eyes, eyes that I knew were those of the angel of death, his right hand came up in a salute of exaggerated respect. He handed me my documents and as he pointed in the direction of the train I was to take, he wished me a good day.

I walked toward the train and was stopped again by another Gestapo officer, with exactly the same results. Nazis were saluting me. The Gestapo was guarding every door to the train. As I attempted to board, I was stopped again, and once more my papers were returned with a respectful salute. Though I was being given such honor, I could not dispel the terror of looking into the Gestapo agent's eyes while he inspected my papers.

Once on the train, I realized that I was the only civilian on it. Now I was literally in the lions' den, one lamb among hundreds of ravenous lions. As the train moved through the countryside, soldiers got on and off and the Gestapo conducted periodic inspections of my documents. And though each ended in similar fashion, I felt as if I was in grave danger with each inspection. As always, I had a plan to escape. I tried to stay within a few strides of the car door at all times. I reviewed the training I had received when I was studying at Nitra. Fortunately, I did not have to leap from a speeding train.

Some hours and many salutes later, the train reached Svetkrisenteronim. This town also served as headquarters for the German Army for the region. Here too, there were soldiers everywhere. I felt it was very dangerous to wait around the city any longer than absolutely necessary, so I set off immediately in the direction of the bridge over the Hron River. As I looked toward the bridge, I was aware of the Tatras Mountains rising majestically on the other side of the river.

I had just spent hours in total abject fear. As I gazed at the mountains, I knew that the partisans lived there. I imagined these were special, powerful men who were not afraid of the hated Germans, and soon I would be one of them. As I walked toward the last checkpoint at the foot of the bridge, I prayed: "O, G-d, help me to make it across alive."

"Halt! Don't move! No civilians can pass!" The shouted orders of a German SS border guard interrupted my prayer and

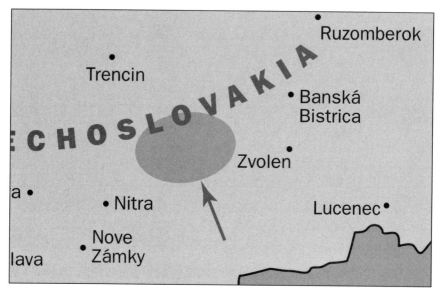

The arrow shows where I crossed into partisan territory. The circled area indicates the partisans' sphere of command.

jolted me back to the reality of the Nazis. After a myriad of document inspections by the Gestapo, this was the first time that I was looking down the muzzle of a machine gun. I calmly handed him my travel order and almost instantly his entire demeanor changed. He said, "It isn't often that I meet a secret agent who is risking his life to go into enemy territory to infiltrate the partisans." This, of course, explained the Nazis' respectful salutes. The partisans were so feared by the Nazis that any one who was being sent behind enemy lines to spy on them and sabotage them was held in the highest esteem by the Germans.

He continued talking without waiting for any comment from me. All I could think about was that at any second a Gestapo agent could come running toward the bridge screaming about my real identity, that I was a partisan and should be killed immediately. Still, the checkpoint guard went on telling me that the German troops were deathly afraid of the insurgent fighters. He told me about the many casualties they had suffered at the hands of the hit-and-run partisan bands. He went on, with his voice raised in anger, "How dare they challenge the Third Reich!"

All the while I listened with feigned sympathy. "What chutzpah!" I was tempted to say, but I thought better of it, Nazis were not known to use such jargon.

When the SS guard seemed to be finished, I started across the bridge and never looked back. About halfway across I could hear the guard call out to me, "Good luck. Don't get caught."

I chose not to respond to the guard's good wishes. The knowledge that the Germans were running scared thrilled me. As I neared the far end of the bridge, I thought, "G-d has kept me alive this day." And I prayed, "May He keep me alive to see their final downfall."

Once on the other side, my objective was to reach a little village called Dornosdena. I had been told to follow the only road, which I found was little more than a narrow snow-covered mountain trail. The walk was only about two kilometers. However, the trail was so rough and steep that I was forced to walk very slowly; and even then I was afraid that I would slip off the path and freeze to death.

As I struggled along the route, I was greatly surprised to hear someone shout, "Hey! You are not from around here." I looked in the direction of the voice and I saw a burly peasant who was standing a few meters to the side of the trail. If he had not called out to me, I would have walked right past him.

He continued, "Watch out for the partisans. If they catch you, they will kill you." I should have been frightened by this assertion. Instead, I was again reassured that I was now in territory where it was the partisans who were feared more than the Germans. He told me that the village was now only a ten-minute walk away.

As I entered the little town, an old peasant woman came up to me and commented that I must not be from this region. I told her that I was from Pressburg. "You had better get to your destination before dark," she warned ominously. "It's not safe to walk around the town or on the roads at night. It is very dangerous. The partisans shoot at anything that moves."

With nightfall within two to three hours, I did not have to worry. However, this message was the cause of great satisfaction for me. This was the happiest moment I had experienced for a long time. It was a great relief to no longer be frightened of the Nazis.

When I had first received my travel order, I was also given a series of passwords to use when I made contact with the partisan guide. It was this old woman who directed me to the house where I would make my first contact with the partisans.

I knocked and the door opened immediately. The residents were not frightened to answer my knock; they were not expecting to find a Gestapo agent when they opened the door. They were not living with the pervasive fear that I had endured for so many years.

I greeted the peasant who opened the door. He gruffly asked me what I wanted. I repeated the password that I had been given and without saying anything, he winked at me. Turning, he closed the door, leaving me outside in the cold. Though he had said nothing, I felt that he had understood my secret and that I had made my contact.

Within a few minutes, that same peasant came around the side of the house with a boy and a horse. He told me that the boy would show me the way to the next village, a place called Hornosdena. This trip would be longer and more difficult and I would need a guide. I was told that in Hornosdena I would find a man named Nemchok, who would bring me to the partisans. Nemchok, a peasant living in the village, was on very friendly terms with the partisans and provided them with information on German troop movements on almost a daily basis. I would eventually find out that a network of these villagers was a key factor in the partisans' success. Not only did they provide information that allowed the partisans to attack the Germans in positions where the terrain favored the partisans, but also the information that the partisans received from the villagers about the movement of the German troops made it impossible for the Germans to ambush them. As a result, a small group of very aggressive partisans with excellent intelligence could wreak havoc on the larger, better-equipped German army.

The boy, who looked to be about 13, climbed onto the horse and offered his hand to help me up. The trail was narrow and steep and as a result we traveled very slowly. After a few hours we reached Hornosdena. The boy took me directly to Nemchok's house.

Nemchok was waiting impatiently inside. I expected to be questioned about why I wanted to join the partisans and what I knew about being a soldier. Instead, all he wanted to talk about was news from the city. He wanted me to tell him everything I knew. I told him as much as I knew about conditions in Pressburg. Most of my information was about Jews who were taken by the Nazis and he listened to me with obvious disinterest. However, when I began to relate what I had seen of troop movements, Nemchok became attentive. He was very interested in my observations of the troops heading out of the city toward Svetkrisenteronim and asked many questions about the numbers of troops, the arms they were carrying and where they detrained.

We spoke for at least half an hour, then Nemchok fed me supper. I was so tired from the rigors of my trip that I had no trouble falling asleep afterwards. At daybreak, I was shaken awake. As I finished breakfast, there were noises from outside the house. I could hear the sound of horses walking and neighing. Suddenly, there was a loud pounding on the door that startled me. Nemchok must have been expecting the knock because he jumped up and quickly opened it without hesitation.

The blast of cold air made me realize how warm and comfortable I felt in Nemchok's house. But nothing could have prepared me for what followed that cold wind into the room. Two of the tallest, largest men I had ever encountered walked in. Aside from their immense size, their appearance was fierce. Their eyes were hard, and glowed with the fire of unbridled anger. These were men who had long been removed from the civilizing effects of normal social contact. I thought to myself that these two certainly would have no problem killing a man when the need arose. The thought sent chills up and down my spine. This was the first challenge to my romantic notion of the partisans. The obvious hardness and ferocity of these men conveyed an undeniable sense of the reality of life as a partisan.

As I sat there, a boy too frightened to move or say a word, Nemchok conversed with the two men. There was a good deal of laughing and joking, so I concluded that they must be friends. After 5 or 10 minutes of this bantering, they seemed to come to some sort of agreement. Abruptly, Nemchok turned to me and announced with authority: "You're going with these men."

Just months earlier, I had been living the life of a *yeshiva bachur* (schoolboy) sitting at my bench, filling my mind with the holy Scripture. As I stood next to the horses, I realized that I was placing my life in the hands of two strange men who were very different from the people whom I had trusted in my previous life. "Are these two killers a vision of my future?" I wondered. Even though I had great misgivings, I knew that I had no choice. I could only go forward; returning to my past life was impossible.

Gathering all my courage, I climbed onto the horse in front of me with an outward confidence that I feigned. We left the village traveling in single file along a snow-covered trail that led toward the mountains. It was not necessary for me to direct my horse because he was following the horse in front of me. The totally white world that we had entered and the steady rhythm of the horses were hypnotic. With nothing to do, my mind began to wander and soon I was lost in my thoughts.

Surely the partisans knew of all the good work I had done for their people in Pressburg. The partisan leadership would be very grateful and I was certain that they would greet me with an honor guard and music. I would receive a hero's welcome. I thought about how wonderful it would be to be able to rest for more than a few minutes at a time. I could begin to recover from the effects of all the troubles I had endured. The thought that they would give me a nice room in which to sleep called to my mind a vision of a warm, soft bed with thick blankets and luxurious pillows. I would spend days in this wonderful bed as I waited for the end of the war in peace and tranquility.

A loud snorting and whinnying of a horse awoke me from my daydream. As I looked around, the second horse and then my horse repeated the protest. I realized that we were beginning to climb into the mountains and that the trail would become more treacherous than it had been. This trip would be more difficult than I had anticipated. And I would have to pay attention to the erratic movement of the horse as he ascended this trail or I could easily be thrown. Nevertheless, I realized that this suffering was but a small hardship to endure to reach my freedom and a more normal life. The honors that I would receive from the partisans would be a pleasant bonus.

We traveled for hours, the horses plowing through half a meter of snow that covered the trail. Most of the time the path wound through dense forest with tall trees on either side within a meter or two of the path. The trees were shrouded in white, giving a feeling of traveling through a tunnel of snow. When the wind would pick up, the snow swirled down from the tree branches to white out all the details of the forest. Sometimes, even my companions were cloaked in this whiteness and disappeared from my view. When we reached a high point along the trail, I could see snow-covered mountains in every direction. Under more normal circumstances, the scene would have been exhilarating. But for me, it only served to emphasize the fact that I was removed from all civilized society.

Occasionally, I caught a glimpse of a deer or a fox through a break in the trees. But for hours on end I saw little sign of life and absolutely no human life, and for the entire time, my companions uttered not even a word. It was as if the two partisans were no longer human and I was totally alone with no connection to anyone. This dire feeling of isolation and loneliness devoured me.

My companions had stopped next to a tree and were dismounting. The one who had been in the lead position looked up at me and announced, "We're here!" These were the first words I had heard since we left Nemchok's house. I looked around excitedly. I looked in every direction, but saw nothing but snow and trees.

I immediately reverted to the defenses honed by my years of experience with the Nazis. I was instantly alert. This must be a trap, an act of treachery by my companions. I had no weapon. No one would know that I had been murdered in this desolate spot. I was trapped, one young teenager against two seasoned killers. My only hope was to run back over the trail that I had just traveled. I was about to prod my horse when the leader called to me. "Come on. We're taking you to central command."

The other partisan brushed aside the snow revealing a board set at a 45-degree angle lying on a hill that was directly behind a cluster of trees. The partisan lifted the board and revealed an opening to a cave. The second partisan told me that he was remaining outside to take his turn on guard. He pointed toward the cave in a way that I understood as a direct command to go inside. I crouched down and entered the cave with the other partisan behind me.

The large cave I had entered was at least three meters wide and two meters high. Only lanterns and two campfires provided light. To breathe, I had to remain stooped over because smoke hung in the upper quarter of the cave. Along both sides of the cave was planking set up off the dirt floor and I could see that there were patches of cut straw lying around. As we walked toward the back of the cave, we passed a number of partisans cleaning their weapons. No one so much as looked up to see who was coming by; not a single word of greeting was proffered. The tunnel was about 20 meters long. When we reached the end, we came to a heavy wooden door. My escort knocked on the door and was given permission to enter. He went in alone, closing the door behind him. I was greatly relieved by the totally unexpected level of military decorum and respect shown by my escort. Almost immediately, I heard him say in a respectful tone, "I brought the boy from Pressburg."

"Bring him in!" a second voice commanded.

At last! I was about to speak face to face with the commander of the local partisans. My heart was filled with excitement and anticipation. Surely, he would know of all the bold and dangerous exploits I had carried out for the underground. I was certain that the commander would welcome me with open arms and would praise my courage and resourcefulness. I expected that after we talked he would introduce me to the other soldiers who made up this brigade, singing my praises to one and all.

The door opened, my guide emerged, but said nothing to me; he only waved his arm toward the door, motioning me to enter. I concluded that he meant for me to go into the commander's room. Expecting the best, I walked confidently through the doorway. The bang of the door as it slammed shut behind me made me jump. However, nothing could shatter my happiness. I had waited for this dreamed-of moment for so long.

Standing stiffly inside the command room, I faced a heavy table made of rough, unfinished wood. Behind the table sat another very large, imposing figure, dressed like a soldier. His face was etched with deep lines. It was hard, as were his eyes, though they had the light of intelligence. His shoulders were wide and his arms heavily muscled. Altogether he had the appearance of a man of dauntless determination and iron will. I thought, this is a man who could lead other men into battle. I jumped again as the commander yelled in my direction, "Do you want to join us?"

I was shaken by the harshness in his voice. Before I could form the words for a response, my head meekly nodded yes. The commander reacted with an even louder question: "What is your name?"

"Avrohom Cohn," I answered proudly though my voice was shaking and I could feel my knees knocking. Again he yelled, but this time so loudly that his voice seemed to reverberate in the room. Again I answered, but this time with much more humility. "My name is Avrohom Cohn."

My partisan commander Jan Husik

I was shaking with fright. I had goose bumps all over my body. This was hardly the greeting one would expect for an honored hero. However, I did not have much time to brood over the impoliteness of my reception.

"Give me your papers!" The commander bellowed.

I was not sure I would be able to

extend my hand to give him my papers. Somehow I managed to control my shaking arm and placed the papers in his outstretched hand.

He looked at my papers for a moment and then thundered, "It says here that your name is Jan Kovic, liar!" He slammed his hand heavily onto the tabletop with such force that the room seemed to quake; cups, pencils and paper flew off the table. He roared at me again, "Your name is Jan Kovic! Do you understand?"

My eyes were wide in terror. I am sure I looked like a child who was convinced that there was a monster hiding under his bed. I thought now I was among friends and I did not have to hide my real identity. Before I could explain my answer, he screamed at me one more time. "Get out of here and go get yourself a gun! Here you don't get food for nothing!" This time his eyes were dark and hard with anger.

The commander did not want his men to know I was a Jew for there could be partisans who were anti-Semitic.[1] He could not have infighting among his men. The last thing he wanted was intrigue and dissension. He wanted a unit of men who trusted one another. Therefore, I was Jan Kovic, a gentile, end of topic.

A movement at the far end of the table caught my attention and for the first time I realized that there was another partisan in the room. My attention had been so riveted on the dominating figure and personality of the commander, I had not noticed the presence of the second partisan. This one seemed

---

1. Though some partisan units included Jews, the partisans not only did not welcome them, they were often rabidly anti-Semitic, going as far as to expel them from their units (which meant certain death in the forest) or to murder them outright. Non-Jewish commanders would justify their refusal to accept Jews into their fighting units on the grounds that the peasants and townspeople on whom the partisans relied for information would begin to think of the partisans as defenders of the Jews, and so be less inclined to help them. Kowalski, *Anthology of Armed Jewish Resistance*, Brooklyn, 1985, pp. 117-20. Shalom Cholavsky, *Jewish Resistance During the Holocaust*, Jerusalem, 1971, pp. 323-8.

to be another battle-hardened warrior. He was not as physically imposing as the commander but still looked like a man who could kill when the time came. I would later learn that he was in fact the second in command. He grabbed my left arm and steered me toward the door. Pushing it open with his free hand, he shoved me through, back into the main, large room with the partisan soldiers. I stumbled clumsily feeling shamed and disheartened. I had fully expected to be appointed an officer at some level, with honor and respect. Instead, I had been treated with total disdain; it seemed that it was with great reluctance that they allowed me to stay.

My eyes were drawn from one partisan to the next. Each had been distracted from his individual chores by my unceremonious entrance. I stood, dumbfounded, with no idea where to go, where to get food, where to get an assignment, where to sleep or where to get a gun. I looked at the partisan nearest to me and asked in a feeble voice, "Where do I get a gun?" The question came out before I realized what I had said.

Though I had barely whispered, every man in the room burst into hysterical laughter. Again, I was totally humiliated. Moreover, I was perplexed by their reaction. Why were they making fun of me? They were showing me no respect, treating me as if I was simply a silly child of no importance. And no one gave the slightest impression that he intended to answer my question. I walked to the front end of the cave and asked again where I could get a gun. Once more, they all wildly laughed at me. I walked around the cave and repeated my question several times and received the exact same response.

I looked from face to face, unable to understand why no one would answer me. I noticed that one of the partisans was wearing what looked like a regular army uniform, with the emblems of an officer on his shoulders. I decided to try to explain my situation one more time in the hope that this real soldier might be different, in the hope that he would help me.

I walked over to him: "My name is Jan Kovic. I have just arrived to join the partisans. The commander agreed to take me, and told me to get a gun. But no one will tell me where they are stored. Whenever I ask for a gun, everyone laughs at me."

He told me what the commander meant, why everyone was laughing. They had each killed a German to get a gun.

When I heard this, my heart sank. My earlier glory-filled fantasies paled when confronted by reality. I had never learned from my teachers at yeshiva how to kill another man. And though I had experienced great violence and had seen Jews killed brutally, I myself had never acted violently. The entire idea was utterly foreign to me. I was bewildered, confused. I had no idea where I could turn.

In yeshiva, for one to raise a hand against another was unheard of, to even say or think anything negative was considered a terrible transgression. We learned humility, consideration for others, love of mankind and of G-d. We would go through great personal discipline to etch these character traits into our personality. Rising at 5 o'clock in the morning, retiring at 11 o'clock at night, we devoted the whole day, every day, to our studies. On Thursdays we stayed awake the entire night preparing for our weekly exams. Yes, we ate and slept, but our concern was to keep our bodies healthy in order to serve G-d more effectively, and grow spiritually.

To be thrust into a world at war, in which I was among those who could kill with their bare hands without a second thought, made my head reel. The officer must have sensed my despair. He arose from the wooden bench where he was sitting and instructed me to follow him. As he led me out of the cave, I thanked G-d that I had found at least one man who seemed more civilized than the others.

After a short walk, he bent down next to a tree and brushed away the snow to expose a small piece of wood. I saw as he moved more snow aside that it was a handle attached to a much bigger board. He stood up, pulling on the handle and as the board moved I could see that it was in fact a door, and underneath there was another cave. The officer crouched down to enter and I followed.

I was hoping that the cave would be a storehouse for guns. To my dismay, this cave was also being used as a bunker. A cloud of smoke hung near the ceiling, making it nearly impossible to see. I could tell that the ceiling was slightly lower than an average man's height and I could see it was less than half as large as the first cave. As my eyes became accustomed to the dark, I counted 10 partisans who were much like the men in the first bunker; these too were coarse, brutish and dangerous looking. They were all dressed for the winter cold. There was no furniture, no chairs or tables or beds. Everyone sat directly on the floor. The fire that they had made to cope with the fierce cold had filled the top third of the cave with smoke and it was only possible to breathe under this cloud. As I looked around, I noticed that their guns hung on pegs that they had driven into the earthen walls. I could imagine that each man never moved more than a few feet from his own gun.

To my surprise, the partisan nearest to me asked me my name and where I was from. This small display of normal civility gave me encouragement. I joined the men sitting on the floor, ready to relate the story of my exploits with the pride they warranted.

I announced that I had been involved in the resistance in Pressburg and that I had recently come from that city. There were no questions about details or conditions in the city; instead, to my horror, when they heard that I had just come from Pressburg, they pounced upon me, taking my bags. They retreated with all my worldly possessions like a pack of snarling dogs, discarding whatever they did not want onto the floor of the cave. I imagined that I heard the sound of growling as they tore through my things. The food I had for my trip was devoured. One of the scavengers of the pack found a bottle of after-shave lotion and before I could say a word he took a long drink and then passed it to a friend who also took a swig. The lotion was passed from partisan to partisan like a bottle of prized whiskey. The empty bottle was thrown to the floor. I sat there in stunned silence. I had not been prepared for this. This was not the way I expected to be treated by my comrades in arms. These people might be soldiers, but they acted like primitive savages.

I noticed that one of the partisans had not joined the group. He was sitting on the floor near me looking through his own clothing. When he glanced at me, I asked him what he was doing. His expression changed to a look of amazement. "What? Don't you have any fleas or lice in your clothing?" he asked.

In all innocence, I responded, "No, I certainly don't."

Another of the men screamed at me: "Liar!" He leaped up, grabbed the front of my shirt and repeated, "You're a liar!" He tore open my shirt, ripping off all the buttons. He began to examine my chest looking for fleas and lice. "I don't believe it," he muttered incredulously. Turning towards his friends, he announced loudly for all to hear: "He doesn't have any lice!"

Without another word to his friends and with no sign of an apology to me, he went back to his place on the floor. This brute acted as if he had done nothing unusual. This is a nightmare, I thought to myself. I prayed to G-d to deliver me from this hell.

Though I had only been with them a few hours, I was beginning to understand something of how the partisan army was structured. I soon learned much more. The vaunted partisan soldiers were mostly local peasants who had little or no education and who were accustomed to a relatively primitive lifestyle. These fierce warriors who engendered fear in the German war machine were common farmers fighting for their homes. Most of the soldiers were Slovaks, the rest were Czechs. In contrast, the officers were not recruited from the area's farmers. Generally, they were trained military men. Some were officers who had been separated from the regular army in the course of the war. Others were officers who had been dropped behind the German lines specifically to organize the partisan resistance. For instance, General Kustechenko, who was the chief commander for the region, and General Cherpansky, his second in command, were both officers from the Russian paratroopers. Likewise, the officer who brought me to the second bunker was a lieutenant from the Yugoslavian army. Consequently, the officers tended to be more standard military types; they were more civilized, more cultured and not nearly as crude as the other partisans.

The Yugoslavian officer called me over and whispered, "Do you understand why these men act this way?" I had no idea why any human being would choose to act like these men. The perplexed look on my face encouraged him to continue: "They are confined to this cave with nothing to do except clean their weapons day after day. They are not allowed to go out and walk around, to get exercise or even to visit their families. If they did, the Nazis would discover our location. And if we had to fight the Germans on their terms, we would be annihilated. So, the men have to sit around here doing nothing until they get an order to go out and fight. Sometimes, they have to stay confined to these caves for days at a time. On top of that, many of the men have lost family members or comrades to the Nazi butchers. When they seem like they have lost all semblance of humanity, I'm not surprised."

I could understand that these men were living under the worst hardships and I had great sympathy for their plight. Even so, I could not bear the thought of living with them in a cave under such terrible conditions. The lieutenant must have discerned from the expression on my face the battle that was raging in my mind. Again he leaned over and whispered, "On the other hand, my men do not have to live this way."

Without waiting for any response from me, he went on: "I lead one of the patrol units. Every day my soldiers go out in groups of two and scout through the mountains and valleys all around us. Their objective is to gather information about the position and movements of the German army. It is a difficult and dangerous assignment. Each patrol usually covers about 20 kilometers a day and there is no shelter from the winter cold. It is essential that the patrol not lead the Germans back to the camp. And occasionally, the scouts are unable to avoid direct confrontation with the Germans."

He continued, "If you joined the patrol unit, at least you would not be confined with the men in the cave waiting for something to happen. Most of the time you would be out on patrol."

I did not have to think long to make my decision. I told the lieutenant that I wanted to join his group. He must have felt guilty taking advantage of my state of mind to recruit me because he tried to dissuade me. He provided me with a series of graphic descriptions of the terrors I could encounter on patrol. They included freezing to death while asleep, being ambushed by the Germans, stepping on a mine and getting lost in the mountains. He informed me that his patrol unit had by far the highest casualties of any partisan unit.

But I had made my decision. "I don't care," I said. "I'm going with you. I'm not afraid." The macabre atmosphere in the bunker was enough to make me set aside my fears of the dangers I would encounter in the field.

But I had another motivation. With my most determined voice I said, "Besides, my only wish is to be able to fight the Nazis."

I found my bags, collecting the few belongings I could find after they had been picked over during the partisans' rampage, and walked back to where the lieutenant was sitting. All I could think about was getting out of this awful place.

I was relieved to see that he had a slight smile on his face. "Our bunker is on the next mountain," he said as he turned toward the door of the cave.

He pushed open the door and I followed him outside. After he closed the door, we carefully pushed a thick layer of snow over it. I could see that within minutes the ever-present wind would blow away any telltale signs that we left in the snow and no one would know there was a door to a cave next to that tree.

As we set out through the deep snow, he said, "There are essentially three rules that every partisan must know and follow. First, you must fight the Germans to your very last breath. Second, you must follow every single order to the letter without fail. Third, never, ever, walk outside without a weapon and never let it out of your hands as long as you breathe. Anyone who violates any of those rules will be brought to a partisan military tribunal, which will decide whether you are guilty or not. There is only one sentence for a person found guilty: death by gunshot."

While he spoke, I nodded my acceptance of every point he made. I did not think I would have any problem living up to those rules, and more importantly, the lieutenant was much more civilized than the partisans whom I had left; I assured him that I wanted to stay in his group.

We crossed a small valley to the base of the next mountain. He started up the mountain with me in close pursuit. Having to push through the thigh-high snow while traveling uphill made the last 200 meters very difficult. He stopped near a large boulder. Pushing aside the snow behind the rock where it was embedded in the frozen earth, he exposed a wooden plank about a meter square. As before, he lifted the plank to reveal the entrance to a cave.

I followed him into the dimly lit bunker. This cave was not as smoke filled as the other bunkers had been. There was a low bench that ran continuously along the perimeter of the bunker. There were about 10 partisans sitting on this bench, with a number of guns hung on wall pegs. At intervals on the bench there were piles of two or three travel bags or knapsacks. These bags were the personal belongings of each partisan and marked the portion of the bench which served as a bed for that soldier. Against one of the walls was a small fire that served both as a source of heat and a kitchen. The partisans all appeared to be young men and were dressed like the ones I had met earlier. They were also sitting there doing nothing while a few cleaned their guns.

However, they were not as tightly wound up as the men in the first two groups. When the lieutenant informed the group that I had arrived from Pressburg and was joining them, no one attacked my belongings or me. Two or three asked me a few questions about what was happening in Pressburg, but mostly they were quiet. They were all Slovaks. The one exception was a German Communist who had escaped from

My partisan unit, November 1944

his homeland to fight against the Nazis. I was surprised that the partisans would trust any German. I was not sure that I would ever be able to completely trust this man. In fact during every assignment I always made sure that my back was never toward this German.

From all the partisans I had encountered in these underground bunkers I was by far the youngest. They were all seasoned warriors and, despite my experience outwitting the Nazis, I was still like a little schoolboy compared to them.

The lieutenant asked me if I intended to stay with the group. I answered an emphatic, "Yes!" Though these soldiers were clearly peasants, I did not have the feeling of revulsion that had come over me when I encountered the other partisans. For the first time, I felt that I would be able to stay and fight side by side with the partisans.

The lieutenant seemed satisfied with my enthusiasm. He gave me my first assignment: "Tomorrow you will get your chance to be a partisan soldier. You will go out on patrol with two soldiers who will teach you how to use a gun and show you the way through the mountain paths. They will also show you how to move through the forest without leaving a trail back to the camp."

I thought to myself, "Finally." I looked at the lieutenant and asked, "How do I get a gun?"

I half-expected someone to yell out, "Go kill a German!" But instead the lieutenant only whispered that he could give me a gun and ammunition thus freeing me from my first assignment of having to kill a Nazi. He walked toward the back of the cave, stopping in front of a large wooden crate.

"Mr. Kovic!" I was called to attention by the sharp, loud voice of the lieutenant. I quickly joined him in front of the crate. When he lifted the lid, I was startled to see it contained at least 10 rifles and a few submachine guns. He reached down and pulled out one of the submachine guns and handed it to me. I took it with a confidence that I did not feel. I must have had a bewildered look on my face because he whispered to me, "Don't worry, they will show you how to use it before you leave tomorrow." I nodded in relief.

The lieutenant led me back toward the cave entrance, and pointing toward an unoccupied portion of the bench, told me that this piece of board two meters long and half a meter wide was my sleeping area. I put my bags on the bench; my gun and two bullet clips I placed on top of my bags. I sat down, for I was totally exhausted and famished. The partisans had stolen all of my food. I had to go on my first patrol the next day, so I needed to keep up my strength. I had to make sure that I learned to use the submachine gun. If we encountered the Germans I had to be ready to fight. I did not want a mission to fail because I was not properly prepared.

But what would it be like to shoot at someone who was shooting at me? I began imagining and fantasizing and visualizing what a battle would be like. I was a soldier and I was not afraid to die. I did not want to die like a sheep led to the slaughter. If I was going to die, I wanted to die as a man fighting valiantly against his enemies. If I was going to die, it would be with dignity.

Chapter 15

A Young Boy Fights the Nazis

I t was my being poked by a rifle which caused me to awake. The lieutenant was hovering over me and I leapt to my feet. As my head cleared, I realized that I had fallen asleep. "These two soldiers are going out on patrol," the lieutenant said. "Go with them and pay attention. They will show you what you need to know."

The soldiers walked toward the bunker door. They were to be my comrades, but they did not ask my name and they did not tell me theirs. They were leaving without saying one word to me. The lieutenant whispered to me, "Make sure you keep up with them and do exactly as they tell you." With that he walked away.

I had fallen asleep without so much as removing my coat, so I was all dressed and ready to leave. I grabbed my gun and ammunition and rushed out of the bunker after my comrades. I was relieved to find that they were waiting right outside the bunker. One of them closed the door and told me to cover it with snow. As I did my job, they began to walk away. I finished it quickly and ran after them.

It was a perfectly clear day and the sun had been up for no more than 20 minutes. The cold clean air on my face and in my lungs chased away the drowsiness that lingered from a night in the stuffy, smoke-filled bunker. As we walked, I was exhilarated by the magnificence of the mountain scenery. The early-morning sun reflected on the snow-covered mountains like a kaleidoscope of pale pastel shades. It was hard to believe that this could be the setting for war.

I caught up with the nearest partisan and asked when they would show me how to use the gun. He replied, "Not yet. We're still too close to the bunker to fire our guns. If there are any Germans or informers in the area they will investigate the sounds of gunshots."

I understood his reasoning, but I could not help thinking that we better not run into any Germans. I would be of little

Partisans outside headquarters in the Tatras Mountains

help because I did not even know how to load the submachine gun that I carried. Even if I could get it loaded, I was not sure that I could hit anything if I pulled the trigger.

We continued to march through the snow-covered forest. Most of the time we climbed uphill. After about two kilometers, we emerged from the forest onto a high ridge. The ridge, which seemed to stretch in front of us for quite some distance, was free of trees and the wind had blown away virtually all of the snow. As a result, the surface of the ridge was bare frozen ground littered with rocks and boulders.

The partisan who had taken the lead position as we marched through the forest came over to me and explained in very hushed tones that we were going to walk along this ridge for a few kilometers. Because the ground was frozen we would not leave any tracks. He warned me to be very careful not to walk where there was snow and under no circumstances could I step on any snow along the ridge. There must be no trace of our presence there. He told me that when we finally left the ridge we would erase the marks we made in the snow for about half a kilometer. By traveling this way, if we were ambushed, no one could follow our tracks back to the bunkers. He also explained that they would show me a number of places like this one that were usually free of snow, so that I could travel quickly without leaving any tracks.

He asked me for my gun and an ammo clip. I handed both to him, thinking that I was finally going to shoot my gun. He showed me how to engage the ammo clip and how to move the first round into the chamber. He showed me the safety lock and speaking very slowly, as if he were giving instructions to someone who was not very intelligent, he warned me that the safety lock was to be left on always. "You only take off the safety lock when you are ready to shoot at the enemy. We don't want you killing one of us by accident and we don't want to have your gun going off accidentally giving our position away." I wanted to ask, "What if I have to shoot very quickly?" Something told me, though, to keep my question to myself.

I did ask if I would be able to practice shooting my gun. Instead, the leader informed me in a stern voice, "Do not fire your gun unless one of us gives you a direct order to fire at someone." He explained that when I got that order all I had to do was take off the safety lock, point the gun toward the target and pull the trigger.

The other one added, "Your gun will fire so many rounds so quickly that you will probably hit the target at least once." I was very unhappy to see a condescending smile pass quickly over his face. I felt that they were not taking me very seriously. I was totally committed to fighting beside these men. I wanted to learn to use my gun. I needed to be ready. When I encountered the Germans, I wanted them to face a soldier, not a little boy on an outing with grown-ups.

They both set off along the ridge. We had not gone more than a few hundred meters when I noted that we were not walking along the top of the ridge. Rather, we were walking three or four meters below it. I deduced that this way we could never be seen against the clear blue sky. I was beginning to understand that I had to be very observant to learn all the tricks I would need to survive, to catch on to the subtle survival skills that they might forget to tell me about.

I had never handled a weapon, so I had no idea what it would be like to carry a submachine gun for any distance. We had been walking for hours and all the while I had been loaded down by the heavy weapon on my shoulder. As the hours passed, I became extremely tired. At one point, I thought that I could not go any further. I had not eaten for about 24 hours and felt like I might pass out at any moment. However, I was certain that if I did faint, my comrades would leave me to freeze to death. But again, G-d must have given me extra strength because somehow I managed to keep up with them. Never once did I so much as fall behind.

After about two kilometers, we left the snow ridge and again began to walk through the deep snow. For about half a kilometer, we used branches from pine trees to wipe out our tracks. This worked fairly well because there was always enough wind to help blow the snow about. By the time the Nazis covered all the territory between our present location and the other side of the ridge looking for our tracks to start up again, the wind and new snowfalls would have completely covered the tracks that led back to our headquarters.

We had been walking for more than three hours without seeing any sign of the Germans or, for that matter, any indication of human life. My concern, that I would not be ready to shoot my gun if we were attacked, was beginning to seem unfounded. I was relieved.

We would go on daily patrol before daybreak.

It was early afternoon when we moved out of the forest into a clearing on the side of a mountain. Just a few paces into the clearing, the first partisan stopped and was joined by the second. When I came up behind them, I could see for the first time why they had stopped. We were looking out over a small valley. At the far end of the valley, I could see the rooftops of a small village. A narrow road led to the near end of the valley and wandered in and out of a patchwork of open fields and small stands of trees until it reached the village. As far as I could tell, this was the only road to the village.

I found out later that the road continued through the village and exited the valley at the other end. This road was of critical importance to the partisans. The Tatras Mountains, where the partisans hid and roamed freely, formed a long chain that ran roughly in an east-west direction. There were extensive railroads and highways that skirted the mountains but only this one road penetrated the mountains and ran roughly through the middle of the chain. To attack the partisans, the German Army had to either walk into the mountains from the outside or to come into the mountains on this one, narrow road. In the first case, the terrain was so rough that the Germans would have to leave all their heavy equipment behind and walk through the forest for miles. If the Germans took the road into the heart of the mountains, they could not move large numbers of soldiers quickly. The road was so narrow that the column would have to spread out and could not sneak up on the partisans. In addition, on this winding road, it was possible for small groups of partisans to hide very close to the road, hit the column with concentrated fire and then escape quickly over the steep, rough terrain. In both cases, the terrain favored the partisans and their hit-and-run tactics. When the Germans did follow, it was easy to pick off individual soldiers or small groups. The horrible fate of these soldiers at the hands of the partisans was the main reason the partisans were so feared by the Germans.

Without saying anything, the lead partisan moved behind a pile of rocks and boulders about 20 meters further into the clearing. Immediately he motioned for us to join him. As we crossed the clearing, I crouched down, moving along close to the ground like a seasoned commando. By the time we reached the rock pile, my heart was pounding. Suddenly I had the feeling that something was going to happen. Looking around, I could no longer see the road or the village. Then I realized that this meant no one on the road or in the village could see us.

"Kovic! We are going to move down to a spot along the road where we can wait in ambush," the lead partisan said. I had not seen any sign of the enemy so I could not understand why we were going to set up an ambush.

I asked, "Aren't we going into the village?" I assumed we could ask the villagers for any information that we needed. They would be happy to see us and would probably offer us food, I thought.

The partisan looked at me with angry, hard eyes. "You had better pay attention and do exactly as you are told." Before I could respond, he continued, "If you make any mistakes out here you are going to die and you will probably get us killed too. We have procedures that have to be followed exactly." He stopped to let this sink in. I could see that he did not like having to train me. When I looked over to the other partisan, hoping to get some support, I saw the same look of impatience and anger. I was about to open my mouth to defend myself when the ranking partisan began again.

"Now listen. We never walk into a village until we make sure that it is safe. You cannot assume that the villagers will protect us. If the Nazis are around, the villagers will do whatever it takes to survive. That includes hiding German soldiers in their houses or even turning a partisan over to the Germans."

He continued, "We do this in two ways. If we have the time, we watch the village from a hiding place. You will eventually learn what the normal activities are in a village, how the people act and move about. You become able to sense when the Germans are around by the way the villagers act even if you don't see any soldiers.

"Today, we are in a hurry, so we are going to set up a trap along the road outside the village to capture a villager to interrogate. When we do this, we have to be very tough with the villagers. We must be sure that they are telling the truth." I nodded as if I understood everything he was saying while he gave me my orders.

"You will be hiding behind a tree right next to the road. We will be hiding about 20 meters closer to the village. We will let the villager pass us. When he comes near you, I will whistle to signal you to jump out in front of him. You must hold your gun out in front of you so he can see it. He will turn to run. Do not shoot, no matter what! Do you understand? As soon as he turns to run, we will step out from our hiding place and the villager will be trapped."

I had not expected that my military career with the partisans would begin with an operation against unarmed peasants. But I was not about to voice any objection to these two. "Yes, sir," was all I could say, and that is all they wanted me to say.

We moved down to the road and they found perfect spots to set up our trap. There was enough brush around the tree where I was hiding that I could look out to see the road without anyone seeing me. As I waited, it occurred to me that they must have used this place for an ambush before. Within half an hour, I could see someone coming along the road from the village. I pulled my head back behind my tree and waited. After one of the longest minutes of my life, I heard the whistle. Without any hesitation, I jumped into the middle of the road, waving my gun.

With a look of terror in his eyes, the peasant turned to run. My comrades calmly stepped out from their hiding place and the villager stopped stone dead in his tracks. As we closed in on him I could see the poor soul was shaking uncontrollably with fear. I soon learned that this was the essential component of the entire operation. One of the partisans grabbed the villager by the arm and dragged him off the road into some nearby cover. He screamed at the villager that we wanted information about German troops in the area and in the village.

Through his terror, the villager managed to answer, "Yes, I understand." He told us there were no Germans in the village and they had not seen any for over a week.

One of the partisans pulled out a knife and held it to the peasant's throat. "How do I know if you are telling me the truth?" he screamed.

The peasant begged, "Please don't kill me. Why would I lie? I hate the Germans."

"We were informed that you're a German sympathizer. You give information to the Germans and we're going to kill you!"

They were going to make this man so frightened that he would not dare to lie.

"Are there any Germans in the village?"

"No!" the villager answered with stark terror in his eyes.

"If we have to, we will kill your wife and your children, too," the other partisan roared at his response. "We want the truth. Who is hiding German soldiers?"

"No one, sir," he quaked, shaking like the proverbial leaf.

The first partisan put his gun against the villager's head and asked, "When did you see the Germans last?"

"Not for two weeks."

The first partisan explained to the villager, "We are going into the village with you in front of us. If it's a trap, you will die first. This is your last chance to tell us. If there is an ambush, my comrades will come back and kill your entire family. Do you understand?"

The villager was so horrified that he could barely nod "yes". Even I was certain that the villager was telling the truth. As we entered the little hamlet, I could completely understand the logic of this tactic. Though we had not hurt this man, the interrogation had been brutal. I had no doubt that the villager was telling us the truth and that we were entering the village safely. Still, I was not sure that I would be able to carry out such an intense and brutal interrogation.

We walked into the hamlet with the villager leading the way. There was no sign of the Germans. Instead, a number of villagers rushed out to welcome us. We were taken to the home of a man who seemed to be in charge of the village. Here we were fed. After we had eaten, the "mayor" told us that a few villagers had information about movements of the German Army in the area. One of the villagers had seen some soldiers on the other side of the mountain, north of the village. He had only seen a patrol of five or six soldiers, but he could see smoke from at least four campfires, which would indicate that there were many more soldiers at the camp.

While our leader talked to the villagers, the other partisan explained the situation to me. He assumed the demeanor of an elementary schoolteacher instructing a new student on school etiquette. "You must learn to question the villagers carefully and to listen to everything they say. Information from these villagers is one of the most important sources we have. We must know the exact location of these troops, how many there are, how they are equipped, and in which direction they are moving. With this information, we could make sure that these soldiers would never find the partisans. If the group of Germans was small enough or if we could wait for them in an area where the terrain favored us, we could ambush these soldiers and possibly kill them all. It might even be possible to capture one or two soldiers."

I was told that captured Nazi soldiers were the best possible source of information. I remembered how effective my comrades had been when they interrogated the villager. I shuddered to think how they would loosen the tongue of a Nazi soldier. However, I realized that if I lived long enough I would see this procedure firsthand. I asked, "How do you know that the German Army camp is not a trap? There might be a larger group of soldiers waiting in hiding and using the camp as bait for the partisans."

To my complete surprise, I saw a slight smile appear and disappear in an instant. "If you are suspicious of everyone, you might survive in this business," he complimented. "Don't worry, we will make sure that there is no trap."

Our group leader called me over to the table where he had been talking with the villagers. Food had been piled on the table; loaves of bread, cheeses and dried meat. He told me to put the food in our knapsacks. We would be bringing it back to headquarters.

It would be getting dark within an hour or so. I expected that we would stay the night in one of the houses. If we went out so late in the day, we could never make it back to the bunker before nightfall. As I was thinking about getting a good night's sleep, my comrade announced, "Get ready. We're going to check on those German troops."

I knew better than to object, but as we prepared to leave, I thought of the warm beds in those little cottages. When we opened the door, visions of warm houses and comfortable sleep were driven from my mind. A winter storm had begun, with a cold wind blowing snow in every direction. I was worried that it would be impossible to find the German camp under such conditions, though at least we would not have to worry that they would see us as we moved about. I was also reassured by the obvious confidence of my two companions.

We set out on our mission, leaving the north side of the village and walking up into the forest. As we moved up the mountain, one of my comrades walked beside me and told me we would be climbing to the top. There we would find a lookout post that provided a complete view of the next valley. We would be able to observe the Germans without being discovered.

Though I was uncomfortable in the severe winter weather, for the moment I was happy. This was the first time that either of my comrades had treated me with any respect. However, my happiness was displaced by the realization that we would not be able to see anything before daybreak and that we would be spending the night outside in the storm.

Though the uphill hike to the lookout post was extremely difficult, my comrades had no problem finding their way. Their knowledge of the terrain was amazing. After about two hours, we reached the summit, but we were unable to see the Germans. The combination of darkness and falling snow made it impossible to see more than 5 or 6 meters. Under these conditions it would be extremely dangerous to move around, for we might inadvertently walk right into a campsite or a soldier on guard duty.

One of my team suggested that we should get some rest. Since I could see no cabin or shelter, I concluded that we were going to sleep out in the snow. While I was contemplating this, my comrades walked off into the storm. In near panic, I ran after them. I caught up quickly because they were waiting for me next to a cluster of pine trees. They lowered themselves under the bottom branches of one of the trees, and I did the same. The area under these branches was dry, for the branches were dense enough to catch the snow. Though it was extremely cold, well below freezing, this would provide some measure of protection. Within a few minutes I was asleep.

I was shaken awake before daylight. We moved back to the lookout point and waited for dawn. During last night's march, snow had gotten inside my boots and melted. Then, while I was sleeping, my socks had frozen solid. Even though I had only walked a few meters, my feet were beginning to hurt badly. I had no dry socks to change into, so I decided I had no choice but to tolerate the pain.

With the first rays of dawn providing the dimmest of light, we used our binoculars to look for the German campsites in the valley below. Sometime during the night the snow had stopped so that visibility was optimal. We could see four camp sites forming a triangle about 15 meters on a side. Within 15 minutes there was movement in the German camp. We could see two men standing guard at opposite ends. There seemed to be three soldiers assigned to each tent, a total of 12 in all. They were armed with the standard rifles and a few submachine guns. We watched this group for two hours and saw no evidence that there were any other German troops nearby.

Once we were sure of the situation, we had to decide on a plan of action. Our group leader felt that if we ambushed the Germans, we probably could not kill the entire group. (I had a feeling that this was because I was so inexperienced.) Therefore, he decided we should return to headquarters to report our information. The commander would decide how to handle the situation.

We started out about 11o'clock in the morning. As had been the case the day before, we were concerned with obscuring our tracks on our return leg. We did not want to be followed back to our headquarters. This time I walked in the middle. They wanted to make sure I did not accidentally leave any signs that would allow the Germans to follow us.

The pain from the ice in my frozen socks increased to totally unbearable levels. By afternoon, it felt like the ice was cutting my feet to shreds. I simply could not go on. I fell to the ground, unable to take another step. My companions looked at me with utter disdain.

The lead partisan coldly told me, "We can't stay here with you and wait until you feel better. That's out of the question." He continued, "If we leave you, the Germans will capture you and torture you until you tell them everything you know. Besides, it's against the rules."

He ordered the other partisan, "If he can't keep up, shoot him." The partisan asked me if I was able to walk as he removed his gun from his shoulder and began to take off the safety lock. I pulled myself up with all my strength and continued marching even though I was suffering enormously. I never said another word of complaint to my comrades. I know that this was another miracle; G-d granted me the strength and will to take one excruciating step and then another, until we finally reached our bunkers.

Partisans wait to ambush the enemy

We returned directly to the command bunker and reported all that we had seen to Commander Cherpansky. After we finished our report, we handed over all the food we had collected in the village.

Only when we had finished all our duties did I return to our sleeping bunker to attend to my tortured feet. My boots and socks were still frozen solid and my feet hurt so much that I could not take my shoes off. After holding my feet near the fire for about 20 minutes, the ice finally melted. With the help of my partners, I was finally able to pull my boots off. I had frostbite on both feet and each foot had a number of large bleeding wounds. I was amazed that I had managed to walk so far on feet that were so badly wounded. With my shoes off, I could hardly walk at all. I was told to eat and get some sleep. The commander ordered me to stay in the bunker the next day to allow my feet to recover.

I awoke before sunrise the next morning; my first thought was of my painful feet. As I tried to stand, I thought I would pass out from the pain. I had been determined to rejoin my patrol group when it went out at sunrise. But the pain was so intense that I realized that I would be of little use to the unit. The lieutenant agreed that I could not go out and ordered that I spend the day resting.

At first light about 20 men went out to set an ambush for the German platoon that my patrol unit had observed. The group was made up of men from the first two bunkers I had visited on my first day with the partisans. Men from my patrol unit were not included in this group. They were sent out to search for other units of the German army that might be in the area.

The operation was a victory for the partisans. When they returned to the bunker 24 hours later, the platoon had killed all 12 of the German soldiers. Two partisans had been killed and two had been wounded in the battle. There were other rewards gained from the battle in addition to the number of dead Germans. The unit brought back guns, ammunition, hand grenades, food and tents. This was the first time I had to think about the fact that my partisan comrades might die in these encounters. I was surprised that there was no discussion about the dead men. The partisans only sat in the smoky bunker and talked about their killing of the enemy and the supplies they had captured. I had expected formal ceremonies to mark the sacrifice these brave fallen partisans had made. However, everyone soon returned to their bunkers and fell asleep.

Some time later, my group leader roused me from a sound sleep with a rough shake. He told me that we would be going out on patrol at first light. As I put my feet on the floor, the intense pain reminded me that my wounds had not healed. However, the look on the face of my comrade made it clear that I would be going with them. As we climbed to the first peak I was sure that I would never make it. But again, G-d extended a hand to help me and gave me the strength to keep going.

As we had done on our previous patrol, at each village we captured and interrogated a resident. By the second village, I was already experienced in the procedure. There were no Germans in any of the villages and they had not reacted to the ambush of their platoon. However, my comrades told me that we could expect that the SS would retaliate, probably against the village that had told us about the patrol but not because it had given us information. The SS had no way of knowing that the villagers had helped us. Rather, they would take hostages from the nearest village and kill them as an example to everyone in the area. Often, they would include very young boys, very old men, women, girls and even babies. There was not the slightest concern with punishing those who were guilty of giving information to the enemy. This was not about punishment. This was about terror.

We made it clear to the villagers that we would deal with any Germans that came into the area. However, for us to help and protect them, they would have to tell us when they saw any German soldiers. Of course they could not know where to find us. We would contact them on a regular basis. It was made clear to the villagers that if they betrayed us, they could expect to be punished.

For the first few weeks, my two companions used our patrols as training exercises for me. I learned how to move through the forest without leaving tracks and to move through the forest in such a way as to leave tracks to lure the Germans into an ambush. I learned to observe a village without being seen and to question a villager in a way that would procure the truth. Though it was all less glamorous than I had anticipated, I was in control of my own life. This was what I liked best about life with the partisans. I was as happy as I had been in a long time.

With each passing day, I felt I was becoming an accepted member of the patrol unit. Though I was the youngest member of the partisans, I had shown them that I could carry my weight. I had managed each situation as it arose. Other members of the unit were talking to me; asking me questions about our last patrol or telling me something I needed to know or to look for. I was very pleased that they were including me.

One day, as we were leaving to go on patrol, I saw a horse tied to a tree near the bunker. When I asked one of my new "friends" whom the owner might be, I was told, "Janko, the horse is yours!"

I was delighted. Some of the partisans had horses and they were an important status symbol. I walked over to the horse, untied the rope that served as a bridle and jumped onto the back of the animal with the agility of a seasoned rider. However, before I had a chance to secure my seat on the horse, it reared up, went wild and bucked. In an instant, I was thrown from my mount and hit the ground with the grace of a sack of potatoes. As I fumbled to my feet, my friends consoled me by laughing uproariously. My first thought was to get right back on the horse and teach it that I was the master. However, before I could remount, one of my comrades informed me that this was a particularly stubborn and mean animal. Many of the men had attempted to tame it, but no one had succeeded in riding it for more than a few seconds. With everyone enjoying this joke at my expense, I tied the horse to the tree and decided that I would train it.

I would use the wisdom from a verse I had learned in the yeshiva: "An ox knows its owner, and a donkey the trough of its master" (*Isaiah* 1:3). Every day, I would pet the horse very gently and put a piece of sugar in its mouth. Within three days, I could see that the horse was becoming more comfortable with my presence. Soon it was looking forward to the treat as soon as it saw me coming. After two weeks I could tell that I was the master. I decided that it was time to test our relationship.

While my horse was tied to a tree, I climbed onto its back and took hold of the reins. My comrades looked up in surprise and in suppressed glee at what they thought would be a repeat comical performance. A crowd soon gathered, relishing the expected amusement. A smirking unsolicited volunteer untied my horse from the tree, and stepped back quickly so as not to be hit by my impending fall. However, to the surprise of my comrades, the horse made not even the slightest protest. As rider and mount strutted about, they could not believe their eyes. Along with the commander, I was one of the very few partisans who owned a horse. I could not help smiling proudly as they all looked at me with a newfound mixture of envy and respect.

My training proceeded similarly. Each day brought new tests and as I passed each one, I was privy to a greater degree of acceptance. Within a short period of time, I felt like a full-fledged partisan soldier.

When I had started going out on patrols regularly, I bought an immense laundry vat and hired an elderly peasant woman in one of the villages to cook for me. She would always wait for me before she would begin and in that way I was able to insure that I did not ingest anything nonkosher.

On patrol everyday, I arranged to pass by this village as a routine part of my tour of duty. One week she would cook beans and the next week, potatoes. I have to say, they were delicious. This gigantic pot contained enough food for the entire week. Since there was no refrigeration the vat was stored in the chimney which was cool enough to preserve the food.

When my partisan companions noted that I did not eat with them, I told them that my stomach was sensitive and I could not digest this meat properly. At first I was surprised at how willingly they accepted this explanation. Then I realized that they figured that if I did not eat, there would be more for the rest of them. I was the only person in the unit who did not suffer stomach and intestinal maladies, another benefit of my

A horse was an important status symbol among partisans.
I was one of the few with a horse of my own.

special diet. They would appropriate a cow from a nearby village, unceremoniously shoot it in the head, and feed the unit from it for weeks. Often the meat was rancid, yet that rarely prevented them from roasting it and devouring it. As a result, these men often became severely ill.

I ate nonkosher food only once and that was the result of a direct order from our commander, Captain Cherpansky. Since he did not speak the local language, the captain always needed an interpreter who could speak both Slovak and Russian. Therefore, he often brought me with him when he met with the mayors, town elders and local officials in the region. At one such meeting, a roasted deer was brought out for the partisan guests. When he saw that I did not take anything, Captain Cherpansky commanded me to eat, barking at me in a voice of great authority, "That's an order!" And gave me a kick under the table which nearly broke my leg. Remembering the rule of the death penalty for disobeying a direct order, I had no choice and I tasted a little. Even then I only chewed it and when no one was looking discarded it without having to actually swallow any of it. It was the only time I did this and I felt that it was necessary to save my life.

My life and training with the partisans had reached a level of mutual acceptance, respect and even normalcy. An encounter with a platoon of ten Germans would bring my training period to a formal close.

Chapter 16

The Battle for Life and Death

It was a routine patrol day and we were about to enter a village which we had under surveillance. It was our intention to capture a villager and interrogate him. As we moved toward the road to set up our usual trap, we could see a small band of German soldiers leaving the village. We quickly decided to ambush and kill them. As we silently ran back into the forest, moving further down the road, I was trembling — this would be my first actual battle. Though I was tremendously excited, I was worried about how I would act. Would I really be able to kill a Nazi?

Within five minutes we were overlooking the road, positioned at a perfect spot for an ambush. About 20 meters from the road to the hills on each side was an area that was free of trees but littered with very large boulders. Two of my comrades hid behind the boulders on the far side of the road while another partisan and I took up a position on the near side.

When the Germans marched down the road they would pass directly between us. We would have them trapped in crossfire with no place for them to take cover. They would not even be able to return our fire.

We were hidden behind the boulders when the Germans approached. They were completely unprepared for our attack. A sharp whistle indicated that our target was in place. All four submachine guns began firing simultaneously. Most of the group seemed to fall at once. They were not able to fire a single shot in return. They did not have any time to even remove their guns from their shoulders.

I had fired my weapon at a soldier. As I stood there trying to comprehend what had happened, I saw a trail of blood leading off the road. Apparently, one of the Germans had only been wounded and had crawled off the road in an attempt to hide in some bushes near the edge of the road. I could not see him but I could hear him moving. Before I could think, I reacted by throwing a hand grenade into the bushes. There was a huge explosion. I could hear the German's screams of pain. After a minute, there was only silence and the movement in the bushes had subsided. We had destroyed the entire group without any loss to our band.

Once a yeshiva boy, now a partisan fighter, and there was no contradiction between the two. In the time of peace a Jew must serve his G-d in one prescribed manner. But at a time of war, in a world gone insane, with the forces of evil running amok, a Jew must serve Hashem differently. My religious duty was to fight the enemy to save my life and to save my family. I was not a killer, but a religious man doing the will of his Creator.

By the winter of '44-'45, the partisans had gained a reputation as fierce and merciless warriors.[1] They were feared by the German army because they had killed so many Nazis and had captured and executed many others. Their attacks

---

1. Gutman, *Encyclopedia of the Holocaust* (New York 1990), p.1372.

were always carried out as ambushes and nearly always against small groups of soldiers. The partisans' strategy was always to have some deciding advantage in every battle. Rarely did they have superior numbers, but they always had the advantage of knowledge of the geography of the mountains and the advantage of surprise. What is more, they nearly always had the sympathy of the local population. Whenever we learned that there were large numbers of German soldiers in the area, we attempted to disrupt their operations. We never launched direct assaults against these large units of the German Army.

Our aim was to punish and slow German convoys by using hit-and-run attacks. We would break up into groups of two-to-four men, each of which would attack the German column in turn, and then disappear into the forest over terrain so rough that the Germans could only follow on foot and only very slowly. They never were able to move as quickly as we could so they were unable to catch us. If the German soldiers did make the fatal mistake of following us into the forest, we would move far ahead of the slower-moving soldiers and set up an ambush. Thus, in this manner, a small group of partisans could destroy a group of 10 to 20 German soldiers, a few Nazis at a time.

Late one afternoon, while my patrol unit was checking one of the passes through the Tatras Mountains, we came upon a fresh trail of footprints made in the snow by a large group of people. Clearly a military column had made these tracks and we estimated that there might be 100 or 200 soldiers in the group. Because this was the only way through the mountains, we were certain that they would stay on the trail and we could anticipate their progress as they moved along the length of the pass. Equally important, there was only one area where that many men could set up camp, so we knew where they would be stopping for the night and we could move ahead of them to set up an ambush.

Immediately, we returned to headquarters so that the commanders could plan an attack strategy. When we were sure that we had traveled far enough from the Germans' visibility, we fired off a series of three-colored signal flares to warn our people at headquarters. We used a prearranged pattern of colors that indicated the presence of large troop concentration. This way the group could make preparations for the attack, checking and cleaning guns, loading extra ammunition clips, and readying explosives.

When we arrived back at camp in the early evening, we headed straight for the command bunker to give our report. We watched as Captain Cherpansky and his lieutenants worked over a large map of the area, planning the details of our ambush. They asked us a few questions about the German column but most of our information was inferred from our observation of the footprints they left. We knew there were at least a couple hundred soldiers, that they were all on foot and that they had only the arms that they could carry.

Captain Cherpansky divided us into fighting groups of three men each. By now, I knew the area as if it were my own backyard, as did each of the partisans. He gave us the details of his plan on the map and assigned each group an ambush point along the trail. We would be spread out about 15 meters apart on both sides. We would not open fire until they were within a few meters. The Germans would have nowhere to hide and could only stumble into each other's way.

We hid behind boulders and trees and dug ourselves into the snow so there would be no trace of our presence. After a few hours, one of the lieutenants came by to tell us that the column was approaching and that we should be prepared, but that we must not fire until the command was given.

As I lay on the frozen ground, covered in snow, I held onto my gun with all my strength. This was the first time I would be confronting a large contingent of German soldiers and I could feel my heart pounding in my chest. My hands tightened on my gun as I thought about what I was about to do with it, a semiautomatic submachine gun, a Mauser, capable of firing 32 nine-millimeter bullets at a clip in less than a minute. I thought of all those Nazis trapped with nowhere to hide while my comrades and I emptied the ammo clips we had readied for this battle. They would not be as vicious and fearless as when they terrorized Jews in the streets of Pressburg.

With a start I realized that I could hear the Germans coming. My heart began to beat faster and harder. Its pounding was so loud that I was afraid it would burst out of my chest. I was startled to hear the command, "Fire."

As I sprang up from my hiding place there was a roar of gunfire from every direction. I looked out from the boulder in front of me and I too began to fire my gun. In an instant the clip was empty. I ducked behind my boulder while I replaced it with a new one. We were all firing down on the confused German column. They were taken totally by surprise. It was impossible to aim at any one German soldier. We were all shooting into the milling crowd. There was no place for them to take cover so they could only retreat in panic into their own column, making their disorder even worse. There was no dignity or power or ferocity to be seen in this group of Nazis. There was only terror. They were hardly able to fire back at us. Within a few minutes, they were in a totally disorganized retreat back down the trail. About 10 partisan soldiers pursued the Nazis, firing into what was left of the column as they ran for their lives. It was part of our battle plan to keep after them to prevent them from stopping their retreat and regrouping for a counterattack.

This battle lasted less than ten minutes. They gave us almost no resistance and more than 100 Germans were killed. As far as we could determine, there were a few survivors who made it out of the forest. As we emerged from behind our hiding places, each partisan was totally alert. We could hear the cries of pain of the wounded Germans and pleas for mercy. These same men who, when little children, women, or the elderly cried for mercy, only laughed as they intensified their sadistic viciousness. These Nazis crying for mercy were to me pathetic and infuriating. The slightest movement by a fallen Nazi elicited a burst of gunfire from the nearest partisan and sent the rest of us diving for cover. No prisoners were taken after this battle. The dead were everywhere. I walked through the carnage feeling a sense of power and strength. I was thankful that I was still alive and I tried to remember all the Jews that I had known whom the Nazis had killed. When I witnessed the terror they inflicted upon the weak and helpless Jews in the cities, these same monsters had seemed invincible, a power beyond comprehension. These Nazis, slaughtered in the forest by a handful of partisans, did not seem so fierce. When confronted by soldiers who could fight back, the Nazis showed how cowardly they actually were.

Those of us that stayed behind had work to do. We moved among the corpses that littered the trail, looking for anything that was in usable condition. We went over each body and collected coats, boots, gloves, hats, scarves, guns, ammunition and grenades — anything that might be useful. The spoils of an effective ambush were the main source of our supplies. If we did not capture arms and materials, we went without. As we walked among the bodies, we found more supplies than we could carry. The spoils of this battle would keep us supplied for weeks. As we left the dead behind, I felt immense satisfaction at having inflicted at least some small damage upon our wicked enemy. Fully loaded with as much as we could carry, we made our way back to our bunkers.

Once there, we took stock of the materials we had rescued from the dead Germans. We had retrieved all of their boots and everyone found at least one pair that fit. Hats, scarves and gloves were distributed to everyone, and we had plenty of food. Most important, we now had a surplus of guns, ammunition, explosives and grenades. For the time being, we could exploit every opportunity to ambush any Germans who might venture into our mountains.

We believed that a few soldiers had survived and had made it back to the road and the trucks that had carried them into the mountains. Experience had taught the partisans that the Germans would be back. The unit we had attacked was from the Wehrmacht. We could be sure that the soldiers who returned would be the fiercest in the German army.

Knowing this, Commander Cherpansky had stationed lookouts at key points on all the roads so that we would have advanced warning of approaching German soldiers. We immediately began to prepare an ambush for the impending attack.

We did not have too long to wait. One of our lookouts returned to the command bunker and reported that a column of Waffen SS had come into the mountains. These soldiers were feared as crazed killers; they were known to pursue their prey with suicidal fervor.[2] We were certain they were looking for us to exact revenge for the slaughter of their comrades and that they would chase us until they caught up. We had a plan to take advantage of their eagerness for revenge.

Along the road the SS was traveling there was an ideal position from which a group of snipers could fire down. We intended to have five or six men fire on the approaching SS using submachine guns. They would be firing from within the

---

2. The SS were the Nazi elite, an order within the Nazi party that came to have a great deal of power. The Waffen SS were "fanatical in spirit ... not always particularly obedient ... becoming a kind of fire-brigade for critical points on the front." Eager to recruit volunteers they were touted as 'the shock troops of the new order." Gerhard Weinberg, *A World at Arms*, New York, 1994, p. 458. Michel, *The Second World War*, New York, 1975, p. 282.

forest, making it impossible for the Germans to determine how many partisans were present. It was our hope that the SS would think they had encountered the main group of partisans and that they would jump at the opportunity to destroy our entire unit. Our people would immediately retreat at top speed through the woods to a trail that they would follow for about three kilometers. We had already taken more than 50 partisans over this trail, so that it appeared that a large unit had moved through the area.

The trail led to an ambush site that was perfect for trapping a large group. When the SS came out of the forest, in hot pursuit of our bait, they would come to a wide meadow. On the far side of the meadow there were rugged mountains separated by a hill that was about 200 meters high. This hill was clear of trees and rocks. Compared to the surrounding mountains, passage over this hill would be rather easy. Our unit had made a trail in the snow indicating the passage of a large group of partisans through the woods, across the meadow and up and over this hill.

When our attack group opened fire from the woods, the plan was set into motion. The German SS column halted abruptly, the soldiers leapt from their trucks and barreled into the forest. By the time they got into the forest, the partisans had disappeared. All the Nazis could find were spent shell casings and hundreds of footprints. In their eagerness to wreak vengeance, the SS troops streaked through the forest hot on the trail for blood, exactly as we had hoped and planned.

The hill, with a meadow behind and rugged mountains on either side, was the perfect trap. We set up two heavy machine guns in the woods about halfway up on each side of the hill. The four guns had a clear sweep of the entire field and would catch the Germans in crossfire. Just over the crest of the hill, partisans with submachine guns were hiding under the snow.

When the SS came out of the forest, they crossed the meadow without hesitation and started up the hill. As they approached the top, we opened fire. They were taken totally by surprise. Because there were so many of them, perhaps they had felt the puny partisan army would never stand and fight. However, fight we did, with an unrelenting barrage of automatic fire which drove them back. Once they began to retreat, all four machine guns opened up. The SS troops were in total chaos. There was no possibility of any cover and gunfire was coming from every direction. They were unable to mount any organized return fire. In desperation, all they could do was flee back across the meadow, only to find more partisan gunners waiting for them in the trees. A few managed to retreat across the meadow into the woods and back along the trail, but more than 200 Waffen SS died in this ambush. The dead and wounded were everywhere; there would be no SS survivors. I could hear the Nazi soldiers crying out in pain. I could hear the wounded pleading for mercy. Their cries and pleas were mixed with the sound of gunfire. The most seasoned partisans executed the wounded on the spot. The snow on the hill and much of the meadow was stained dark red with the blood of the German soldiers. We incurred limited casualties, a few wounded and three killed. It was the last time the Germans would send a large force into the forest in an attempt to stamp out the partisans.

This was a spectacular victory for our unit. We now had more supplies than we could ever use. It would take us two days to strip the battlefield of all the materials that were useful to us and to place our supplies in safe hiding places. The effect of the battle on our unit's morale was wonderful. We felt powerful and in control of our mountains. Every few days we heard stories of German defeats. It was clear that the end of the Nazi nightmare was approaching. Our unit felt great pride that we too had inflicted such a resounding and brutal victory over the vaunted and hated SS. These monsters had inflicted so much pain, suffering and terror that each of us felt some measure of relief in proving that the Germans could be terrorized.

Within two days we had resumed our normal routine of daily patrols. Though the Germans had suffered a major defeat in the mountains, they did not give up their efforts to destroy the partisan army. They simply changed tactics. Rather than using large regular units to chase us, they switched to using crack commando units from the SS, special forces who were willing to infiltrate the region and make the supreme sacrifice for the Führer. These soldiers were trained to fight as we did; laying sinister traps and ambushes for the partisans. This approach resulted in many partisan casualties. Many of the men in my unit died. To my horror, I also fell into one of these traps.

One afternoon I was a member of a four-man patrol that was moving through the forest toward one of the villages we had under surveillance. As was our normal procedure, we were watching the village for signs of the Nazis, always careful to move quietly without leaving any trail. Suddenly, there was a burst of gunfire from our left and from our right. We had stumbled into an ambush. My three companions, who were ahead of me, were killed instantly by the first burst of fire. I realized that a bullet had hit me in the knee. I managed to stand up hidden behind a large tree and though my wound was extremely painful I was able to put my weight on it and move. I knew that I would die if I stayed and returned the fire of the Germans. Instead, I ran for my life.

I had been told many times that if I came into close proximity with the Nazis, I should never retreat toward the bunker. However, I was still very inexperienced and all I could think of was to run as fast as I could. Running away from the ambush meant that I was running in the direction of the command bunker. The Germans, who were experienced commandos, were able to stay on my trail. As I ran through the woods, I could hear them firing at me. Every few minutes, bullets would cut through the branches over my head or ricochet off a tree trunk or boulder. I had completely forgotten about the pain in my knee as I used every ounce of strength to run. Although I knew the area well, and I took advantage of the areas where the trees were the thickest and where the terrain hid me, I was not able to lose them. As I was running, I realized that I had made a serious mistake. I came out of the forest into a glen, a hollow, bare of trees for more than 100 meters. I could not go back because I could hear the commandos firing as they closed in on me. The terrain on either side was too rough to try. I could only go forward. I was sure that this would be the end of me.

I bolted into the clearing, running as fast as I could, feeling the enemy right behind me. As I crossed that field I had only one refuge. I asked my G-d to save me. It was at this moment that I merited to see the fulfillment of the verse: "Even as they are yet speaking, I will hear" (*Isaiah* 65:24). Immediately, I felt as if I was floating through the air, angels carrying me across the glen on their wings. Miraculously, in a flash, I had traversed the meadow and was safely on the other side within the protection of the trees, bullets whistling around me left and right.

I stood there trying to catch my breath. At this moment, I realized the hidden meaning of another verse: "It is a time of trouble for Jacob, but from it he will be saved" (*Jeremiah* 30:7). The very danger through which I had just passed now became my salvation. The Germans had stopped on their side of the clearing. They were afraid to cross the glen themselves for fear that I would now have a clear shot at them. Thus, my life was spared again, even with a bullet lodged in my knee.

When I reached the bunker, everyone was amazed by my miraculous escape. While I told the story, the "medic," a student who had taken a course in first aid, attended to my wound. He had only two medications in his dispensary: one, syrup for diarrhea and stomach ailments, and the other, aspirin which he used for everything else. Any partisan who fell ill was given one of the two medications: If one was wounded, he received both.

The medic cleaned my wound with vodka and discovered the miracle within my miracle. The bullet had penetrated the flesh and missed the bone by a single millimeter. That was why I had been able to run; otherwise, I would have fallen and died at the hands of the Nazis as had my companions.

Again, I had been delivered from the clutches of the angel of death. I was certain that there was some reason for this; I understood in a special way that my life was in the hands of G-d and that there must be some work or service that I still had to complete. In this frame of mind, my wound healed quickly and I was back on patrol in two or three days.

As I mentioned, our outfit had one German Communist who I never trusted and was meticulously careful never to turn my back to, especially when we went out on patrols. For it is relatively easy to be killed by one's own comrade. During battle, with gunfire exploding everywhere, when one is hit by a bullet, was it the enemy who shot him or a comrade?

Yet, suddenly this German became overly friendly, becoming too interested in my welfare for my comfort. Continually he approached me, engaging me in unnecessary conversation, constantly asking me about my family and myself. It was obvious he suspected me of being Jewish. Even though he was fighting the Nazis, that meant only that he opposed their oppressive Fascist ideals, preferring the oppressive Communist ideals in lieu, not that he disagreed with the Nazis commitment to exterminate G-d's Chosen People.

In the past few desperate years, if there was any skill I acquired, it was the ability to detect when my life was in danger. To me, it was no longer a question of if he would try to kill me, but of when. I had to protect myself; I had to take action, but how? A plan came to me a few days later.

Since a surplus of ammunition was hardly ever a reality, target practice for the partisans was a rare event. However, because of our recent overwhelming victories and the resultant excess booty we garnered from the Nazis, our commanders announced that the following morning there would be target practice.

I remembered that during one of my patrols a few weeks prior, I had discovered in a tangle of overgrown bushes a forgotten 9mm-magazine ammo clip. However, to my disappointment the bullets were rusted. Not only were rusted bullets worthless, they were extremely dangerous. A rusted bullet would explode in the chamber. Still I kept them thinking that perhaps they could be of use somehow. They remained in the bottom of my pack.

In the middle of the night before target practice, with the German sleeping a safe distance away from me in the bunker, I silently crawled toward his rifle propped up against the back wall. In the pitch-black darkness, as everyone snored exhausted from the rigors of the day, terror pulsed through my veins for the fear of someone awakening and discovering me. I clicked opened the chamber of the German's rifle and placed in two or three of those rusted bullets I had saved. In front of them I placed good bullets, so that his first few rounds would go off smoothly.

The next day, during target practice, an unfortunate accident occurred. The German was rendered incapacitated when the chamber of his rifle exploded. Now this German had more important things to worry about than me. And now I could worry about different things, other than him.

Within a week another incident occurred that had a profound impact on me. I was on patrol with a partisan Franti Cek. We had taken up a position overlooking one of the roads through the mountains. From our vantage point, we could observe all traffic on the road for a kilometer in each direction. Within an hour, we saw two German soldiers walking on the road toward us. We could see that they were alone so we decided to move ahead of them and set up an ambush. It would be easy to surprise them.

We moved quickly through the forest to a point about half a kilometer ahead of the two Germans, each hiding on opposite sides of the road. Within a few minutes, our targets came strolling down the road, each with his gun slung over his shoulder as if he were out for a weekend walk. When they were parallel to our position, we jumped from behind our cover screaming, "Hands up!"

They threw up their hands in terror, neither reaching for his gun. They stood there frozen in fear until we told them to drop their weapons on the road. They did as they were told. I tied their hands behind their back while Franti stood guard over them with his submachine gun. Once I had them securely tied up, I blindfolded each prisoner and we took them off to our commander.

Captain Cherpansky congratulated us on our good work. Prisoners who were in good health were a valuable source of information. Every unit had at least one "specialist" who could effectively interrogate Nazi soldiers. I knew that the interrogation of these prisoners would not be a pleasant experience. Each of us understood that capture and interrogation was a fate worse than death. It would be no less for these two Nazis.

Two days later Franti and I were called to the command bunker. When we approached the bunker I was surprised to see one of the two prisoners bound and blindfolded standing next to Captain Cherpansky. He informed me that the prisoner was being returned to us. We were to be given the honor of executing him. Before I could say anything, Franti stepped forward, grabbed the German by the arm and pushed him to get him moving. I realized that Franti had just accepted this honor for the two of us. I walked alongside him as he shoved the German into the forest.

As we walked, Franti reminded me that this was a great honor for the unit to give to such a new recruit. As he talked, my mind raced back through all the suffering the Germans had inflicted on my family, on me and on so many other Jews. I realized that even if I killed all the Nazis in the world, I would never have satisfactory revenge. Nothing could ever avenge the pain and suffering inflicted by these evil people. Killing this German would be only a very hollow symbol of my revenge. He could only represent the monsters who had killed my mother, my sisters, my brothers and all the others Jews.

I was nearly overcome with a soul-wrenching sadness over all I had lost. Franti yelling my name jolted me into the present. He had secured the prisoner to a tree, so that he faced us with his hands tied around the tree. Franti reached out and pulled the cover from the German's face revealing eyes filled with stark terror. How many times had this German seen that look in the eyes of defenseless women and children? Was he ever moved to show compassion for their suffering?

I looked into his eyes and he began to plead pathetically, "Please don't kill me." He cried. Tears streamed down his cheeks.

He was pitiful. He was a study in cowardice as were all his comrades. The Nazis had tried to masquerade as fearless soldiers and conquerors led by some exalted vision. In reality, they were cowardly butchers, predators on the weak and defenseless. They killed old men, women and children and those who were unable to fight back. There was no mighty hero here; there was no almighty conqueror, only the terror of cowardice.

"Jan, the honor is yours," Franti informed me with mock formality. In front of the entire partisan company that had assembled for the show, he instructed me in the proper procedure for this ceremony. The Nazis were such monsters, such cruel beasts that they did not deserve the dignity of a bullet that was reserved for a true soldier. This Nazi was not worth wasting a bullet on. Therefore, he would be killed with a knife. Tradition dictated that he have his belly slit open and be left to die slowly and painfully. As Franti gestured with his knife, the prisoner whimpered and began again to plead for mercy. There was no honor in this desperate animal.

Standing in front of the prisoner, I thought again of my mother and my family. I felt the terrible pain of all that I had lost. This act would be a small return for all the suffering that the Nazis had inflicted. I reached down for the knife that I kept inside my boot. As I pulled the knife out, I could see the faces of my mother, sisters and my brothers. All I had to do was use the knife and I would have some measure of revenge. Looking at this whining creature though, something in me recoiled and I was repelled by the whole idea. I knew that I could never kill this way. I could not become the beast that I hated.

I turned to Franti and handed him my knife. All I could say to him was, "You can have this honor." As I walked away, screams of pain and anguish told me that Franti had accepted.

I was shaken by this incident. Through all that had happened to my family, with all I knew about the horrible things that the Nazis had done to other Jews and to me, I had been sustained by thoughts of fighting back. This was the first time that I had to consider whether there was a limit to the level of brutality to which I could be driven. I had fought furiously in battle without regret. But I learned that day that I could not lower myself to brutally slaughter that pathetic animal no matter how much he deserved it, no matter how much I hated him and the horrific philosophy for which he stood.

Chapter 17

The War Finally Ends

With the arrival of spring, Passover was soon approaching. I had no calendar by which to determine the exact days. I did the only thing I could do. I began to watch the skies at night. When the moon was full, I knew we had reached the 15th of the month, the first night of Pesach, and I stopped eating bread. However, the next night, the moon seemed fuller than the night before, so I decided that this night was the 15th. The same thing happened on the next two nights. As a result, I ended up observing what I could of Pesach for 12 days instead of eight.

The fact that I was the only Jew in the unit made the observance of Pesach even more vital for me. During my time with the partisans this was how I maintained a connection with my faith and myself. I could not don *tefillin*, nor could I wear *tzitzis*. I could not keep Shabbos, its observance would have endangered my life. When I would pray, I would utter my supplications under my breath by heart as I trudged through the mountain paths on patrol. What I could observe of my faith I did earnestly. Like a starving person treasures his last morsel of food, like one who has not seen his loved ones treasures every glance at their photo, so too did I take solace and refuge in my secret rendezvous with my G-d. I steadfastly held onto my own identity and though I suffered many unbearable experiences, through adhering to my beliefs I was able to retain and maintain who I was.

By the end of Pesach, 1945, the Germans were suffering one major defeat after another. Dresden was destroyed, Danzig captured, Berlin under siege, Auschwitz, Buchenwald and Bergen-Belsen liberated.[1] What had seemed to be an invincible army was being driven into cowering retreat on every front. Large numbers of German troops were retreating from the front toward the mountains. When we would receive reports that a group of German soldiers had taken refuge in one of the villages we patrolled on a regular basis, we would surprise them with a raid in the middle of the night. This was an effective strategy that enabled us to kill many Germans.

Toward the end of April, one of our patrols received information from a villager that some Germans soldiers had found a safe haven in one of the towns to the east. Apparently, the Nazi soldiers had entered the village from the other side of the mountains. Because they had reached the village without crossing through the area we dominated, they entered undetected by us and we knew nothing of them. Before we could challenge them, we needed to have some basic information about them. It would have been suicidal to attack without knowing something of their numbers, how they were armed and what type of unit they were.

Another partisan and I were ordered to scout the village to get the information we required about these German soldiers.

1. Gutman, *Encyclopedia of the Holocaust* (New York, 1990), p. 189, pp. 256.

To reach this hamlet, we had to climb a long distance up the slopes until we reached a ridge that we followed for five or six kilometers. We could just barely see the village from our vantagepoint, and even with binoculars we were not able to ascertain much about the activities of the German occupiers. It was clear that we would have to get much closer to the village. However, I could see that the cover between the village and us was minimal. If we attempted to move any closer, I worried that we would not be able to conceal ourselves effectively. We decided to wait for a peasant to come out of the village, to be captured and interrogated.

However, after about four hours not one person had left the village. We decided that we had no choice. We would have to enter the village ourselves.

I suggested to my friend, "If the Germans see us with guns, they'll grab us and we'll be dead men. Instead, we should conceal our rifles under one of the bushes, take some poles over our shoulders and act like we're just two teenage boys coming into the village to buy food."

My comrade agreed with my analysis of the situation. As we made our way toward the road, we found a secure place under some brush where we hid our weapons. We both knew that the care of one's gun was a most solemn duty. The penalty for its loss was court-martial and execution. Certain that our guns were safely out of sight, we continued down the slope until we reached the road. As was our practice, we hid among the trees to make sure that no one was on the path and then set off along the road to the village.

We walked along the narrow, winding road toward the village, confident that we were indistinguishable from the villagers living in the area. We had walked about 1,000 meters along the road when we were startled by a shout ordering us to halt. Before we could move a muscle, 10 German soldiers surrounded us. They had concealed themselves behind some large trees along the side of the road and we had been totally unaware of their presence. Had we been armed, they would have killed us on the spot. Fortunately, we both had the presence of mind to act like timid and frightened provincials. The Germans began to question us immediately. They shouted questions and pushed both of us around until we each fell terrified to the ground. Our fear was only partially an act. We knew that the Nazi soldiers needed little excuse to kill a peasant. One of the soldiers accused us of being partisan spies. The instant he mentioned the partisans, we both began to curse the partisans and complained about the harm that the rebels had caused our families. They had stolen our oxen, our horses and our crops. They even took what little money we had. The partisans stole from us without regard to our needs. They terrorized our village and we hated them.

Our act was effective enough to prevent them from shooting us on the spot, but not convincing enough for them to let us go. We explained that we were traveling to the village to buy food to replace the supplies that the partisans had stolen from us. As we finished our story, one of the soldiers told us that they were taking us to the village. Another of the soldiers bound our hands with handcuffs. I was certain that the Germans were going to execute us. Next, we were thoroughly searched. Fortunately, we never carried any form of identification. To our relief, we were marched off in the direction of the village.

It took only about half an hour to reach the village. There was no activity in the street. It was like an abandoned town. No one came out to see us and I did not see anyone looking out of the windows. We were taken to an old mill. One of the soldiers called out, the front door opened and a German soldier with a submachine gun at the ready stepped out. We were shoved through a door and pushed down some stairs. In the basement, they chained us to poles and left us there in total darkness without any mention of our fate.

In the darkness, it was easy to imagine how the Nazis would torture and kill us. Every time we heard someone move about in the house, I thought it was the noise of the soldiers finally coming for us; but no one came into the basement for two days.

During the morning of the second day, we heard yelling and then there was a barrage of gunfire. The gunfire continued for an hour. Then as suddenly as it had begun, the gunfire stopped. We were startled when the door to the basement was opened without warning by a partisan soldier. We were told that the partisans had attacked the German unit in the town and that the Germans had surrendered.

We were amazed when the partisan who had discovered us left without freeing us. I figured that he must have been so happy to find us alive that he was not thinking clearly. About 15 minutes later, he returned with the company commander. He began to question us about how we had been captured. We explained in great detail. It was clear that the commander was not happy with our story. He asked us what we had done with our weapons. As soon as he heard our explanation, the commander ordered that we be placed under arrest.

The partisan soldiers unchained us, but we were to return to our base camp to face a partisan military tribunal. We were informed that we were being charged with a capital offense — we had given up our weapons.

Nonetheless, we traveled back to our command bunker thinking that we were going to be merely reprimanded for our carelessness. When we arrived, we were taken inside. We waited there as one by one the officers of the unit joined us in the bunker. One officer stepped forward and announced that he was the prosecutor for the tribunal. He declared with a grim expression on his face that he was calling for the death penalty because we had violated one of the cardinal rules of the partisan army.

"A partisan must not abandon his weapon as long as he breathes!" he shouted at the officers of the tribunal. "This is a vow that we all made when we joined the partisan army. We all swore on our honor and on our life!" The prosecutor was totally consumed by the righteousness of his argument. As I listened, I could not believe this was happening. He could not be serious about such outlandish charges.

We attempted to defend ourselves. We explained why we left our guns hidden in the forest. Had we entered the village with our weapons, we would have been shot immediately and our mission would have certainly failed. Hiding our weapons and entering the village in disguise was a superior way of carrying out our mission. It was only bad luck that had brought us in contact with the German patrol. Though we argued with great conviction, the officers sitting in judgment rejected our argument.

The commander heading the tribunal looked at each of us. "It is part of the duty of a partisan to fight with his weapon until death," he declared as he stared at us. "Placing yourself in a position where you could be captured without a fight is the worst thing you could do. The Germans would have eventually tortured you and you would have given them all the information they wanted. Everything, the entire unit, would have been lost. It would have been far better if you had been killed in battle." His words had the tone of a final decision.

The tribunal's sentence was unanimous. We were guilty and were to be executed by a partisan firing squad. The dread and gloom that seized me was indescribable. I had made it through the Nazi terror in the cities and through the battles with Nazi soldiers, I had survived all the brutal attacks of the enemy and the severe conditions in the mountains, only to be put to an ignominious death at the hand of my own comrades? Surely, G-d had not spared me simply that I should die in this manner. So many times I had barely escaped the claws of the beast, to be delivered by miraculous intervention. Now I was to be dragged out before my comrades, bound hand and foot, to be shot like a common criminal. Through my entire ordeal as a partisan I had been sustained by the thought that I would not die meekly like a lamb, but would die fighting. I was not afraid to die, but I wanted to die like a man, with honor. I decided I would not allow them to shoot me like an animal.

Although we were not kept under guard, it was clear that it would not be possible to simply walk away from the camp. I began to plan an escape. After a few hours we were called to appear before one of the officers from the tribunal, who told us that we had been granted a reprieve. I silently said, as I had so many times during the past seven years, "Thank You, G-d."

The officer told us that after some discussion the tribunal had decided to wait with our execution. Since the war would soon end, they did not want to take such serious action. When the war ended formally, all the partisans would be gathering in Koshice; the final disposition of our case would be determined there. With a certainty that I had experienced few times in my life, I understood that the hand of G-d had delivered me one more time.

A few days later, the partisan in charge of our radio came out of the command bunker yelling that the war was over. My comrades and I had long been preoccupied with the war's imminent end, but it still seemed too wonderful to be true.

For most of us, our first impulse was to visit the friends we had made in the villages we patrolled. The people were celebrating in the streets with unbounded joy and we were happy to join them. We were all survivors of indescribable horrors, stalked by death and torture at every turn. And now the monster had been defeated. It was hard to believe it had finally ended.

"The war is over." It was too simple a phrase to signify an end to the enormous trial that I had endured. For years, unending fear, brutality, terror and consuming sorrow had defined my life. Suddenly a stranger walks up and says, "The war is over." It was hard to comprehend. Along with the joy, my heart was filled with pain. "Is it possible? Can this nightmare end?" The faces and the suffering of those that I had lost were as real in my memory as they had been during my childhood. The war might be over, but their loss would be with me as long as I lived. The pain would never leave me.

The partisans were jubilant. We had helped to defeat the Nazis, so we felt we had every right to celebrate. However, we had paid dearly for the victory. At the beginning of the Slovak rebellion against the Germans, Commander Cherpansky's group had numbered 250 soldiers. At the end of the war only 32 remained and this included a number of later recruits like myself. Every one of us had received at least one serious wound. We all had some significant frostbite injury. We all had suffered some sickness from the harsh conditions we endured. Of our 30 horses, only two survived (mine being one of them). Even though each of us bore severe scars of one type or another, we were happy to be alive to see this moment. After a few days, the local people began to reestablish their everyday lives. All the partisans were leaving for their big celebration in Koshice. With the rest of the country having been occupied by the now-retreating Nazis, Koshice had been the temporary seat of the Czechoslovakian government-in-exile, and hence where the commander of the Armed Forces, Commander Svoboda, ordered us to convene.

As we inched our way out of the mountains, we were welcomed in every village and treated like national heroes. After half a year as a partisan, I thought of myself as a victorious liberator jubilantly returning from the war. Despite the harsh conditions[2] and the danger of battle, the time I

---

2. For example: when we were on patrol into the night, we would dig out a narrow catacomb for ourselves in the hillside, crawl into our snug cubby-hole, snow and branches would be piled over the entrance to mask our whereabouts, and there we would stay until dawn. If there was nowhere to burrow a hole for ourselves, we would sleep right out on top of the snow.

After the war, I wanted to return to normalcy, but life would never be the same again.

endured with the partisans was my most triumphant. Not to be a sheep led to slaughter, not to die by the cruel Nazi tortures, to fight back, to thwart those who sought to destroy my people and me. I was filled with a sense of pride, of glory and of a destiny fulfilled. The sense of power associated with defeating the enemy of G-d was exhilarating and intoxicating. To me it was a spiritual triumph. The welcome given us by the grateful and exuberant villagers fed this feeling.

Even though I was still formally charged and convicted of abandoning my weapon, I realized, to my great relief, that it was a mere formality. My conviction was only to satisfy the tenets of the partisans. However, since the war was over, no sentence would be meted out against me. I would not be punished at Koshice but I was to receive an honorable discharge, awarded for my heroism, and decorated. However, I was not interested in celebrations or decorations; what I wanted most was to find my mother, father, brothers and sisters again.

This would be impossible to overemphasize: The reunion with my family encompassed all my thoughts, it is what kept me alive. As I would laboriously march on patrol through the monotonous white mountainside I would fantasize and daydream of being reunited with them. Repeatedly I would imagine the sweetness of being embraced by them. With the greatest, most intense yearning my heart burned to be with my family again. There was nothing else in the entire world that mattered to me; I had to find my family!

As I parted from the victorious caravan, the illusion of power and triumph of being a partisan died a sudden unexpected death. It vanished the moment I encountered the first Jews returning from the death camps.

Chapter 18

Returning of the Dead

While using all my wits to survive as a Jew hiding in the midst of the Nazi killers, I witnessed the most extreme demonstrations of wickedness. During my time with the partisans, I was able to slay the monsters that had inflicted such evil. I was a soldier fighting against evil; I had been willing to put my life on the line to destroy the enemies of humanity. The horrors that I witnessed and endured were burned into every part of my being and I understood that I would never be able to erase those images. They would haunt me for the rest of my days. I came to understand that I could survive my memories only through prayer and faith.

My time with the partisans made it clear to me that I must always fight against evil. I knew that I had to do so without compromise when evil first made itself known no matter how inconsequential the affront or injustice; Jews must never endure such suffering again. This was my state of mind in the late spring of 5705 (1945) as the dusty, creaking transport truck bounced and rocked as it sped down the narrow mountain road.

As the partisans went their way to Koshice, I hitched a ride with Russian soldiers who were headed, I hoped, in the direction of my last real home, Pressburg. I sat in the back of the covered vehicle with my legs dangling over the edge of the truck, my rifle still slung over my shoulders. I spoke very little with my hosts, as the soldiers who were inside the truck conversed in their usual raucous manner. I was still lost in my ever-present dream of the moment I would see my father again, of the moment I would embrace my sisters. It was my sweet painful dream that took me out of the world and placed me with my family even though I was alone.

I was jostled out of my reverie as the lumbering vehicle slowed to a stop. We had reached an intersection, a fork in the road, which in those days was treated like today's highway rest stops. The soldiers piled out to stretch their legs and I followed.

As I walked toward the front of the armored truck, my eyes swept over the panorama of the mountain countryside. I could see the iced mountaintops that had been my frozen home for the last six months. As my eyes scaled the mountain, they alighted upon a closely clustered group of five men perched and huddled together, sitting or squatting on the bare earth. They wore striped uniforms, uniforms I had never seen before and was unable to identify.

I was nearly 17 years old and I had lived through experiences that the worst nightmare could not equal. However, nothing I knew about or had ever imagined could have prepared me for the sight of these men.

Their appearance was beyond shocking. They resembled bodies exhumed from the grave. They were emaciated, possessing no flesh. Their skin, which resembled the texture of old, dried paper, was stretched taut over their bones. They were so frail that their bones appeared to move without any muscle. Their skin was a uniform ashen gray. It seemed that if you touched them, their skin would crack and they would collapse in a puff of dust.

It was the appearance of their faces and the look in their eyes that disturbed me the most. Their faces were death masks, without expression or life. The eyes were unresponsive, looking straight ahead, locked in an unwavering, dazed glare. Though these bodies were still alive, if only technically, these souls had been murdered. While the other soldiers ignored them or laughed at them, going off to smoke their cigarettes and lie in the grass, I approached them.

I spoke to them, cautiously at first, for I had never seen human beings reduced to such a pitiful state. As they slowly turned their heads toward me, I saw that sorrow and anguish shadowed and cloaked their every move and expression.

I asked them who they were, where they came from, what had happened to them, and, to my horror, in their weak and wavering frail voices they said that they were Jews who had survived the death camps. My heart fell to the floor, my knees began to buckle and I had to catch myself.

They spoke feverishly now for they saw from my reaction that I too was Jewish. Their words rapidly tumbled out of their mouths in desperation to tell their story, for soon I was to depart. They unburdened themselves and tears welled in their sunken, near-dead eyes. They told me of the concentration camps, they told me of the extermination camps, they told me of the gas chambers and they told me of the crematoriums. My head was spinning. I had to use my rifle as a crutch to hold myself up. We knew tragedies were taking place, we knew that the Nazis and their lackeys were plumbing the depths of human cruelty and that people were being killed, but to actually see it was too much. I could not grasp it now.

In a daze I parted from them as they returned their gaze to the horizon, stoically awaiting their transport. I slumped in the back of the truck: Gone was my bravado, gone was my glory. I was once so full of myself, but now I was deflated.

As the truck rumbled off, a verse occurred to me and in my remorse I repeated it to myself as tears cascaded into my mouth, "All her people are sighing, searching for bread. They gave away their treasures for food in order to remain alive. See G-d, and behold, what a glutton I have become!"[1]

And then, once again, the dreams of my reunion with my family flooded and overwhelmed me, but they had taken on a different twist, the twist of the death camps: "What has happened to my mother," my thoughts screamed, "my sisters, my brothers, my father?"

As I arrived in Pressburg, the first trickle of the death camp refugees began returning to their former homes. There were refugees who were beyond help and they died soon after their return. But some had enough spirit to continue and with help from the few healthy survivors and from public agencies that had been established at the end of the war, these camp survivors gained strength.

These few survivors represented the millions of Jews who had been living their lives in peace before the Holocaust. Millions died by all manner of atrocities — by strangling, shooting, beatings, mass executions, by Nazi experimentation, by starvation, by gas, by all unimaginable torture. All as part of the main thrust of the Nazi's insane evil plan not only to kill the Jew but to drive him from his lofty throne as G-d's chosen to the basest of animals. As the survivors recovered, they told us stories of the Nazi horror, of the men, women, children and babies who were slaughtered without mercy. Having seen so many die, most wondered why they had been chosen to live. Some understood

---

1. *Lamentations* 1:11.

their survival in terms of the need to bear witness to what had happened.

For the first time, I began to grasp the immensity of the Holocaust the Germans had wrought. I was now a tested warrior returned from battle in victory, but my heart was broken by their stories and I cried bitter tears of anger for a long time. Although my tears flowed uncontrollably, mixing with the tears of the other survivors like the waters of a great flood, tears could do nothing to wash away the scars of our suffering. I will never recover from the effect of what I learned during those days.

As I wandered the streets of Pressburg looking for connections to the life that had been taken from me, instinct drew me to the Schierstube, the synagogue where we had prayed before the war. All was quiet. The place that at one time had been packed with devout people was barren and empty. I began to comprehend the enormity of the changes that had taken place in the city.

Before the war, this great city had been a magnificent bastion of Jewish life, of Torah. In every neighborhood, there

The Great Synagogue destroyed

were synagogues packed with Jews engaged in the study of our precious heritage. I passed through streets where I knew the names of the people who had lived in every house. Now, all were empty. As I passed a yeshiva on a corner, I remembered a place that just eight or nine years before had been filled with devout Jews, but now there was no one inside, no students were learning. In each place where there had been Jews, there was only silence.

Those few who survived returned to face a new world alone. No father, no mother, no close family, no distant relatives, no close friends, no community — no one could be found. Where were all the Torah scholars, the devout Jews, the rabbis? We were each like Noah after the flood.

In a remarkably short time, however, signs of Jewish life reappeared as a few survivors began to come together as a community.[2] We began to gather in the synagogue and a small congregation was formed. Rav Moshe Yaakov Weiss served as the rabbi and Dr. Eichler served as the secretary of the congregation. Here, I met several of the people whom I had helped to hide in non-Jewish homes. We rejoiced with each other that we were still alive. And in our joy, we affirmed that we had held fast to our beliefs with a prayer that expressed our deepest feelings: "With all that has happened, we remained loyal to G-d, and our eyes are turned to G-d."

We each recounted the hand of G-d in our lives as we recited the words of King David: "Blessed is G-d, Who did not turn us over as prey to their teeth. Our soul was like the bird that escaped the snare; the snare broke and we remain alive" (*Psalms* 124:6-7).

---

2. "On April 15, 1945, a few days after the liberation of the city, the Jewish community of Bratislava (Pressburg) was reestablished ... In September, Chief Rabbi Markus Lebovic was installed in his post in a ceremony in the only synagogue that had not suffered damage during the war; the first public prayer services were held there also on the occasion of the High Holidays. In 1946 Bratislava became the headquarters of the 42 reconstituted Jewish communities of Slovakia." *Encyclopaedia Judaica*, Jerusalem, 1971, p. 1312.

Like most of the other survivors, I was alone in Pressburg, but I retained the hope that some of my family had managed to survive. Two of my sisters, Hana and Sara, had remained in Hungary and as far as I knew they had never been taken by the Nazis. After about two weeks in Pressburg, I was told by an acquaintance that Hana had indeed escaped the Nazis' clutches and was living in Romania. I was preparing to go bring her back when she arrived in Pressburg herself.

Our reunion was a wonderful, joyous occasion. I had given up any hope of ever being so happy again. Hana, the oldest of my sisters, had matured into a lovely and beautiful young woman. I had feared that she would have suffered the hardships of inadequate food and constant fear that all who hid from the Nazis suffered. She had hidden in Budapest as a young Catholic girl, with her own apartment and job. In addition, my father had made arrangements for her to be able to withdraw money from a bank account set up under her gentile name. She had managed to avoid the Nazis until late in 1944. Apparently, someone turned her in as a Jew in hiding and she was arrested. Hana had already been sentenced to be shot, when she was suddenly released. Gentile friends had managed to accumulate enough bribe money to have her papers reevaluated and she was freed. She managed to hide safely in Romania for the remainder of the war. She had returned to Pressburg hoping to find me alive.

Hana also brought wonderful news that made my happiness complete. She informed me that Sara, the second youngest sister, was definitely alive and well in Budapest. Sara had also been hidden from the Nazis for the entire war. She had been raised by Marishka Kerterz and her family as one of their own children. Marishka was the woman who had been our maid and who had taken Sara through the border checkpoint as her own child.

In our elation over these blessings we both knew that we still had to discuss the great sorrows that had befallen us, but there would be time for that later. Now we had a very important mission to undertake; we had to find our baby sister.

During the last months of the war the Russian army had surrounded Budapest and had placed the city under siege. By the time the war was over, the impact of this had created truly terrible conditions for the survivors. There was little food available even for those who had money. The next morning, I hurried to Budapest to look for Sara.

When I arrived, I was stunned to find that the Kerterz family had already given Sara up to a children's home. Marishka's family had no money to buy food and they knew that Sara would now be safe and would at least get something to eat in the orphanage. They also believed that I had not survived, so they felt they had to place her in a home for orphaned children.

As the war had neared its end, there were many orphans, gentile and Jewish, wandering the streets of every city. Most people had no food and no money, so it was impossible to take care of these homeless children. A few rich individuals and some religious organizations and social agencies established homes to take in homeless children. The Swedish Consulate had been very active in hiding Jewish orphans and Jewish families in the basement of buildings that were protected as part of the embassy compound.[3]

During the war, Marishka had taken Sara to one of these buildings, the Domnikos Estate. I found this orphanage easily and was greatly relieved to be greeted cordially. I was immediately taken to the director's office. I carried

---

3. While many European Jews were denied entry into neutral Sweden before and during the war, the Swedes were able to save many tens of thousands of Jews, including Germans, Finns, Norwegians, Danes and Hungarians, especially through the efforts of a gentile Swedish businessman named Raoul Wallenberg. Wallenberg was sent to Budapest in July 1944 by the Swedish Foreign Ministry to help protect the city's remaining Jews. Wallenberg issued Swedish passports to Jews and set up protective hostels, saving many from deportation and death marches. Niewyk and Nicosia, *The Columbia Guide to the Holocaust*, New York, 2000, pp. 191-2.

with me a shoe-box full of 100 pengo notes which I intended to offer as payment for Sara's stay in the home. Inside
the office, I was totally astounded when I recognized the
director, Dr. Wolf Frey, a family friend from Pressburg. He
recognized me also. He had established this home and had
managed to keep it safe because of his influential friends in
the Swedish Embassy.

Dr. Frey was moved to tears of joy when I told him that he
had been taking care of my baby sister under an assumed
Christian name. He took me to find Sara. I could never convey
the depth of my joy when I saw her and my great relief when
she instantly recognized me. I could only think about getting
her home and to Hana back in Pressburg.

Before we took our leave, I offered the shoebox full of
money to Dr. Frey. He politely refused to take any payment.
For years, whenever I met Dr. Frey, he would refer to that
shoebox full of money. Sara could have been taken to any of
the many orphanages in Budapest; it was a great blessing that
Marishka had taken Sara to the home run by Dr. Frey.

Later, I was to learn that Dr. Frey had acted with extraor-
dinary heroism earlier in the war when the Nazis had finally
reached Budapest. He was able to stay in Budapest because
he had worked with Raoul Wallenberg, the Swedish diplomat
who had done so much to save Jews from the Nazis. Dr. Frey
had realized that there were Jews who were being hidden by
non-Jews in Budapest and that these Jews needed money to
pay their expenses. Dr. Frey, who had access to a virtually
unlimited amount of money, perfected a particularly ingenious
plan for delivering money to those people. He would walk
down Andreas Boulevard dressed as a Nazi officer and whenever he would recognize someone who was Jewish, he would
stop him and ask for his papers. These Jews always carried
papers identifying themselves as Christians. He would hand
back their papers with the money they needed wrapped inside.

It was known in the Jewish refugee community that if you needed money you could go to Andreas Boulevard to be stopped by this Nazi officer.

To have reunions with two sisters over a period of two days was a blessing that would have been unimaginable only a month earlier. Yet, here I was gazing lovingly at a baby sister who had become a little girl and a little sister who had become a young woman. When we were happily home in Pressburg, I realized that I was suddenly responsible for a family and I thanked G-d for such a great blessing. They moved into an apartment with me and we managed to begin to collect furnishings.

I now had to find a way of providing a livelihood and caring for my sisters. This was my primary concern. I had no profession or business experience and the few jobs that were available paid very little, too little to provide a decent living. I would be forced to start my own business, but I had no idea what that business should be.

Again, G-d helped me, by showing me a way to make a living. As I was going to visit a friend, a stranger stopped me in the street saying he wanted to show me something. I stopped without even thinking about what this man might want of me. This would have been unthinkable a few weeks earlier. Before I could say anything, the stranger showed me two bottles of whiskey that he had hidden under his coat. "Would you like to buy these excellent bottles of whiskey, sir?" He asked.

Immediately it occurred to me that there were many people who would pay a great deal of money for whiskey. We agreed on a price and I now became the owner of two bottles of whiskey, which meant that I had "merchandise" for a business. Later that same day two Russian officers approached me and asked if I knew where they could find some whiskey. I told them I could get them a whole bottle of whiskey each and gave them a price five times what I had paid. There was no bargaining; they eagerly agreed to my price. I had increased my investment fivefold and I had started a new business.

I realized that I would have to find my inventory on the street, so I spent time on the street talking to people. The following day another stranger asked me if I would like to buy a piece of "fine soap." I stopped and he took a bar of soap out of his pocket. Before he could say a word, I was enjoying the lovely lavender scent of the soap and thinking how people would treasure the luxury of bathing with fine soap. For a long time, everyone had been forced to use coarse, abrasive soap. We talked and he told me he had two cases of bars of soap. We agreed upon a price and now my business inventory consisted of two cases of beautifully scented soap. Within a day, I had sold the entire lot to someone on the black market for 10 times what I had paid. The next day, someone had yarn to sell and I doubled my money.

A few days later my business expanded to a new level. I heard about someone who had matches to sell. When I found him, he indicated he had an entire truckload to sell. I was not sure how I would sell so many matches but I decided to take a chance and I bought the entire cargo. To sell such a large quantity, I would have to talk to a lot of people. One of these people said that he could not buy the matches because he did not think he could sell them locally. However, if he could get them to Budapest, he could sell them all because there was a shortage of matches in that city.

At that time, society had reached a state of near anarchy. Because I had been a partisan, I knew how to do things that were not possible for the average person, like obtaining a Russian truck by bribing a Russian officer. I now had an inventory that consisted of a truckload of matches and the truck in which I could ship them. A friend by the name of Steinfeld agreed to help me.

We loaded the matches onto my new truck and set off for Budapest. Getting past the Hungarian border guards was still a problem. However, the fact that I had been a partisan again worked in my favor. We stopped at the guardhouse. One of the border guards came out and looked into the truck. He took one look at the machine gun on my shoulder, turned and walked back to the guardhouse without saying a word. Once he was back inside, the guard waved us through. He was happy to be alive. We went on to Budapest without any problems.

In Budapest, I made contact with someone on the black market who introduced himself as a wholesaler. He made an offer that was two times what I had paid for the matches. We bargained and he eventually paid me five times the amount I had invested in the matches. When I drove the truck into the warehouse, I was surprised to see that there were stacks of all kinds of goods. I asked my contact about this and he told me that in general there were plenty of consumer goods available in Budapest, but some essential things were impossible to find. Furthermore, though most people had little or no money, some had plenty of money to buy the goods they wanted. In fact, for the most part the stores were filled. There were only a few things that were scarce, like sugar. This was the final key to my new business. I decided that in Budapest I could load up my truck with consumer items that were scarce in Slovakia, such as soap or cigarettes, and sell them in Pressburg. And in Pressburg I would load up my truck with items that were rare in Budapest, and sell them there.

In Slovakia, the sugar refineries were producing more sugar than the people could use. I would load my truck with a couple of tons of sugar and head back to Budapest. The profits on each trip were enormous. People on both sides of the border also needed a dependable way of getting parcels to friends and relatives on the other side. My truck was much more dependable than any government agency. As a result, my business made money carrying packages back and forth for people. In this way, I began my "export/import business," and thank G-d it became very successful.

My wartime associations, again with G-d's help, were a significant resource for my various business ventures. Though I had refused to take a government position, my partisan friends were happy to enter government service. My comrades were appointed to the top posts in the civilian administration, in the army and in the police. As a result, I had free and easy access to all the state institutions. On top of that, I enjoyed the honor and prestige accorded to all the former partisans by the masses of the population. As members of the partisan army, the country's national heroes, my former companions and I were able to get anything we wanted.

My friends and my status as a partisan together made me very important in the Jewish community. Whenever I came into synagogue, I was surrounded immediately by people requesting favors. One person needed a passport, one wanted an apartment, and another needed some special permission. Because of my contacts I was able to meet these requests quickly. This asset was even more significant in light of the postwar confusion that reigned which sometimes bordered on anarchy. People clambered for the return to normalcy, but, at that point, there was no stability, only disarray.

One of my partisan friends, a man named Barnak, was appointed as Deputy Minister of Police. In those days, with the entire political system in flux, this meant he had tremendous power, but it also meant that it was impossible for the average citizen to reach him. When at synagogue someone asked me for a favor, I went directly to Barnak's office and asked the assistant to let the Deputy Minister know that I wanted to speak to him personally. As I waited, I realized that there were many people in the waiting room hoping for an opportunity to see the Deputy Minister. Among them was Dr.

Eichler from our congregation. I was about to speak to Dr. Eichler, when Barnak rushed into the room, wrapped his arms around me in a great bear hug and said, "Janko! Come, come inside my office where we can talk." We spent a long time talking about the war and old times. Of course, he also took care of my request.

As I left the office, Dr. Eichler came over to me and said, "I've been waiting here for two weeks to ask for some assistance that the congregation needs. Do you think that you could ask the minister for us?" I immediately returned to the office and made my request of Deputy Minister Barnak. He agreed to take care of each item without hesitation. With such connections, my status in the community soared and my business thrived.

My business trips to Budapest and back took me away from my sisters for the entire week, but I always returned to them on Friday to spend the Sabbath. Shabbos with my family was a blessing for which I had prayed for years. The peace and rest I experienced were truly the answers to my prayers. Shabbos also made us remember our father, mother, sisters and brothers and we shed bitter tears for them.

I hoped and prayed that my father was still alive. I knew that he had been subjected to every barbaric torture that the Nazis could inflict. I had been told that he had been taken to Mauthausen, a camp that the SS had designated to be a camp of utmost severity. Conditions at Mauthausen were brutal even by concentration-camp standards and almost all prisoners were either worked or tortured to death. But still I prayed.

Chapter 19

My Father

The prayers for my father's return were ever present on my lips, my first thoughts as I awoke and the last thoughts that lulled me into another troubled sleep. One day as I trudged through the streets passing another broken contingent of concentration-camp survivors, skeletal hulks roaming the streets in search of their lives, in search of their souls, my thoughts turned bitter, "How could the German monsters do such horrid things to another human being? How could they reduce a man to little more than a skeleton and worse?" These questions raced through my mind, reawakening deep-seated feelings of anger and sorrow.

I walked ahead, struggling to keep my mind on the concerns of my business.

"Romi."

My name, barely audible, reverberated in my head like a distant echo of the most wonderful sound of my childhood.

Though the voice was weak and frail, it was my father's voice, exactly the way it had always sounded. I assumed that my desire to see my father again was causing me to hear things.

"Romi." The voice was louder, more insistent.

For two or three seconds my mind raced. Though I knew it was an impossible dream, I turned toward the group of survivors. I stopped in front of the wretched soul whom I had passed. It was my father. The tears burst from my eyes; all the sadness, bitterness, hopelessness, and love I had for him, which had been stifled inside of me, came gushing forth like a geyser.

His eyes were still the clear, lively brown eyes which I could never forget, eyes gleaming with warmth and an overpowering desire to live. They, and his voice, were all that I could recognize. I fell into his arms, both of us weeping uncontrollably. They were tears of joy and they were tears of sadness over what had happened to us and to our family.

His ordeal had left my father extremely weak and on the brink of death. It was obvious that he required care that I could not provide at home. However, I felt that it would not be wise to put him in the hospital. Everyone knew that the general hospitals were very crowded and since my father was so weak I feared he would not receive the special intensive care he needed. Therefore, I took him to a specialized facility, Sanatorium Mraz, a private hospital headed by one of Pressburg's most prominent doctors, Dr. Mraz, a specialist in the fields of digestion and stomach disorders. My father was put in a special treatment program.

At first, he was given only minute amounts of very thin soup several times each day. Over a period of several weeks, the soup's consistency was gradually thickened until he could consume a normal meal. I could only guess what the ingredients of those concoctions were. But their effect on my father was dramatic, as he seemed to gain weight and strength each day. As much as I understood that the medical treatment was responsible for his recovery, I also saw it as G-d's intervention. While my father improved, many of the camp survivors who were taken to that same sanatorium and given the same treatment died. There were some who died that did not seem to be as ill as he had been.

Reb Brudi Stern[1] and Shlomo Brown[2] were also admitted to this exclusive sanatorium. My friend Brudi had to be carried like a little baby into the sanatorium. He had absolutely no strength, neither to walk nor to

My boyhood friend Yisroel "Brudi" Stern in 1945, after his postwar recovery

stand. He was a bundle of bones; he could not even move.

A fourth patient was a fine gentleman by the name of Mr. Coleman who had been the largest manufacturer of pickles and pickled herring throughout the entire country. When it came to pickled goods, Coleman Pickles was a famous trade name. Mr. Coleman, like my father, had been reduced to virtually a human wraith. Along with the extreme mental and physical cruelty the Nazis inflicted on him, he began to suffer from a severe heart condition that was filling his chest cavity with water. They inserted I.V. needles daily into his frail chest in an attempt to drain it. However, despite all of their valiant attempts and care, the sanatorium became resigned to the fact that despite their best efforts they could no longer help Mr. Coleman. He was transferred to a local hospital, and sadly, within two weeks Mr. Coleman was no longer among the living.

---

1. He is highlighted, along with his father, Reb Shlomo Stern, in Chapter 11.
2. He was the concentration-camp survivor Shlomo Brown, who first told me about my father surviving, see Chapter 1.

The porridgelike gruel with whichthey nourished my father with was as flavorless as it was monotonous. We began to smuggle in our own food for my father to eat. This was specifically against sanatorium rules. Stern and Brown's families started doing likewise, as one of them had a relative lower a basket tied to a rope out of his hospital-room window which was then loaded up with food by other family members and then hoisted up. In the middle of the night, the three of them, unbeknown to the nurses, would indulge in these homemade meals.

Within a few weeks, my father had recovered his strength to the degree that he could begin to tell us how he had been miraculously saved. It was a story that was difficult for him to tell, for as he talked, he remembered. It was many years before he was able to relate all of the details.

When he was arrested, he was taken to the local prison where his arms and legs were shackled with heavy iron chains. The cruelty could hardly be described and certainly never understood by anyone who did not experience it. He was not questioned. He had no information that the authorities needed. He was not charged with anything. There was nothing for which he deserved to be punished. He was a Jew. That was all they needed to know. He was beaten day and night by his guards because he was one of G-d's chosen people.

The brutality was well organized. When one guard tired from the exertion of beating the prisoners, a rested guard took his place so that he could continue the torture without respite. My father told me that there were several Jews in his cell who were so battered that every part of their bodies was left bleeding, bruised or broken.

At one point, my father's tormentors took him out of his cell and led him to a room where there were no other prisoners; only other Nazi guards were present as witnesses. They made him stand on a stool and then put a rope around his neck. They tied the rope to an overhead pipe and then announced that he would be hanged. The guards stood around laughing at him as he pondered his last few seconds of life. One of the guards walked over to stand next to him and just when my father thought they would kick the chair from under him to end his life, the guard reached up and removed the noose without a word of explanation. The entire exercise was deliberately designed to torture the prisoner.

Each day brought renewed beatings and psychological terror, treatment so monstrous that the awful living conditions were a routine relief by comparison. Constant cold, too little to eat, food that was spoiled, no water for washing, no sanitary facilities and grossly overcrowded sleeping facilities — all could be tolerated and some prisoners might even survive, but the unending pain and constant fear cannot be described.

After two weeks, they took my father from the prison and threw him into the Serdahel Ghetto. One might think that this constituted a prison release. In reality, the Serdahel Ghetto was the true prison. The Nazis were keeping all those in the ghetto behind barbed wire with the threat of lethal violence. Everyone knew that the only release from the ghetto came in the form of a journey that ended in the death camps. For the Jews imprisoned in the Serdahel Ghetto, the journey ended in Auschwitz. My father could expect no less.

Despite all this, first the police who had arrested my father and threw him into prison and then the Gestapo who confined him to the Serdahel Ghetto never checked his papers or even asked his name. He was just an anonymous Jew to his captors. The supposed sacred civil rights of the Hungarian citizens had ceased to exist. The Nazis could imprison anyone; to be Jewish was the ultimate crime.

Without doubt, my father felt doomed to the most horrible death when he was pushed through the gate of the Serdahel Ghetto. However, an unexpected series of events resulted in his life being spared. While he waited in the ghetto for his turn to be sent to the death camps, the commander of the local army brigade issued a written order to the Gestapo officer in charge of the Serdahel Ghetto instructing that Leopold Cohn was to be sent to a forced labor camp. The labor camps were horrible in their own right. Jews were made to perform extremely strenuous and backbreaking work for long and inhumane hours; they were beaten and whipped mercilessly by their taskmasters. However, if they did not die of malnutrition or disease, they had a small chance of surviving. If my father had remained in Serdahel it would have only been a matter of days before he would have been transported to the death camps.

How the commander even knew that my father was in the ghetto is still a mystery. I do know that my father was held in great respect by what was left of the Jewish communities of Pressburg and Budapest. I suspect that one of the many people whom he had helped came to his rescue and bribed the commander.

What happened to my father at this point is astounding. He was ordered out of the ranks of the ghetto inmates to see the Gestapo officer in charge of the ghetto. The officer told him that he had received an order from the army commanders instructing him to send Leopold Cohn to a labor camp. However, the officer was going to ignore the order. He told my father, "Going to a labor camp would make no difference. All of you Jews are going to end up in Auschwitz anyway." Yet, inexplicably, the Gestapo officer handed the letter ordering my father's release to him and walked away.

As the days passed there were rumors that the Nazis would be transporting the Jews of the Serdahel Ghetto to the death camps. My father realized that the transport day had arrived when he observed the dramatic increase in the number of German soldiers stationed outside the ghetto. Immediately, he hid some food and water in a pile of debris on the roof of the house where he was staying, and as the soldiers began to round up the Jews, my father hid in a pile of straw near the house.

The soldiers, led by their Gestapo superiors, were efficient and within 24 hours had rounded up nearly all the Jews remaining in the Serdahel Ghetto. A significant number of Jews, maybe 300 or 400, had managed to hide themselves in one way or another — on a roof, in a cellar, under a bed, inside a piano, inside a hidden closet, in the toilet; desperation was the designer of all manner of hiding places. However, the Nazis were devoted to the task at hand. They came back after a few days with large numbers of fresh troops and with special dogs to scour the ghetto for Jews. With the dogs pointing the way, the troops used fixed bayonets to explore every potential hiding place. Many Jews died of stab wounds in the very places they were hiding.

My father, still in the same haystack, heard the Nazi soldiers approach. One soldier plunged a bayonet into the pile of straw, and then another. My father knew he had to remain perfectly still and no matter what happened, he could make no noise. As they probed the pile of straw with their bayonets, he was stabbed several times, in his neck, in his arm, in his leg and in his abdomen. Through it all he made not a sound. Thankfully, his wounds were not severe enough for him to bleed to death. If the Nazi soldiers knew there was a Jew in that haystack, they probably figured they had killed him. They did not know Leopold Cohn and they knew nothing of his courage or his will to survive. The hunting parties eventually scoured the entire ghetto, killing or capturing virtually every Jew. When my father finally emerged from his hiding place, the soldiers had left.

However, he was recaptured by the local police and thrown back into the same jail. He was treated exactly as he had been treated the first time he was imprisoned. Again he endured cruel beatings and torture. However, he still had the letter from the army commander. He managed to inform the head guard that he had a letter that gave instructions that he was to be transferred to a labor camp. The guard arranged for him to show the letter to the commander of the jail. The police guards and the commander of the jail were Hungarian citizens, not German soldiers and not necessarily Nazis.

A few days later, a group of four or five policemen removed him from his cell. They beat him and then put him in chains, hand and foot. With no explanation, he was taken out of the jail and moved to a labor camp, an Arbeitslager. Though he was to be treated in the most barbaric way and subjected to the most inhumane treatment, this transfer saved his life. Leopold Cohn would be a slave laborer but he would not be shipped off to the fires of Auschwitz.

I had always felt that my father merited survival because of the exemplary life he had led during the most trying of times. At the beginning of the war when refugees began pouring into Pressburg from Austria, my father was one of the first to step forward to extend a helping hand by taking a family of nine into our home. These people were not only bedraggled and unkempt, they were terribly unclean and had lice. My father was kind and gentle with them, welcoming them into our home and making them feel safe and secure. They were comforted and fed and then they were washed and given new clothing. They received every care and stayed with us until they could provide for themselves.

He told us that body lice had been the most common plagues in the camps. There was not a person whose clothing, hair and body were not infested. But though he worked in close quarters with people who were full of lice and even lived in the barracks with them, my father was spared this affliction. Miraculously, not one louse was ever found on his person or his clothing. He told me that he believed G-d had spared him this discomfort because he had tended to the needs of those Jewish refugees.

As he related his experiences, it was clear that he had suffered greatly but with each atrocity he had been saved. And with all that had happened to him, my father took great joy in the fact that he had been true to his faith throughout. With great humility, mixed with a little pride, he would voice his thanks to G-d that he never ingested nonkosher food during the course of his trials, that he did not so much as drink nonkosher milk. Of the Jews in the death camps, those who were not murdered usually died of disease or starvation. That he survived, limiting himself only to kosher food, was truly a miracle.

How he managed to get kosher food during the time the Nazis held him is also amazing. In the labor camp he was placed in a brigade that was assigned to work for a battalion of the Hungarian Army. As a result he was often working outside of the camp. He had been assigned to clean up after the horses on a local farm when the farmer came in to the barn with dead rabbits that he wanted prepared for supper. As the farmer handed them to him, my father suggested that he could also prepare the fur of the rabbits and make a pair of fine, warm gloves. The farmer agreed and a few days later my father gave the farmer his gloves. The farmer was so grateful that he offered to give my father some food as payment. My father asked the farmer to give him fresh beans, oats and barley. This was the basis of his kosher diet. Word of his expertise with fur and leather spread quickly from farm to farm. Soon he had a reasonable store of grains for himself and others in the labor camp. The grain would last for many weeks and kept him alive. Ironically, even some of the German officers asked my father to make gloves or hats for them. An officer could have him make a hat in the morning and that evening lead a group of soldiers who beat him without mercy.

My father told many stories of hardships and brutalities impossible to comprehend. But with unwavering faith, he would

After the war, I was able to run the family business with considerable success.

end every one of these stories with a vision of the hand of G-d intervening to save him.

With Hana, Sara, my father and I reunited, our lives began to take on a semblance of normalcy as we reassembled the pieces of our Jewish life. Our lives began anew with the same source of strength that had saved us during the Holocaust; our devotion to G-d, our loyalty to Him even in "the valley of the shadow of death" is what saved us.

At the same time, my business activities met with increasing success. We were also building a thriving fur business, including a factory to manufacture fur goods. By late 1946, we were shipping fur products all over Europe. My father had recovered to the degree that he could resume his role as a businessman.

Within a few days of returning to our business, my father asked me to come to his office to discuss the future. At that moment, I made a choice that I have come to regret more than any other I have ever made. He told me that he was fully recovered and could resume his business responsibilities. With great pride and happiness, he said that he could take over my duties so that I could return to my education. I was totally surprised by his suggestion. I had never considered resuming my studies.

As I sat there in silence, many objections raced through my mind. I had been away from school for so long. I enjoyed my place in the world. I was a success; I was becoming a rich man and I had great influence in the community. Also, I could come and go as I pleased and I did not answer to anyone. I knew that I could never return to the disciplined life of a student. I was a soldier who had fought in the war. How could I spend my time in school studying with children?

I did not refuse my father's request. I told him that I would think about it, though I knew that I would not go back. I made my decision, one that I would regret many times in my life as I discovered that all of my worldly accomplishments were worthless compared to what I could have accomplished had I returned to yeshiva.

Chapter 20

We Leave Pressburg Forever

Though we had reestablished our lives, the normalcy was superficial. We had managed to make enough money to become wealthy, but we were not happy living in Pressburg. We could never be at peace in that city. There were too many ghosts. Every landmark was a reminder of someone who had not survived the war. Every house, every seat in the synagogue, every street corner, every park bench, every business, every stranger walking in the street called forth a face or a memory from a terrible past.

Whenever we encountered a non-Jew, our minds were filled with suspicion and distrust: "Did he turn over a Jewish family to the Nazis?" "Did he look the other way when the Nazis came and took a Jewish neighbor?" "Did he assist the Nazis?" "Did he take the property of a Jew?" "Did he do anything to help?" It was the same for all the survivors. We would never trust our gentile neighbors ever again.

We could not stay here. Our future lay elsewhere. By the winter of 1946 we were beginning to talk about starting a new life in the United States of America.

The Communist takeover of Czechoslovakia in 1948 sealed our decision.[1] When the Communists seized power, they first ended political freedom and soon began to eliminate economic freedoms. They began to nationalize all significant businesses. Ours was no exception. I received a letter from the Communist party instructing me to come to the Ministry of Commerce to discuss the status of my fur factory. At the Ministry, I was informed that henceforth the Communist party owned my business. However, because I was an acknowledged war hero, they would allow me to serve as the manager of the factory.

I was totally outraged by the proposition that I would no longer own my own business, that the Communists could simply pass a decree and take my business away. I knew I had to buy some time to plan so I politely declined the position.

True to their threat, the Communists appointed a party member to run my factory. Within a few days, the Deputy Minister who asked me to serve as an assistant or consultant to the manager visited me. He explained that this was my duty to the country and to my fellow citizens. I realized that the wisest course was to agree and help the new manager.

My first priority was to get my family out of the country with as much of our assets as possible. My father, who had recovered physically and had regained his place in the Jewish community, had traveled to the United States as a delegate to the 1948 Agudath Israel[2] Convention. Fortunately, he had taken Sara with him and had left her with

---

1. Gutman, *Encyclopedia of the Holocaust* (New York, 1990), p. 1370.
2. Agudath Israel was founded in 1912 to mobilize Torah-loyal Jews for the perpetuation of authentic Judaism. Today it is the world's largest international Orthodox Jewish organization serving the ever-growing needs of Orthodox Jewry throughout the world.

close friends who lived in Belgium. He was in the United States for one week when the Communists seized power in Czechoslovakia. We were able to cable him that conditions were terrible and he should not return at this time. He understood our message and through some influential friends he managed to stay in the United States as a refugee. Soon, he was able to bring Sara to join him.

Getting our assets out of Czechoslovakia was not going to be easy. I set into motion a plan that would take advantage of the close working relationship we had with an importing firm in Belgium. I made arrangements to have this company place a large order for fur goods. When the manager of my factory received this large order, he immediately brought it to me. With his lack of experience, he had no other choice but to rely on me. I assured him that we could fill the order and that I would make all the arrangements. He was happy to have my assistance.

I had all the merchandise packed into large metal drums that were then loaded onto trucks. Before the drums could be sealed they had to be inspected by customs. Again, my association with the partisans would work to my advantage, for the inspector was a former partisan. I put personal items that I wanted to take out of the country into each of the drums, jewelry, money and other valuables. None of these things appeared on the manifest. The customs inspector made a cursory inspection of the drums and then had them sealed. I thought I was home free. Soon, the trucks with the sealed drums would be on their way to Belgium. However, when I came back that evening to check up on the shipment, no one was watching the drums. I was horrified to see that all the seals had been broken. In this condition, the border guards would never let the drums through the checkpoint. Worse, if they found the items in the drums that were not on the manifest, everything would be confiscated.

I did the only thing I could. I went back to my friend the customs inspector. In total panic, I told him of my predicament. His reaction was not what I expected. He was not at all worried about the situation.

"Don't worry. I'll have someone take care of your problem. In the meantime, let's have a drink," he said. One drink led to another and another and another. I woke up with a terrible headache. When I looked at my watch, my headache became even worse as I realized that it was 11 a.m. As panic pushed aside my headache, I heard my friend laughing at me. While I was attempting to focus my eyes on his face, he explained that the seals had been replaced on the drums. The drums had already passed through the border and were well on their way to Belgium.

Having gotten my possessions out of this Communist country, I still had to find a way to get Hana and myself safely out. Again, it was through the intervention of my partisan friends that I was able to solve this problem.

It was no longer possible for an ordinary citizen to get a passport and travel freely across the border. My greatest worry was that some bureaucrat would connect the shipment of goods from our factory to Belgium to our request for passports. However, a partisan comrade who held a high position in the embassy had no difficulty providing us with passports with no questions asked. Hana left Czechoslovakia the next day.

I had decided that if we left together we might attract attention, so I stayed behind in Pressburg. Furthermore, I had concocted a plan to punish the Communists who had taken our factory. The payment for the shipment of fur goods that we sent to our friends in Belgium was a very large sum of money. I did not want them to get this money.

I returned to my job as assistant to the Communist manager of our expropriated factory. At the same time, I managed to get a letter to our business associates in Belgium asking for their help in implementing my plan. Within a few days, the manager called me into his office to discuss an urgent problem. He had just received a letter from the company in Belgium that had received our shipment. The letter had informed him that the merchandise had arrived in unacceptable condition; many items were damaged and all were of low quality. The letter continued that they would not pay for the shipment and were intending to collect damages in court. The manager pleaded with me, "What should we do? This is a fortune of money to lose."

I responded with as much sympathy as I could feign, "You will have to straighten this out face-to-face or you will lose a fortune for the factory. You should take a plane and leave as soon as possible." It was difficult to keep from laughing as I watched the panic rising in the manager's eyes.

"I'm not an expert. I can't speak with any authority. I don't know what to say to these people!" he said in a voice close to tears.

As I left his office, I looked back at him saying, "You're the manager. This is your responsibility. You must straighten out the problem."

The next day the manager called me back to his office. With exaggerated authority he informed me, "I consulted the Minister of Commerce and he authorized you to go to Belgium to take care of this problem."

I politely refused saying, "This is not my responsibility and frankly, I do not like to travel by plane." With that, I calmly left his office.

The following morning, I was called into the manager's office for a third time. The manager informed me that the minister had declared that I must go to Belgium to take care of this problem. "It is your duty as a citizen. You are an expert in this field and you have an obligation to serve the interests of the state." With exaggerated reluctance I agreed to represent the "Communist-owned" factory. It took great self-control not to laugh out loud as I watched the look of relief spread over his face.

At this point, I informed the manager that I did have one condition for accepting this obligation, "I would like to go by car and drive my own car." The manager agreed without hesitation. He would take care of all the arrangements. It was obvious that he would do anything to fix this problem. The next day, he handed me an international driver's license, a visa allowing me to travel for 10 days and government papers indicating that I was on an official trip as a government representative.

For me this was a great accomplishment. I was committed to leaving the country but I did not want to leave my car behind. For a young man, his first car is very special. This one was magnificent; it was a dark-blue BMW 328 racing model and I loved driving it. I could not bring myself to abandon it.

I packed a small bag with just enough clothing for a trip of a few days. If I was stopped and my luggage was inspected, they would find nothing that would suggest that I might not be coming back. All the important possessions that we wanted to take with us had been packed in the drums with the shipment of furs and were already safely in the possession of our friends in Belgium.

With all the details of my plan in place, I placed my bag in my BMW and set off on the first leg of my westward journey. As had happened so often in the past, I soon found my path to freedom blocked by the gate of a border-crossing guardhouse. The sight of the closed gate conjured so many memories of the terrors lurking in those places that my blood ran cold as I brought my car to a halt. However, this time I was not the hunted one.

The guard's face paled as he looked inside my BMW, frightened by the medals that I displayed proudly on my coat. I could perceive real fear when I handed him my partisan ID.

"Please, wait here, sir," he said with exaggerated respect as he turned and ran into the guardhouse. The partisan ID struck fear in people. Everyone knew that even the Nazis had been afraid of the partisans.

Within a few minutes, he came out of the guardhouse leading the commander of the guard toward my car. At first, I was greatly amused by the fact that the commander looked even more nervous. With a great show of politeness, the commander invited me into his office. Once inside he handed me a piece of paper that he requested I read. It was an order from the military command that required all who passed through the border checkpoint to be thoroughly searched. He was very apologetic, saying, "I don't want to offend you, but I am required to search you." He then proceeded to pat me lightly on the shoulders and arms. I could see that he was very nervous and greatly embarrassed as he said, "That will be all. You may pass." He stamped my passport and handed it back to me with exaggerated politeness. The entire time he never took his eyes off my medals.

As I walked back to my car, I could hardly conceal the conflict I was feeling. I was no longer amused. Having spent so many years living in fear that I would be grabbed and killed by a Nazi soldier or a Gestapo agent, I should have been delighted by the reversal. The sight of this guard quaking in fear of my wrath should have made me very happy. Instead, I had had enough of fear; I could only think of getting past the symbol of that gate and finding a place where I could live in peace and freedom.

My attention was fixed on the gate as I sat in my car. The sound of the guard's cough startled me back to attention. "Excuse me, Mr. Cohn," he said. When I turned toward him, he continued. "With all due respect, I think that your partisan ID might cause you some problems. If the Americans ask for your papers, they might feel your partisan ID means that you are a Communist."

"I'm not a Communist," I replied with a start as if he had thrown cold water on me.

"But the American military police might suspect that you are a Communist. They would probably hold you while they check your background and that could take days or even weeks." Before I could react he continued, "If you like, I could mail your partisan ID to your home in Pressburg. You will have the ID when you return. That way, you would not have to take the risk."

My first reaction was that this was a ridiculous idea. However, I realized that the guard might be correct. The Americans were worried about the Communist threat to Europe and everyone knew that some of the partisans had been Communists before the war and others had become active supporters of the Communists after the war. I quickly decided that the safest thing was to follow the guard's advice. I handed him the ID knowing that I would never see it again. I would never return to Pressburg and its memories.

The commander of the guard took my ID, assuring me that he would handle this service expeditiously. He gestured toward the guardhouse and the gate was raised. The door to a new life had been opened and all that was left was for me to drive through. In an instant, my mind jumped back to Pressburg, the city I was leaving behind. Just as quickly, I pulled my thoughts back to the open gate in front of me. I turned the key to start the engine. The car roared through the gate and I was on my way to a new life.

It took me two days to reach Antwerp. I went directly to the people to whom we had sent the shipment of furs. They greeted me as if I was a long-lost relative. The next day, after a wonderful night's sleep in a safe home in a free country, my hosts handed me a manifest of the merchandise that they were holding in a warehouse for me. My first order of business was to recover the money and family treasures that I had hidden in the drums. When these were safely stored, I arranged to sell the fur goods. In reality, these goods were of the finest quality and I was able to sell them for the highest prices. When the money was safely deposited in the bank, my plan had been carried to completion. It had been a total success.

The thought of the "manager" explaining the state of the factory inventory to his Communist superiors was very amusing. No doubt, his "management skills" would prove to be valuable to the Communist economy.

The sale of the huge shipment of furs made my family and me wealthy. I was in a free country. I could walk on the street safely as a free man.

Within a few days I was reunited with my sister Hana. When my 10-day pass had expired, I easily got permission to stay in Belgium as a refugee, as did Hana. And even as a refugee, I was soon able to reestablish an export/import business.

Shortly after I had been granted refugee status, the Consul General of Czechoslovakia visited me. He tried to convince me to return to Czechoslovakia. Displaying his most officious manner, he declared, "You must return to your homeland. You have an obligation to your fellow citizens to use your skills to serve your country." I did not respond but only gave him the most skeptical expression I could muster. He softened his tone and tried a more emotional appeal. "How could you live in a foreign country as a refugee? You are a stranger here. In Pressburg you are a hero and you will be treated with great homage and respect."

Was it possible that this man had already forgotten all that had been done to the Jews in our homeland? Did he not know the non-Jews who stood by while the Jews were killed in the street, while babies were murdered in front of their mothers, and families were taken away to the death camps? These were the only people left. The people who would call me a national hero were the very ones who had witnessed our plight and done nothing. The Consul General might have conveniently forgotten, but I had not. Was it possible that he did not see the ghosts of the dead on every street and in every window? I would always see these ghosts at every moment, awake or asleep. "I will never return to my homeland," was the only response I could manage, and I wished him good day.

Though we were determined to immigrate to the United States, it was necessary to stay in Belgium for a while. During this time, I was able to travel around Europe to pursue business. On one of my trips through France, I was able to see in a small way the mind of one of the Nazi leaders who created the monsters that had stalked us in the valley of death.

While in Paris, one of my business associates mentioned that the French had captured a Nazi war criminal whom they were about to send back to Czechoslovakia. He told me that the prisoner was the Nazi who had destroyed Lidice, a small village near Prague.[3] Early in the war, on May 27, 1942, two anti-Nazi agents had bombed the car of Reichsprotector Reinhard Heydrich, killing him. The Gestapo, under the command of this Nazi criminal, had been ordered by Hitler to execute all those living in the village. One hundred ninety-two men were shot and 71

---

3. On June 10, 1942, this small village in Czechoslovakia was destroyed and its inhabitants murdered (192 men and 71 women) as part of the German retaliation for the assassination of Reinhard Heydrich who had been installed by Hitler as the governor of the Protectorate of Bohemia and Moravia. Heydrich was killed on orders from the Czech-government-in-exile and the official reason given for the mass murder at Lidice was that the villagers had helped the assassins – an allegation that had no basis in fact. Gutman, *Encyclopedia of the Holocaust*, New York, 1990 pp. 870-2. For an autobiographical account, see Zena Trinka's *A Little Village Called Lidice*, Lidgerwood, 1947.

women and 103 children were sent to death camps. I wanted very much to confront this Nazi monster. Within two days it was arranged.

I remember that his first name was Max. I had planned to have something profound and eloquent to say to this man when I confronted him. Instead, what I said was, "You look like an intelligent and educated man. How could you do what you did to the Jews?"

He looked at me with very sad and almost begging eyes. He told me he regretted what he had done, but I continued to press him. "You knew that what you were doing was evil, yet you did it anyway. Why?!" I demanded.

He pleaded, "Let me explain. If you had met Adolph Hitler, you would understand. When you looked into his eyes, you lost your will. You would do whatever he asked. The man psychologically controlled us all. I did not think. All I could see was his vision for us. Each of us would have given up everything for him, even our own families."

Did this man expect me to believe that he was not responsible for his deeds?! His excuse was that he was powerless to resist Hitler and his nightmarish vision for Germany! It was too much to accept. I was totally repelled and disgusted by this man. I could no longer tolerate being in the same room with him. Shaken, I turned away to leave. He begged me, "I'm sorry. Please forgive me and give me your blessing before you leave."

As I walked away, I could hear him sobbing uncontrollably. When I reached the door, I turned and said, "If you are innocent, that will be your blessing."

The encounter with this Nazi war criminal made me remember the faces of the people who had been torn from my life since 1939. I controlled my grief and forced myself to remember the faces of the loved ones to whom I could still return.

For a moment, my mind wandered to a new life that would begin in America. But my thoughts were quickly pulled to the memory of those who once made up my life. As I drove, I recalled a certain Jewish prayer which best expressed my feelings:

> *Father of Compassion, Who dwells on high,*
> *In His profound mercy,*
> *He will be compassionately mindful of*
> *the pious, the upright, and the blameless ones;*
> *the holy communities who gave their lives*
> *for the sanctification of the Divine Name.*
> *They were beloved and pleasant in their lifetime,*
> *and in their death are not parted (from Him).*
> *They were swifter than eagles and stronger than lions*
> *to do the will of their Possessor*
> *and the desire of their Rock.*
> *Our G-d will recall them favorably*
> *together with the other righteous of all time.*
> *And He will avenge the blood of His servants*
> *that has been shed.*[4]

---

4. From the Sabbath morning prayers

Chapter 21

The Conclusion and a Continuation

We had hoped that leaving Pressburg would bring this tragic period of our lives to a close. By going to a new land, to America, I was starting a new life. I hoped that it would be like being reborn. And in a way it was. I began a successful home construction business and married early and happily. My sister Sarah graduated from Hunter College in Manhattan with a Masters in Psychology and worked as a guidance counselor. Eventually she moved to Israel where she became a still-life artist. Hanna married a fine young man who became the head of the Statistical Bureau for the United Nations. Hanna is now a grandmother many times over. My father remarried and had another large family, two sons and four daughters, with his second wife. His sons and sons-in-laws are all scholars, happily married, with families of their own. My father past away at the age of 96.

My sister Sara in 1958

However, in a very different vein, America has not been a rebirth, for the vestiges of my previous life pursued me. For years I suffered from terrible nightmares. Two or three times every week, I was carried back to the most terrifying and horrible experiences that I had endured during the war. The dreams were so real that I relived those monstrous events.

I would wake up screaming or shaking in uncontrollable fright, lying on sheets that were saturated with my sweat. In each of these nightmares I suffered as intensely as I had during the actual experience. The sense of fear cannot be described. Screams of pain and terror came from those who were being dragged away or beaten by the most ferocious of Nazi monsters. The tears of my mother, the fright of my sisters and brothers, and the pain of my father were all revisited in my nightmares and brought unremitting suffering to my life.

Though the Nazis did not kill me and their savagery could not break my spirit, the nightmares often made me feel that I would not survive.

As the years went by, I felt compelled to keep myself as busy as possible. I immersed myself in business, my family and my faith. With time, the nightmares diminished in frequency. Eventually they stopped and I managed to suppress all thoughts of the Holocaust.

All of this changed, when I began to hear the voices of hate-filled pseudohistorians who were attempting to rewrite history; watering down the evil that the Nazis had committed, even denying that the Holocaust had occurred at all. This was unthinkable! I had lived through the Holocaust and it was more horrible than anyone could imagine.

I summoned forth my buried memories and began to relate to other people the stories of the Holocaust. These were bits and pieces of my life, disconnected from each other. And though they were moving and often brought tears to the eyes of my listeners, they never conveyed a sense of the immensity of the disaster I had suffered through.

I realized that I did not want my experiences to be forgotten. Those that suffered and died cannot be forgotten: mothers, fathers and children. So many Jews, so many families;

My father, Leopold (Yom Tov) Cohn, (right) at the age of 94. I am beside him.

hundreds and thousands and millions of people gone forever, killed in the name of a monstrous belief that is now despised throughout the world.

More and more I find myself worrying that our children and their children will forget what happened. Surely, if they do, the Holocaust could be repeated. Not only must we remember that it happened, but we must also understand how it happened and why it happened.

Certainly, there are still people that hate and fear the Jewish people. I doubt that we will ever be able to convince all of these hate-filled people of the error of their ways. Nevertheless, they must never have the power to turn their views into deeds; they must never be allowed to recreate the monsters that stalk in the shadows of the valley of death. I know that we can be vigilant and we can make sure that the events that led to the Holocaust are never repeated. To guarantee that the beast will never be loosed again, we must recognize the first insidious erosion of our rights as human beings. We must refuse to tolerate these injustices, fighting them with all our courage and all the resources at our command.

But still we ask, "Why? Why did it happen?"

"And nations will walk by your light and kings by the brilliance of your shine" (*Isaiah* 60:3). This means that the Jewish people are a light to the nations, but only if they cling to His teachings. Then through their exemplary conduct the people of the world will emulate them and adopt these ways making this world a better place. As it states, "When they (the other nations) hear all these statutes (of the Torah) and they will say, 'Certainly a wise and understanding people is this great nation'" (*Deuteronomy* 4:6).

Before World War II, the Jewish people, first in Germany, and subsequently, throughout all of Europe, were abandoning the Torah and assimilating at a terrifying rate, thus frustrating G-d's grand plan for the world, causing Him to intercede.

Twice daily we recite this exact sentiment: "You should love the L-rd, Your G-d with all your heart and with all your soul and with your resources…" (*Deuteronomy* 6:5). This is our mission; this is what we are asked to do. "Beware lest your heart be seduced and you follow the idols of others and bow to them,"

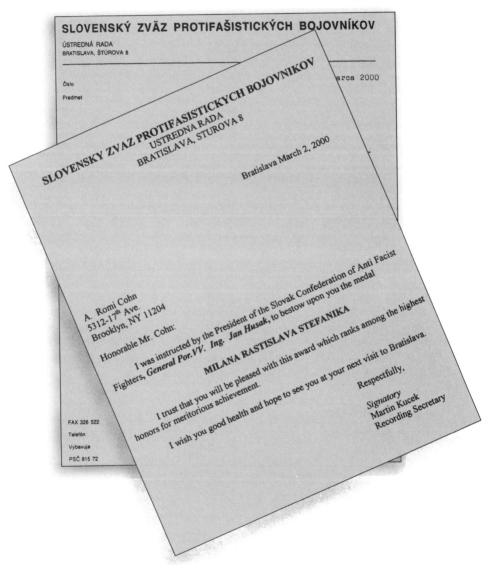

I received numerous medals after the war, including this award.

whether it is the idol of Socialism or Communism or the Enlightenment. However, if we do bow down to them? "Then the anger of G-d will blaze against you ..." (*Deuteronomy* 11:16-17).

Throughout history we have witnessed that when there is destruction and devastation the righteous are punished along with the wicked. Not only that, but they suffer first. Why? For the righteous are willing to sacrifice themselves for the good of the people. Perhaps this will assuage the anger of Hashem and He will take pity on us and forgive our shortcomings on their behalf.

However, why did I survive?

Perhaps it is to tell this story, bringing the horrors and the triumphs of so dire a period to the conscience of a world

The medals I was awarded for his heroism during World War II when I fought with the partisans against the Nazis

that is being falsely seduced into believing that the Holocaust did not even take place, that the victims of the Holocaust are the liars.

We must never let anyone forget nor can we stand by idly when the Holocaust-deniers promulgate their false doctrine. We must resist when society tries to revise history, whether in the form of monstrous lies or seemingly trivial inaccuracies, whether in the guise of public policy or personal ignorance. We must pray, increase our devotion to Hashem and beg Him to prevent this from occurring again. We must cling to and wholeheartedly serve G-d and not to wage war against Him.

More than simply "remember the Holocaust," we must remember the lessons of the Holocaust!

Bibliography

Berenbaum, Michael and Gutman, Israel. *Anatomy of the Auschwitz Death Camp*. Bloomington: Indiana University Press, 1994.

Cholavsky, Shalom. *Jewish Resistance During the Holocaust*. Grubsztein, Meir (ed.). Jerusalem: Yad Vashem, 1971.

Dawidowicz, Lucy. *The War Against the Jews*. New York, Holt, Rinehart and Winston, 1975.

Friedman, Philip. *Roads to Extinction: Essays on the Holocaust*. New York: Conference on Jewish Social Studies, 1980.

Gutman, Israel. *Encyclopedia of the Holocaust*. New York: Macmillan, 1990.

Hecht, Ben. *Perfidy*. New York: Messner, 1961.

Hilberg, Raul. *The Destruction of the European Jews*. New York/Holmes & Meier, 1985.

Jelinek, Yeshayahu. *The Parish Republic: Hlinka's Slovak People's Party, 1939-1945*. New York: Columbia University Press, 1976.

Koch, H.W. *The Hitler Youth: Origins and Development, 1922-1945*. London: Macdonald and Jane's, 1975.

Kowalski, Isaac. *Anthology of Armed Jewish Resistance*. Brooklyn: Jewish Combatants Publishers House, 1985.

Le Chene, Evelyn. *Mauthausen: The History of a Death Camp*. London: Methuen, 1971.

Levin, Nora, *The Holocaust*, Schocken Books, 1973.

Michel, Henri. *The Second World War*. New York: Praeger Publishers, 1975.

Nicosia, Francis and Niewyk, Donald. *The Columbia Guide to the Holocaust.* New York: Columbia University Press, 2000.

Rosten, Leo Calvin. *The Joys of Yiddish.* New York: McGraw-Hill, 1968.

Rothkirchen, Livia. *Rescue Attempts During the Holocaust: Proceedings of the Second Yad Vashem International Historical Conference.* Gutman, Israel and Zuroff, Efraim (eds.). Jerusalem: Yad Vashem, 1977.

Smith, Marcus. *The Harrowing of Hell: Dachau.* Albuquerque: University of New Mexico Press, 1972.

Toth, Dezider. *The Tragedy of the Slovak Jews.* Banska Bystrika: Datei, 1992.

Trinka, Zena. *A Little Village Called Lidice.* Lidgerwood: International Book Publishers, Western Office, 1947.

Weinberg, Gerhard. *A World at Arms.* New York: Cambridge University Press, 1994.

About the Author
A. Romi Cohn

A native of Pressburg, Romi Cohn spent the years of World War II keeping one step ahead of the Nazi juggernaut, managing not only to survive but to help other Jews hide from the Nazi onslaught and escape certain death. When, eventually, his own life was so endangered that he was forced to entrust his *Hatzalah* activities to others, he joined the partisans who fought the occupying Germans from hideouts in the surrounding mountains.

At war's end, Romi Cohn made his way to Canada, where he helped organize Zeirei Agudath Israel in Montreal, continuing to help preserve Jewish life and *Klal Yisroel's* legacy.

Though a businessman by profession, and a highly-respected one by merit (having even served as the director of the Staten Island Chamber of Commerce), Reb Avrohom Cohn's dedication to *Torah u'mitzvos* is legendary. Nothing could likely express that dedication as trenchantly as his well-honed expertise in *milah*. For over two decades, he has practiced *milah* without remuneration, trained numerous *mohalim* and earned a sterling reputation among local doctors and surgeons. Having surgical privileges in several hospitals, Reb Avrohom has performed *brissim* on countless *ba'alei teshuvah*, and immigrants from the Soviet Union. His renowned sefer on the subject, *Bris Avrohom HaCohein*, a truly comprehensive text endorsed by some of the highest rabbinical authorities of our time, is a well-utilized resource for *mohalim* around the globe.

Another noteworthy aspect of Reb Avrohom's Torah activism is "Kerem Avrohom Cohn," which he established eleven years ago with the support and commendation of a broad range of *gedolei* Torah and *roshei yeshivos*. each year the Kerem chooses two awardees from hundreds of nominees to receive the prestigious five-year grant for *talmidei chachamim* of truly impressive character and remarkable ability, an award that has been called "the Nobel Prize in Torah."

A powerful enhancer of Kovod haTorah and a wellspring of tomorrow's *gedolei u'manhigei Yisrael*, "Kerem Avrohom Cohn" has set high standards and continues to sow the seeds of the international Torah community's future, a true tribute to the foresight and insight of its founder.